SUFFERING AND THE CHRISTIAN LIFE

SUFFERING AND THE CHRISTIAN LIFE

Edited by
Karen Kilby and Rachel Davies

LONDON • NEW YORK • OXFORD • NEW DELHI • SYDNEY

T&T CLARK
Bloomsbury Publishing Plc
50 Bedford Square, London, WC1B 3DP, UK
1385 Broadway, New York, NY 10018, USA

BLOOMSBURY, T&T CLARK and the T&T Clark logo
are trademarks of Bloomsbury Publishing Plc

First published in Great Britain in 2020
Paperback edition first published 2021

Copyright © Karen Kilby, Rachel Davies and contributors, 2020

Karen Kilby and Rachel Davies have asserted their right under the Copyright, Designs and Patents Act, 1988, to be identified as Editors of this work.

Cover design: Terry Woodley
Cover image © Isle of Skye, Scotland/Wanda Thompson

All rights reserved. No part of this publication may be reproduced or transmitted in any form or by any means, electronic or mechanical, including photocopying, recording, or any information storage or retrieval system, without prior permission in writing from the publishers.

Bloomsbury Publishing Plc does not have any control over, or responsibility for, any third-party websites referred to or in this book. All internet addresses given in this book were correct at the time of going to press. The author and publisher regret any inconvenience caused if addresses have changed or sites have ceased to exist, but can accept no responsibility for any such changes.

A catalogue record for this book is available from the British Library.

Library of Congress Control Number:2019949297

ISBN: HB: 978-0-5676-8723-4
PB: 978-1-4411-6532-9
ePDF: 978-0-5676-8725-8
eBook: 978-0-5676-8724-1

Typeset by Deanta Global Publishing Services, Chennai, India

To find out more about our authors and books visit
www.bloomsbury.com and sign up for our newsletters.

CONTENTS

List of Contributors   vii

INTRODUCTION   1
    Karen Kilby and Rachel Davies

Chapter 1
SUFFERING, SIN AND DEATH IN PAUL   3
    Dorothea H. Bertschmann

Chapter 2
GIVING THE SELF THROUGH DEATH: A CRUCIFIED CHRIST AS GIFT
IN GALATIANS   23
    Logan Williams

Chapter 3
GREGORY OF NYSSA ON PAIN, PLEASURE AND THE GOOD: AN EARLY
CHRISTIAN PERSPECTIVE ON REDEMPTIVE SUFFERING   33
    Siiri Toiviainen Rø

Chapter 4
GREGORY OF NAZIANZUS ON THE ROLE OF SATAN IN
HUMAN SUFFERING   43
    Gabrielle Thomas

Chapter 5
SUFFERING, DERELICTION AND AFFLICTION IN CHRISTIAN MYSTICISM   55
    Bernard McGinn

Chapter 6
PROTEST THEISM, AQUINAS AND SUFFERING   71
    Rik Van Nieuwenhove

Chapter 7
SUFFERING AND THE DESIRE FOR GOD IN JOHN OF THE CROSS   87
    Edward Howells

Chapter 8
STOP KISSING ME: READING MOTHER TERESA WITH BONAVENTURE'S HELP
Rachel Davies — 95

Chapter 9
'THERE IS STILL A LOT OF POLLUTION IN THERE': UNDOING VIOLENT IDEOLOGIES, UNDOING THE SELF
Heather M. DuBois — 105

Chapter 10
READING SIMONE WEIL IN EAST LONDON: DESTITUTION, DECREATION AND THE HISTORY OF FORCE
Anna Rowlands — 113

Chapter 11
REFLECTIONS ON SUFFERING AND BIPOLAR DISORDER: THREE FORMS OF SUFFERING
John Swinton — 133

Chapter 12
SHOULD I LOVE MY TUMOUR?
Andrew Graystone — 147

Chapter 13
DEPRESSIVE SUFFERING AS TRAGIC SUFFERING: THEOLOGICAL INSIGHTS AND TRAJECTORIES
Jessica Coblentz — 155

Chapter 14
THE SEDUCTIONS OF KENOSIS
Karen Kilby — 163

Chapter 15
ON VULNERABILITY
Linn Tonstad — 175

Chapter 16
LIVING SACRIFICE: IS THERE A NON-PATHOLOGICAL WAY OF LIVING SUFFERING AS SACRIFICE?
Paul D. Murray — 189

Index — 207

CONTRIBUTORS

Dorothea H. Bertschmann is Tutorial Fellow of Biblical Studies at the College of the Resurrection, Mirfield, and Honorary Fellow in the Department of Theology and Religion, Durham University, UK.
d.h.bertschmann@dur.ac.uk

Jessica Coblentz is Assistant Professor of Religious Studies at Saint Mary's College (Notre Dame, IN), USA.
jessica.coblentz@gmail.com

Rachel Davies is a research fellow in the Institute for Religion and Critical Inquiry at Australian Catholic University, Australia.
rachelannemariedavies@gmail.com

Heather M. DuBois is Gannon Post-doctoral Fellow at Florida State University, USA.
hdubois@fsu.edu

Andrew Graystone is a visiting fellow at St. John's College, Durham, UK.
andrew@mediafutures.info

Edward Howells is Senior Lecturer at the University of Roehampton, UK.
eddie.howells@roehampton.ac.uk

Karen Kilby is Bede Professor of Catholic Theology in the Department of Theology and Religion at Durham University, UK.
karen.kilby@durham.ac.uk

Bernard McGinn is Naomi Shenstone Donnelley Professor Emeritus of Historical Theology and of the History of Christianity in the Divinity School and the Committees on Medieval Studies and on General Studies at the University of Chicago, USA.
bmcginn@uchicago.edu

Paul D. Murray is Professor of Systematic Theology in the Department of Theology and Religion at Durham University, UK.
paul.murray@durham.ac.uk

Rik Van Nieuwenhove is Associate Professor of Medieval Thought in the Department of Theology and Religion at Durham University, UK.
rik.van-nieuwenhove@durham.ac.uk

Anna Rowlands is St Hilda Associate Professor of Catholic Social Thought & Practice in the Department of Theology and Religion at Durham University, UK.
Anna.rowlands@durham.ac.uk

John Swinton is Chair in Divinity and Religious Studies at the University of Aberdeen, UK.
j.swinton@abdn.ac.uk

Gabrielle Thomas is Lecturer in Early Christianity and Anglican Studies at Yale Divinity School, U.S.A.
Gabrielle.thomas@yale.edu

Siiri Toiviainen Rø is a post-doctoral researcher at the Centre of Excellence in Reason and Religious Recognition, University of Helsinki, Finland.
siiri.toiviainen@helsinki.fi

Linn Tonstad is Associate Professor of Systematic Theology at Yale Divinity School, USA.
Linn.tonstad@yale.edu

Logan Williams is a PhD student and teaching assistant in the Department of Theology and Religion at Durham University, UK.
Logan.williams@durham.ac.uk

INTRODUCTION

Karen Kilby and Rachel Davies

Is suffering a topic for reflection in Christian theology? It is familiar as part of the territory of philosophers of religion as they wrestle with the problem of evil and of pastoral theologians writing about mourning, lament and the accompaniment of those who are afflicted. But when one turns to the central themes of systematic theology – themes like sin, grace, creation, salvation, eschatology, Trinity, Christology and so on – suffering is not typically on anyone's list.

This volume is motivated by the belief that Christian theology can benefit from paying more direct and explicit attention to suffering, in part because implicit construals of the nature and value of suffering and loss may already be shaping theological positions in significant and unacknowledged ways. The aim, then, is to consider afresh the problem of how to think about suffering, its status in Christian thought and theology, and where it belongs in relation to such things as love, grace, God and meaning. We hope this volume will take the discussion beyond both familiar concerns with theodicy and well-worn debates around divine impassibility, and that it will do so through a variety of lenses, drawing on biblical, historical, practical, political and systematic theology.

The book can be divided into two broad sections. Chapters 1–8 represent a roughly chronological series of essays on specific theological texts and figures, beginning with the New Testament (Bertschmann and Williams), and continuing through the patristic period (Toiviainen Rø, Thomas), and the medieval, early modern and modern periods (McGinn, Van Nieuwenhove, Howells, Davies). Main figures discussed include Paul, Gregory of Nyssa, Gregory of Nazianzus, Aquinas, Bonaventure, John of the Cross and Mother Teresa, while McGinn offers a helpful overview of figures from the seventh century onwards.

Chapters 9–16 deal with more political, practical and systematic concerns. DuBois and Rowlands explore concepts of asceticism, purgation, affliction and decreation in relation to political theology. Swinton, Graystone and Coblentz focus on first-person narratives of mental and physical illness and examine ways of interpreting experiences of suffering. Finally, Kilby, Tonstad and Murray explore how the uncritical affirmation of certain theological tropes and intuitions can inappropriately valourize suffering, and they argue for more cautious thinking about kenosis (Kilby) and vulnerability (Tonstad), and a fundamentally reimagined conception of 'offering up' suffering (Murray).

The volume is anything but comprehensive. It is not a handbook so much as a series of explorations. As one might expect with a group of explorers, furthermore, we are not all going in the same direction, and we do not all necessarily agree with each other. As editors we are confident, however, that the diversity of views combined with the fundamental intellectual and spiritual seriousness of our contributors come together to produce a rich and stimulating whole.

This book has its origins in the Love and Suffering Project, an initiative sponsored by the Congregation of La Retraite in England and Ireland and headed by Karen Kilby, Bede Professor within the Centre for Catholic Studies at Durham University. As part of the project, an international conference was organized at Ushaw College, Durham, in January 2018, entitled *Suffering, Diminishment and the Christian Life*. The present volume offers a selection of papers from the conference in expanded form. The editors offer their sincerest thanks to the Congregation of La Retraite, the Centre for Catholic Studies at Durham University, the staff of Ushaw College and all those who presented papers or assisted with the conference in practical ways. They also wish to thank Wanda Thompson for providing the cover art, Joshua Mobley and Fiona Bradley for their assistance in preparing the final manuscript, and Chris Brennan for his help with the index.

Chapter 1

SUFFERING, SIN AND DEATH IN PAUL

Dorothea H. Bertschmann

Paul is famous for his work not only as a missionary and apostle to the Gentiles but also as the apostle of suffering, who endured great hardship for the sake of the Gospel.[1] Paul talks about these sufferings from the first to the last of his letters.[2] He mentions the θλίψεις, the tribulations, which threaten to unsettle his young converts in Thessaloniki (1 Thess. 3.1-5), and he talks about the privilege of being able to suffer for Christ to the church in Philippi, especially in Phil. 3.10-11, where he states, 'I want to know Christ and the power of his resurrection and the sharing of his sufferings by becoming like him in his death, if somehow I may attain the resurrection from the dead.'

In 2 Corinthians we see Paul defend himself against charges of being a less-than-impressive apostle, afflicted with numerous sufferings and weaknesses. In a paradoxical move he wears these hardships and sufferings as a badge of honour: they reflect and embody his proclamation of the crucified Lord. All the floggings, beatings, shipwrecks, dangerous journeys, sleepless nights, all the hunger, thirst, cold, the destitution ('nakedness'), pressure, persecution and worrying about the churches (cf. 2 Cor. 11.22-33) arise from Paul's unique vocation as the apostle to the Gentiles.

But how does Paul make sense of the sufferings his converts undergo? In Phil. 1.29 Paul calls suffering for Christ a privilege graciously granted by God. But could suffering also be good for something in an instrumental sense?

---

1. This fact is preserved and remembered in later traditions about Paul beginning with Acts, where at Paul's conversion and calling God says to Ananias: 'I will show him (Paul) how much he must suffer for my name' (Acts 9.16).

2. 1 Thessalonians is almost universally assumed to be Paul's first letter, written between 49 and 52 CE. His last letter might be Philippians, which was possibly written from a prison in Ephesus or Rome, with Paul awaiting his verdict in the early 60s. The tradition of the suffering apostle is continued in the letters whose authenticity is disputed (cf. Col. 4.18, or the striking statement of 'completing what is lacking in Christ's afflictions for the sake of his body' in Col. 1.24 as well as 2 Tim. 2.9).

Various traditions have related suffering to the growth of ethical qualities or virtues.[3] In an important variation of this, the Christian spiritual tradition sometimes sees suffering as a painful but benevolent divine intervention which leads to the *mortification of the flesh*, where the flesh is seen as the site of sinful desires. We already find this notion in 1 Pet. 4.1, where the author writes, 'For whoever has suffered in the flesh has finished with sin.' The notion of suffering as παιδεία, as fatherly discipline, which is necessary for growth, is related to this motif.[4]

We might expect Paul, who seems to have a critical view of the 'flesh, and its passions and desires' (Gal. 5.24, similarly Rom. 13.14), to have a close affinity to this mortification of the flesh tradition. In this study I will test this proposition by looking closely at Paul's participation language of 'dying with Christ' and 'suffering with Christ' respectively, focusing on Paul's letter to the Romans. I will conclude that Paul's 'dying with' discourse must not be fused too quickly with his 'suffering with' discourse. In a second step I will argue that the ongoing susceptibility of the body to sin and death *might* open the door more widely to notions of mortification. In a final section I will argue, however, that this possibility is ultimately not followed up by Paul. Instead he discusses suffering within a discourse of tragic mortality and hope. Put differently, Paul does not follow the route towards a concept of mortification, despite some elements in his theology pointing in that direction.

Before we turn to our key texts, a brief comment on Paul's participation language is needed.

'Dying with' and 'suffering with'

Paul is famous for his dense statements about the death and resurrection of Christ on behalf of humanity. There is something in these salvific events which is universal and cosmic and precedes an individual's response.

Within the letter to the Romans, which is our special focus, Paul unfolds this especially clearly in Romans 5, where he stresses that Christ died for us 'when we were still sinners' (5.8), or died for us 'when we were still enemies' (5.10), and where he paints Christ with cosmic brush-strokes as the last Adam, who undoes the fall of the first Adam and brings about a new humanity (5.12-21).

But successive waves of scholarship have recognized that Paul has a further mode of speaking of Christ's death and resurrection, speaking of them as something

---

3. Cf. D. H. Bertschmann, '"What Does not Kill Me Makes Me Stronger" – Paul and Epictetus on the Correlation of Virtues and Suffering', *Catholic Biblical Quarterly*, forthcoming 2019.

4. We find an explicit reference in Heb. 12.3-11, where the author comments on Prov. 3.11-12 approvingly in vv. 5-6: 'My child, do not regard lightly the discipline of the Lord, or lose heart when you are punished by him; for the Lord disciplines those whom he loves, and chastises every child whom he accepts.'

believers share in and partake of. This way of talking about a very personal union between Christ and the believer has sometimes been labelled Paul's mysticism, as in Albert Schweitzer's pioneering work, and has been more recently discussed in terms of 'participation language', 'conformity' and even 'theosis'.[5] In this chapter, I will use what I take to be the least charged term, namely 'participation'.

Participation language in Paul is indicated by the Greek prefix συν in the text, meaning 'with' or 'together'. Paul famously talks about being co-crucified, or crucified with Christ, in Gal. 2.19. In Romans 6 and 8 he talks both of 'dying with Christ' and of 'suffering with Christ'.[6] These statements clearly have in common that they both describe an aspect of union with Christ. Furthermore, they have similar structures: identification with Christ in something negative leads on to identification with Christ in something positive, with a certain inner dynamic expressed in conditional or final constructions. In Rom. 6.8 this is stated as, εἰ δὲ **ἀπεθάνομεν** <u>σὺν Χριστῷ</u>, πιστεύομεν ὅτι καὶ <u>συζήσομεν</u> αὐτῷ (if we have died with Christ, we believe that we will also live together with him). Romans 8.17 reads, εἴπερ συμπάσχομεν ἵνα καὶ συνδοξασθῶμεν (since or if we suffer with him, so that we will be glorified with him). But are these structural parallels akin to mathematical parallels, which never meet? Or do we have overlapping and intersecting concepts? Is *dying with* expressed and lived out through *suffering with*?

Both great pioneers of Pauline Christ-mysticism/participation language, Schweitzer and Tannehill, indeed see 'suffering with' as synonymous with 'dying with'. Schweitzer dedicates one chapter in his influential *The Mysticism of St Paul* to 'Suffering as a Mode of Manifestation of the Dying with Christ'.[7] He states that 'the dying which the believer experiences with Christ is made manifest in suffering which destroys, or tends to destroy, his life'.[8] Schweitzer furthermore

---

5. Cf. A. Schweitzer, *The Mysticism of Paul the Apostle*, trans. William Montgomery (London: Black, 1931) and E. Schweizer, 'Die "Mystik" des Sterbens und Auferstehens mit Christus bei Paulus', in *Beiträge zur Theologie des Neuen Testaments* (Zürich: TVZ, 1970), 183–203 for some older and classical contributions. Michael Gorman has utilized notions of conformity and theosis in his work to describe Paul's theological vision (e.g. M. J. Gormann, *Cruciformity: Paul's Narrative Spirituality of the Cross* (Grand Rapids: Eerdmans, 2001; M. J. Gormann, *Inhabiting the Cruciform God: Kenosis, Justification and Theosis in Paul's Narrative Soteriology* (Grand Rapids: Eerdmans, 2009). An important voice is G. Macaskill, *Union with Christ in the New Testament* (Oxford: Oxford University Press, 2013), who gives much needed theological clarification to the concepts of participation and theosis. See especially his first chapter for a helpful overview of Pauline scholarship on participation language. For another important proposal, compare D. G. Powers, *Salvation through Participation: An Examination of the Notion of the Believers' Corporate Unity with Christ in Early Christian Soteriology* (CBET 29; Leuven: Peeters, 2001).

6. Cf. the classical study of R. C. Tannehill, *Dying and Rising with Christ* (BNZW 32; Berlin: de Gruyter, 1967).

7. Schweitzer, *Mysticism*, 141–59.

8. Ibid., 141.

explicitly claims that 'Paul treats all suffering as dying, and characterizes it by that term.'[9] Tannehill refers to 'dying with' as the once-and-for-all starting point of the Christian life, whereas 'suffering with' describes the daily outworking of grace in a believer's life. According to Tannehill, 'The past dying with Christ and the present dying with Christ in suffering are not two unrelated things, but the same thing taking place on two different levels.'[10]

Against these weighty voices, in this chapter I want to suggest that though these concepts are indeed not unrelated, they are not synonymous either; that while Paul might treat all suffering as dying, he does not treat all dying as suffering, at least not in Romans 6 and 8.

Romans 6.8: 'Dying with'

In Rom. 5.12-21 Paul has sketched how Adam's trespass resulted in the universal rule of sin, which leads to death: ἐβασίλευσεν ἡ ἁμαρτία ἐν τῷ θανάτῳ (sin ruled as a king through death) is how Paul sums it up. This is contrasted with the rule of grace through righteousness, which leads into (εἰς) eternal life through Jesus Christ (5.21). The same opposites of death and life, with their associates sin and grace or sin and righteousness, continue to structure chapter 6. Paul writes in Romans 6:

> What then are we to say? Should we continue in sin in order that grace may abound? ² By no means! How can we who died to sin go on living in it? ³ Do you not know that all of us who have been baptized into Christ Jesus were baptized into his death? ⁴ Therefore we have been buried with him by baptism into death, so that, just as Christ was raised from the dead by the glory of the Father, so we too might walk in newness of life.
> ⁵ For if we have been united with him in a death like his, we will certainly be united with him in a resurrection like his. ⁶ We know that our old self was crucified with him so that the body of sin might be destroyed, and we might no longer be enslaved to sin. ⁷ For whoever has died is freed from sin. ⁸ But if we have died with Christ, we believe that we will also live with him. ⁹ We know that Christ, being raised from the dead, will never die again; death no longer has dominion over him. ¹⁰ The death he died, he died to sin, once for all; but the life he lives, he lives to God. ¹¹ So you also must consider yourselves dead to sin and alive to God in Christ Jesus.[11]

The text presupposes an understanding of baptism as the individual believer's identification or unification with Christ. Participation is expressed in two ways

---

9. Ibid.
10. Tannehill, *Dying and Rising*, 117.
11. All biblical quotations are taken from the NRSV.

here. On the one hand we have vocabulary which compares or identifies the believers' fate with Christ's: believers are experiencing and embracing patterns of death and life *just like* Christ (ὥσπερ...οὕτως, v. 4.); they share in the likeness/ ὁμοίωμα of his death (v. 5); and just as Christ died once for all and lives now to God (οὕτως in v. 11), believers have to consider themselves dead to sin and alive to God. On the other hand, the union of believers with Christ is expressed in σύν-language. They are said to have been buried with Christ (συνετάφημεν, v. 4), and they are grown together with him (σύμφυτοι) and co-crucified (συνεσταυρώθη, v. 6). They have died with him and will or may live together with him (ἀπεθάνομεν <u>σὺν Χριστῷ</u>; <u>συζήσομεν</u> αὐτῷ, v. 8).[12] All these layers of sharing in Christ's death and life are predicated upon the fact that believers have been baptized *into* or *onto* Christ (v. 3).[13]

What then does the identification or unification with Christ's *death* mean? It seems reasonably clear that believers die symbolically or sacramentally in baptism, whereas Christ's death includes the physical, biological reality. The concept of death, like the concept of life, is complex and multi-layered throughout Romans 5–8, and we next have to look at the various meanings of death and life in the text.[14]

De Boer concludes his study in Jewish Apocalyptic Eschatology by distinguishing three levels of 'death'. The first is physical demise, the end of a human life. In continuity with Old Testament notions of death, the separation of a dead person from God's presence is underlined. De Boer rightly states that 'all other meanings that death may have are predicated on this primary understanding of death'.[15] Secondly, death can have moral connotations. A person can be morally or spiritually dead, even while they are alive.[16] This notion is well known in wisdom literature, where 'the ways of death' are contrasted with the 'way of life'.[17] The third level of understanding, in de Boer's taxonomy, is 'eternal or eschatological

---

12. A minority of manuscripts have the subjunctive instead of the future form.

13. For a defence of *onto* Christ as shorthand for 'in the name of Christ', compare M. Wolter, *Der Brief an die Römer* (EKK VI/1: Röm 1-8; Neukirchen-Vluyn/Ostfildern: Neukirchener/Patmos, 2014), 371.

14. A lot of scholarly interest has been generated by the different temporal layers of life: Should this new life in the here and now be understood ethically, as the verb περιπατεῖν /to walk in v. 4 seems to suggest? Or is it the bodily resurrection life, as implied in v.5? Compare, for example, J. D. G. Dunn, *Romans 1-8* (WBC 38a; Dallas: Word Books, 1988), 330-1.

15. M. C. de Boer, *The Defeat of Death: Apocalyptic Eschatology in 1 Corinthians 15 and Romans 5* (JSNT Supp 22; Sheffield: Sheffield Academic Press, 1988), 84.

16. Wolter rightly points out that Paul settles for the more conventional 'conversion language' of life and death in Rom. 6.13 where, unlike in Rom. 6.3-11, Paul describes the old pre-Christian life as death (Wolter, *Römerbrief*, 391).

17. Compare de Boer, *Defeat of Death*, 61. De Boer lists among others Sir. 15.15, 17; Prov. 2.18, 14.12, 21.6; Jas. 1.15; Matt. 7.13.

death'. He stresses that in apocalyptic dualism, 'physical death and moral death are prefigurations of perdition, of eschatological death'.[18]

Clifton Black offers a similar and nuanced range of options of interpretations of 'death' and 'life' which, he claims, are all present in Romans 5–8 in various combinations: broadly speaking death can be seen as either completion or depletion, both in the Jewish and Graeco-Roman world.[19] Seen as depletion, death can be understood as a consequence of or punishment for sin, increasingly so in inter-testamental writings.[20] Death can encompass physical, mythological and metaphorical levels.[21]

If we make use of this taxonomy in our reading of Romans 5 and 6 it first becomes clear that for Paul, language about Christ's death and life points to the concrete events of crucifixion and resurrection. But this is not the only level of meaning. These events within time and space also have far-reaching eschatological and cosmic reverberations, which transcend the physical demise and restoration of one individual. This far-reaching dimension of Christ's death and resurrection is spelled out particularly clearly in Paul's thought about Christ being the second or last Adam.[22] But in what way does Paul use Christ's death in a moral or spiritual sense? Within Romans, 'death' has so far been introduced as the penalty for sin (1.32). Christ's death, or rather, perhaps in metonymic speech, his blood, has some atoning or sacrificial function (3.25), and Christ is characterized as having died for the godless and for enemies in 5.6 and 5.10. There is clearly an element of vicarious substitution in the latter two texts.[23] How then, do believers identify with or participate in Christ's death, which happened on behalf of, or even as a means of substitution for, them? It is possible to explain this identification, as enacted in baptism, as an identification with God's verdict expressed in Christ's death.[24] But

---

18. de Boer, *Defeat of Death*, 84.

19. C. C. Black II, 'Pauline Perspectives on Death in Romans 5-8', *JBL* 103, no. 3 (1984): 413–33 (418–19). The paradigm of completion tends to see death as natural, or as release from suffering, or opportunity for witness and heroism. Death as depletion regards death as something secondary to God's good design, as a powerful mythical ruler and as the diminishment of life.

20. Among many other passages, Black mentions Wis. 2.23-24 where the author states that 'God created man for incorruption and made him the image of his own eternity but by the devil's envy death came into the world and those who belong to his party experience him'.

21. Black, 'Pauline Perspectives', 419.

22. Compare Paul's Adam–Christ typologies in Romans 5 and 1 Cor. 15.42-49 as well as statements such as 2 Cor. 5.14: 'One has died for all, therefore all have died'.

23. Compare S. Gathercole, *Defending Substitution: An Essay on Atonement in Paul* (Grand Rapids: Baker Academics, 2015), especially chapter 3. Black notes both the 'Semitic conception of death as payment owed to God for sin' and 'the classical Greek motif of the Heroic death' (Black, 'Pauline Perspectives', 420).

24. Paul hints at Christ's death as being God 'condemning sin in the flesh' in Rom. 8.3.

then we would somehow expect Paul to say, 'Christ died for you so that you will no longer have to die.' Instead Paul emphasizes that *Christ* who has been raised from the dead dies no more (6.9).

Paul is interested in the mutually exclusive notions of death and life in this chapter. He gives the received tradition of baptism as dying and rising with Christ a twist by stressing the notion of death *to sin* as the radical and irreversible separation from sin. While the notion of Jesus having to die to sin or needing to be justified or released (δικαιόω, v. 7) from its power through his death is awkward from a Christological perspective, death serves as the perfect paradigm of radical separation from one power, the power of sin, in order to live in another, namely righteousness.[25] Just like Christ, who died ἐφάπαξ, once and for all (v. 10), believers have died once and for all with Christ to sin.[26] Just as Christ, who died and was raised, 'dies no more' (v. 9) and is no longer under the power of death, believers, too, cannot return to the realm of sin and death anymore.

When Paul uses participation language in the first part of Romans 6, he is precisely interested in the *result* of the 'dying with', which was enacted in baptism with great finality, and precisely *not* in a process of ongoing dying, which might be understood as having been inaugurated in baptism. Dying and living are construed as *simultaneous but mutually exclusive relational realities*: Believers are dead to sin and alive to God (v. 11). Death with Christ closes the door 'once and for all' to death, sin and the law and opens the door to life, righteousness and grace.

It is certainly no accident that instead of using 'drowning' metaphors Paul reuses the expression of 'co-crucifixion' (compare Gal. 2.19 and 4.25) in Rom.6.6 to talk about this radical 'either-or' reality of the believers. 'The fact that the old human being must "die" or be crucified with Christ (Rom. 6.6), in order to inherit the new, points to the absolutely mutually exclusive nature of the old age of sin and death and the new age of righteousness and life as well as the radical discontinuity between them.'[27]

'Dying with Christ', read as 'dying to sin', thus marks out radical separation from the rulers of the old age so vividly characterized in Romans 5: sin and, by implication, death. Like two negatives resulting in a positive, death to the negative power of sin is a good death. It simply bangs the door shut in the face of bad death, read as separation from God.[28] *This* death separates from death in all its forms: spiritual, moral and eschatological, and ultimately physical death, by moving the believers on the right side of the eschatological balance sheet. All these aspects fuse, from this perspective of being simultaneously 'dead to sin, alive to God'. As

---

25. The word ἀποθνήσκειν followed by a dative expresses separation and definitive termination (cf. the examples in Wolter, *Römerbrief*, 369–70.

26. Note the burial image in v. 4, which underlines the finality of death.

27. de Boer, *Defeat of Death*, 176.

28. Paul will do a similar thing later on in Romans 6, when he plays with notions of freedom and slavery, intrinsically good and bad respectively, and states that there is a 'good slavery', understood as slavery to God (Rom 6.15-23).

de Boer has argued powerfully, 'Believers are not put on the way *to* life, but on the way *of* life.'[29]

All this resists the notion of reading 'dying with' as a continuous and life-long linear process, which eventually leads to (eternal) life. Paul does not, in other words, counsel a daily death to sin, a thing which may or may not include suffering to assist with that purpose. On the contrary, all that is needed is a firm cognitive alignment to this new reality, itself a given: 'Consider yourselves as those who are dead to sin, but alive to God' (Rom. 6.11).[30]

This 'aliveness' has an ethical dimension in the present (Rom. 6.4b) and is ordered towards eternal life as the charisma, the gracious gift of God (Rom. 6.23). But this ethical aspect is not unfolded in a linear way as a cause which leads intrinsically to eternal life.[31] Instead we have a juxtaposition at every step of the way in Paul: If you are in one sphere, the sphere of righteousness and life, you cannot be in the other any longer.

In short, the notion of 'dying with Christ' as a radical once-and-for-all event in the past makes it harder to understand 'suffering with Christ' as the continuous outworking of this death. It is not the notion of 'diminishment' which is foregrounded, but the notion of 'separation', which is in turn specified as separation from a negative.

Romans 8.13: 'Putting to Death'

In the second half of Romans 6 Paul goes on to spell out the consequences of this good death with its simultaneous 'good life', understood as life for God, by sketching out Christian existence as wholehearted, embodied and exclusive

---

29. de Boer, *Defeat of Death*, 175.

30. For propositions of a gradual moral improvement and process from death to life, compare I. A. Morales, O. P., 'Baptism and Union with Christ', in *"In Christ" in Paul*, ed. M. J. Thate, K. J. Vanhoozer and C. R. Campbell (WUNT 2 384; Tübingen: Mohr Siebeck, 2014), 157–79; and B. Byrne, 'Living out the Righteousness of God: The Contribution of Rom. 6.1-8.13 to an Understanding of Paul's Ethical Presuppositions', *CBQ* 43 (1981): 557-8. The linear view has a strong foothold in Paul's statement that the advantage of slavery to God is sanctification, whose *telos* is eternal life (6.22). But this statement is instantly clarified by Paul's assymetric formulation that 'the wages of sin is death, but the free gift (charisma) of God is eternal life' (6.23).

31. Paul is not troubled by the ongoing reality of physical death at this stage nor does he feel a need to dampen believers' enthusiasm. It is as if Paul is looking out from a British manor house, where the viewer's gaze is seamlessly drawn from the park and garden to the meadows outside it, thanks to an invisible boundary between them (a ditch called the 'ha-ha'). Paul is not denying that the ditch of physical death is still there, but in the grip of life in Christ and for God, even the distinction between being physically dead and alive is greatly relativized (Rom. 14.8).

service for God, where believers present their members to God as instruments of righteousness (6.13). The either-or structure is kept in place all the way to the end of the chapter.³² In Rom. 7.1-6 Paul continues to play with the notion of death and life through the example of a married wife who gains freedom from her husband through his death (vv. 1-3). In a somewhat demanding mental leap, he portrays believers as those who themselves have died to the law, in order to belong to 'another one', Jesus Christ, who was raised from the dead, so that they might bear fruit for God (v. 4). Death is once again a good death, read as liberation from 'what held us captive' (v. 6), with an emphasis on separation, not diminishment or mortification.

The rest of the chapter, 7.7-25, is devoted to an excursus explaining why God's holy law could work death for human beings. The reason is sin, which hijacked and abused the law in its service, disabling human agency altogether, despite human goodwill: 'I was once alive apart from the law, but when the commandment came, sin revived and I died, and the very commandment that promised life proved to be death to me' (7.9-10). Despite all the paradoxes of the 'liveliness' of sin bringing death, death and life are used in a more conventional way as far as the human agents are concerned. It is not the 'good death' as separation–liberation which is emphasized here, but the moral and ultimately eschatological death read as diminishment and separation from what is *good*, most of all God.

The person sold into slavery under sin (Rom. 7.14) experiences the terrible dilemma that they can will what is good but not do it (7.17). The section culminates in the cry of despair: 'Wretched man that I am! Who will rescue me from this body of death?' (7.24).³³

It is the σῶμα, the body, which brings a note of complexity in the clear-cut landscape of either-or, of the simultaneously existing states of 'dead to sin but alive to God' (6.11), which lead to mutually exclusive allegiances: the body, which has died to the slave-master of sin, is now in the service of God, as Paul is at pains to explain in 6.15-23. And yet while the 'body of sin' was destroyed (6.6) in a once-and-for-all action, Paul still feels a need to exhort his congregation not to

---

32. In the personal experience of Christian converts, this 'either-or' structure presents itself as 'once-now' structure (cf. Rom. 6.17-18).

33. For an intriguing reading of this much-discussed passage, compare Beverly Roberts Gaventa, 'The Shape of the "I": The Psalmist, the Gospel, and the Speaker in Romans 7', in *Apocalyptic Paul: Cosmos and Anthropos in Romans 5-8*, ed. B. R. Gaventa (Waco: Baylor University Press, 2013), 77–91. Gaventa suggests reading the 'I' as the 'I' of the psalms, especially the psalms of lament, which invite identification. Eastman further develops this into a reading of the passage as performative speech, where the audience is drawn into reliving their hopeless situation apart from Christ (Susan Eastman, 'Strengthening the Ego for Service: The Pastoral Purpose of Rom. 7.7-25', paper given at the Colloquium Oecumenicum Paulinum, Rome, 11–15 September 2018). Used by kind permission of the author.

let sin reign in their mortal bodies, which are the seat of passions (6.12). Like the 'body of sin', the 'body of death' in the cry of despair (7.24) must be understood as relational: we should not understand it as being inherently sinful or inherently dead, but as being in the service of and under the power of sin (ἁμαρτία) and its ally death (θάνατος). In Rom. 8.3, Paul describes how God has dealt decisively with sin, by 'sending his own Son in the likeness of sinful flesh, and to deal with sin' (8.3b). 'He condemned sin in the flesh' (8.3b). Sin is mentioned one last time in 8.10. After this, it does not make an appearance again in the letter.

But one problematic category continues to make an appearance in juxtaposition with πνεῦμα (spirit), and this is the σάρξ (flesh). I quote chapter 8.1-14 in full, highlighting the juxtapositions of death/life and flesh/Spirit, as well as the rare uses of σῶμα (body):

> There is therefore now no condemnation for those who are in Christ Jesus. ²For the law of the **Spirit** of **life** in Christ Jesus has set you free from the law of **sin** and of **death**. ³For God has done what the law, weakened by *the flesh*, could not do: by sending his own Son in the likeness of *sinful flesh*, and to deal with **sin**, he condemned **sin** in the *flesh*, ⁴so that the just requirement of the law might be fulfilled in us, who walk not according to *the flesh* but according to **the Spirit**.⁵ For those who live according to the *flesh* set their minds on the things of *the flesh*, but those who live according to the **Spirit** set their minds on the things of **the Spirit**. ⁶To set the mind on *the flesh* is **death**, but to set the mind on **the Spirit** is **life and peace**. ⁷For this reason the mind that is set on *the flesh* is hostile to God; it does not submit to God's law – indeed it cannot, ⁸and those who are in *the flesh* cannot please God.
>
> ⁹But you are not in *the flesh*; you are in **the Spirit**, since **the Spirit** of God dwells in you. Anyone who does not have **the Spirit** of Christ does not belong to him. ¹⁰But if Christ is in you, though <u>the body</u> is **dead** because of **sin**, the **Spirit** is **life** because of righteousness. ¹¹If the **Spirit** of him who raised Jesus **from the dead** dwells in you, he who raised Christ **from the dead** will give life to your <u>mortal bodies</u> also through his **Spirit** that dwells in you.
>
> ¹²So then, brothers and sisters, we are debtors, not to *the flesh*, to live according to the *flesh* – ¹³for if you **live** according to *the flesh*, you will **die**; but if by the **Spirit** you **put to death** the deeds of <u>the body</u>, you will **live**.

σάρξ is not synonymous with the σῶμα, but also not completely independent of it either. As Susan Eastman points out, the body 'is qualified both negatively through affiliation with death, sin, the flesh and positively through affiliation with Christ and the "body of Christ"'.³⁴ 'Flesh', on the other hand, 'is closely allied with bodily

---

34. Susan Grove Eastman, *Paul and the Person: Reframing Paul's Anthropology* (Grand Rapids: Eerdmans, 2017), 86–7.

life, usually (but not always) in a negative sense'.³⁵ The counterpart of the flesh is the Spirit, the πνεῦμα. This πνεῦμα is God's gift. It is both the new context the believers inhabit and the divine power dwelling in their concrete, mortal bodies, enabling them to obey God's commandment by walking or reasoning according to the Spirit (κατὰ πνεῦμα).

When Paul juxtaposes walking/περιπατεῖν or reasoning/φρονεῖν according to the flesh or Spirit, he uses the concepts of Spirit and Flesh almost as two spheres, which dominate and shape the human being, their thoughts and deeds, in a way which leads towards either death or life.³⁶ Death and life are once again deployed in their comprehensive moral and eschatological sense: bodies, which follow the lead of 'death', morally understood, are moving towards ultimate, eschatological death. But while Paul upholds his stark either-or language by correlating Spirit with life and juxtaposing it with flesh and death, there is a more ambiguous category, the body, which remains linked to the 'weakness of the flesh', both in its moral and physical sense.³⁷

While in a sense the body shares and expresses the fundamental reorientation of the person as 'alive to God' (Rom. 6.11) and with its members being 'slaves of righteousness' (6.18) after having died to sin (6.8), it remains vulnerable to death and sin – indeed it can even be said to be 'dead on account of sin' (8.10).³⁸ This is because the existence 'according to the Spirit' is lived out 'in the flesh'.³⁹

---

35. Ibid., 89: 'In all these instances – physical existence, kinship, and human limitation – *sarx* participated exclusively in what Paul calls 'the present evil age' (Gal.1.4). 'Through such participation, *sarx* denotes a realm of existence that is doomed to pass away'. Σάρξ in Paul denotes the earthly existence of living human beings, with a focus but no exclusive limitation to the physical aspect (cf. ThDNT, E. Schweizer, σάρξ, pp. 124–51 [125].)

36. Schweizer rightly points out that the dualism is never total by stating that 'the σάρξ never occurs as the subject of an action where it is not in the shadow of a statement about the work of the πνεῦμα, while the πνεῦμα on the other hand is often presented as an acting subject with or without σάρξ in the context' (ThDNT, σάρξ, 132).

37. The ἀσθένεια of the flesh can point to the limited human horizon of understanding (cf. Rom. 6.19), but the flesh can, more gravely, weaken and indeed disempower the law (Rom. 8.3a). Compare Matt. 26.41: 'The Spirit is willing, but the flesh is weak.'

38. This difficult phrase is much disputed. I follow Barclay's proposal to translate Paul's dual statement as *simul mortuus et vivens* in a significant alteration of Luther's famous statement (J. M. G. Barclay, *Paul and the Gift* (Grand Rapids: Eerdmans, 2015), 502). Barclay understands the Pauline 'on account of sin' in 8.10 'as a residue of their Adamic heritage' (ibid., 501); sin is 'not the believers' own present sin … but the sin of Adam and of their past, in a cosmos infected by sin and thereby doomed to death (5.11-21; 7.5, 7-11)' (ibid., 502, no. 15).

39. Note how for Paul the life ἐν σαρκί (in the flesh) (Gal. 2.20) can go together with the statement 'I have been crucified with Christ: it is no longer I that live but Christ in me' (Gal. 2.19b, 20a). Paul repeats the crucifixion statement in Gal. 5.24, saying that 'those who belong to Christ have crucified the σάρξ and its passions and desires'. But compare Rom. 8.9, where life 'in' the Spirit is set in juxtaposition to life 'according to the flesh'. In the latter case Paul wants to further emphasize the sense of flesh and spirit as separate spheres.

As Susan Eastman puts it, 'Bodies per se are not sinful, but insofar as bodily existence enmeshes persons in the realm of sin and death, it renders believers vulnerable to the power of sin.'[40]

Christian believers have thus died once and for all to the cruel slave-master sin and its ally, death. Their bodily existence within the body of Christ is the realm where their new allegiance and obedience is necessarily expressed.[41] But life in the body remains mortal in the sense of experiencing the physical weakness and pain of 'the flesh', read simply as human and finite existence, as well as remaining susceptible to the call of 'the flesh', read as the subject of sin. It seems that the incompatible realities of flesh and spirit are played out in the coexistence of the mortal body and the πνεῦμα, the latter inhabiting the former and assuring it of the promise of future resurrection life (Rom. 8.11): Paul can say that it is the mortal bodies (θνητὰ σώματα) which will be raised by the indwelling Spirit.[42] The fact that the simultaneous and mutually exclusive state of 'dead-to-sin/alive-to-God' is lived out in the highly ambiguous entity of the body, which is 'mortal' and therefore dangerously leaning into the side of sin and death, makes the notion of a continuous process of dying and even the notion of mortification a much stronger possible reading of Paul's discourse of death and life. Paul seems to lead the way in this direction when he counsels 'by the Spirit to put to death (θανατόω) the deeds of the body' (8.13).

Just as there was a good death, the once-and-for-all death to the power of sin, there is a good 'putting to death', which deals continuously with the allurement of life according to the flesh on the site of the body. It is astonishing that Paul counsels believers to kill the deeds of the body, without further qualification. In the context of Romans 8 these must refer to the body paying heed and expressing the patterns of the sinful flesh, not to any and all bodily activities.[43] But could this bring us close to a notion of mortification? Romans 8.13 certainly offers interpretative space to imagine both mental and ascetic practices in reining in the body.

40. Eastman, 'Strengthening the Ego for Service'.

41. 'The opposite of such fleshly existence is not a dematerialized "spiritual" life but bodily participation in the "body of Christ"' (Rom. 12.4-5; 1 Cor. 6.15; 12.12-27) (Eastman, *Person*, 91).

42. 'The crucial difference between the "body of death" in 7.24 and "mortal bodies" in 8.11, however, is that the Spirit of God who raised Christ from the dead dwells *corporately* among the community of believers, and therefore also in their mortal bodies (8.9,11)' (Eastman, 'Strengthening the Ego for Service').

43. 'In any case "body" has to be understood here as more or less equivalent to "flesh"' B. Byrne S. J., *Romans* (Sacra Pagina; Collegeville: Liturgical Press, 1996), 246. Dunn expresses the same puzzlement at the term σῶμα and suggests to take it as 'stylistic variant for the overloaded σάρξ' (Dunn, *Romans*, 449). Similarly Käsemann suggests that the σῶμα is not identical with σάρξ but 'is threatened by it, since the power of the flesh has a point of attack in our body, which is still dominated by the earthly' (E. Käsemann, *Commentary on Romans*, trans. G. W. Bromiley (Grand Rapids: Eerdmans, 1980), 226.

However, suffering has not been explicitly mentioned, neither in the admonition to 'kill the deeds of the body' nor from 6.1 to 8.11 at all. While Paul has pulled together death and sin very closely, he has simply not mentioned suffering. In fact, from 8.14 onwards Paul further follows the cue of the notion of 'Spirit', but shifts the weight of his discourse from sin, death and the flesh, to suffering and death. Just as their bodily existence renders believers vulnerable to 'the flesh', read as the stronghold of sin, it renders them vulnerable to suffering. Physical death casts its shadows on believers' lives through the painful experience of mortality and through the hostile violence that threatens them. Even if believers have died to sin once and for all they seem to continue to suffer. Could this suffering therefore be read as an ongoing actualization of 'dying with' Christ? On that note we turn to our last section.

Romans 8.17: Suffering with Christ

How is suffering connected with death? And what might suffering with Christ mean, compared to dying with Christ?

In the following we reproduce the text from Rom. 8.14-25. Expressions of 'Spirit', as the key expression in vv. 14-27 are highlighted in bold print. Expressions of participation are highlighted in bold italics. Expressions of suffering and of glory are underlined.

> [14] For all who are led by the **Spirit** of God are children of God. [15] For you did not receive a **spirit** of slavery to fall back into fear, but you have received a **spirit** of adoption. When we cry, 'Abba! Father!' [16] it is that very **Spirit** *bearing* witness with our **spirit** that we are children of God, [17] and if children, then heirs, heirs of God and joint heirs with Christ – if, in fact, <u>***we suffer with him***</u> so that we may also be <u>***glorified with him***</u>.[18] I consider that the <u>sufferings</u> of this present time are not worth comparing <u>with the glory</u> about to be revealed to us. [19] For the creation waits with eager longing for the revealing of the children of God; [20] for the creation was subjected to *futility*, not of its own will but by the will of the one who subjected it, in hope [21] that the creation itself will be set free from its bondage to *decay* and will obtain the <u>freedom of the glory</u> of the children of God. [22] We know that the whole creation has been ***groaning in labor pains*** ('groans together and is in pain together') until now; [23] and not only the creation, but we ourselves, who have the first fruits of **the Spirit**, groan inwardly while we wait for adoption, the redemption of our bodies. [24] For in hope we were saved. Now hope that is seen is not hope. For who hopes for what is seen? [25] But if we hope for what we do not see, we wait for it with patience. [26] Likewise the **Spirit** *helps* ('comes alongside us', *syn-antilambano*) us in our weakness; for we do not know how to pray as we ought, but that very **Spirit** intercedes with sighs too deep for words. [27] And God, who searches the heart, knows what is the mind of the **Spirit**, because the **Spirit** intercedes for the saints according to the will of God.

From v. 14 onwards the πνεῦμα, which was thus far one half of the contrasting pair of πνεῦμα and σάρξ, takes centre stage. Paul describes the πνεῦμα as the 'Spirit of sonship' or 'Spirit of adoption'.[44] This Spirit is both constitutive and expressive of the new status of the believers as children of God.[45] Unlike slaves, the 'sons' do not live in fear but in the assurance of being God's children. This assurance has a future component if the 'sons' view themselves as heirs also. They are God's heirs and joint heirs with Christ, whose sonship 'is presented as inherent, *sui generis*, constitutive of (but not identical to) the adoptive status of believers'.[46] In Rom. 8.16 participation language enters the picture again with its characteristic σύν-constructions, not always visible in the English translations. The Spirit *co-witnesses* (συμμαρτυρεῖ) to 'our spirit' (v.16), believers are *joint heirs*/συγκληρονόμοι (v.17). Paul's train of thought culminates in the conviction that 'if we suffer with him, we will also be glorified with him' (v.17). But what does this mean? Is suffering instrumental in order to reach glory? Is suffering the present expression of 'dying with Christ', giving it concrete shape in the everyday life of believers?

The εἴπερ doubtless expresses nuances of causality: If A is the case, then B follows.[47] However, this need not be read in a strictly conditional sense, which sees sufferings as somehow instrumental for future glory. We have to bear in mind that this is said to Christian believers who were likely familiar with suffering for the sake of their faith. Paul's tone is one of assurance.[48] Very intriguingly there is no object in the Greek, and most translations supply the phrase 'with him'. Such readings are certainly not forced, given the notion of 'joint heirs' at the beginning of the verse. Still, the missing object is intriguing: Susan Eastman suggests translating the verse, 'We suffer together ... so that we may be glorified together' (8.17), adding, 'All of this is *with* Christ. But it is also *with* each other.'[49]

There is indeed a grammatical and theological parallel between the two participation statements, 'dying with' and 'suffering with'. Each statement describes an aspect of the union between Christ and believers, seen as a linear development. But there is also an important difference. In the case of 'dying with', Paul emphasizes the once-and-for-all death *to sin*, which goes together with the continued

---

44. Compare the very similar thought in Gal. 4.6-7: 'God has sent the Spirit of his Son into our hearts, crying Abba, Father.'

45. Paul uses both the male υἱός/son and the more neutral τέκνα/children in vv. 14-17.

46. Macaskill, *Union with Christ in the New Testament*, 223.

47. Compare Blass-Debrunner-Rehkopf § 454. 2 ('kausale Nebenbedeutung').

48. This does not preclude a note of admonition to hold out, as a similar passage in Rom. 5.3-5 makes clear: 'Tribulation works endurance', says Paul – but even here the tone is one of joyful conviction, not of stern exhortation.

49. S. Eastman Grove, 'Oneself in Another. Participation and the Spirit in Romans 8', in *'In Christ' in Paul*, ed. M. J. Thate, K. J. Vanhoozer and C. R. Campbell (WUNT 2 384; Tübingen: Mohr Siebeck, 2014), 103-25 (115). Read this way, the meaning of συμπάσχομεν (suffering together) comes much closer to the only other occurrence of the verb in Paul in 1 Cor. 12.26: 'If one member suffers, all the members suffer together.'

simultaneous life to God – a life which might be accompanied by a continuous 'killing' of the deeds of the body. When Paul speaks about 'suffering with', there is no such simultaneous but mutually exclusive relatedness of suffering and glory: believers are not said to suffer in regard to sin and at the same time to be glorified in regard to God. Unlike 'death to sin', suffering does not become a 'good suffering', but remains negative. However, suffering is already the paradoxical token of future glory, because it is borne in union with Christ and with each other.[50] Suffering is already pulled under the dynamic salvific purposes of God. This dynamic is headed towards life and glory and is virtually unstoppable, just as the union with Christ is unbreakable. In the last and rightly cherished section of Romans 8 Paul revels in this unstoppable dynamic, which is rooted in the unbreakable union of the believers and Christ. When Paul says, 'Those he foreknew, he also predestined … those he predestined he also called, those he called he also justified, those he justified he also glorified' in vv. 29-30, he echoes his statement 'if Sons, then heirs' in v. 17, but roots believers' confidence even more deeply in God's own good pleasure, which will see them through all the way until glorification.[51] At the end of a long list of tribulations and sufferings, which are closely connected to physical death and diminishment, Paul sounds a note of great triumph by saying that 'nothing can separate us from the love of God, which is in Christ Jesus our Lord' (v. 39). Put positively 'all things', be they good or bad, have now been conscripted to serve towards what is good for those who love God (v. 28).

But this brings us back to our question of whether suffering – even if not good in and by itself – can serve some good, and whether this 'good' might be pictured as combatting sin, which still has a foothold in the flesh.

In this last section I will argue that whereas Paul pulled together sin and death very closely in Romans 6, but did not integrate suffering into the picture, from Rom. 8.17 onwards Paul pulls together suffering and death very closely, but leaves sin somewhat un-integrated. In fact, Paul's way of talking about death changes. In Rom. 8.17 he brings in a new key expression, which is δόξα (glory).[52] There is a clear shift in emphasis, away from the ethically coloured juxtaposition

---

50. Though Paul, unlike the author of 1 Peter (3.18), never says that 'Christ suffered for us', he can characterize his own sufferings as the 'sufferings of the Christ' (2 Cor. 1.5) or speak of 'the fellowship of his sufferings' in Phil. 3.10.

51. Scholars are puzzled by the past tense (aorist) of the verb 'glorify', since glory is normally seen as a future reality by Paul. I take it to express the unstoppable dynamic of God's good purposes of salvation.

52. Ben Blackwell distinguishes δόξα as an aspect of social status, read as honour, from δόξα as ontological glory. The latter, which is commonly associated with divine splendour in biblical scholarship, occurs frequently with connotations of incorruption and immortality in Romans (B. Blackwell, 'Immortal Glory and the Problem of Death in Romans 3.23', *JSNT* 32, no. 3 (2010): 285–308.

of Spirit and flesh, towards a lengthy meditation on suffering, hope and glory.[53] Present sufferings are correlated and contrasted with future glory in v. 17. Paul repeats this juxtaposition in Rom. 8.18, which is the opening thesis for a new train of thought: The present sufferings are 'not worthy' compared to the glory, which will be revealed in or among the believers.[54] These sufferings Paul talks about are characterized in v. 18 as the παθήματα τοῦ νῦν καιροῦ (the sufferings of the present time). The νῦν, the now, is the time, where God has acted in Christ (cf. 3.21), but it is also this 'present evil aeon', as Paul calls it elsewhere in Gal. 1.4. The believers' sufferings result precisely from this clash of forces in the last days. We could therefore say that sufferings are broadly connected to sin insofar as they are inflicted by a hostile and sinful world.[55]

We clearly have tropes of an apocalyptic world view, which speaks of 'us' and 'them', of intense suffering before vindication and restoration arrive for the suffering elect.[56] But Paul does not go down this route any further, instead unfolding a deep meditation on believers as sighing and groaning alongside and together with the whole of creation, κτίσις (8.22, 23).[57] Just as the whole creation groans together and is in labour pain together, believers groan too within themselves (8.22-23).[58]

---

53. John Yates writes that from Rom. 8.12-13 onwards Paul's interest 'shifts to focus not on the contrast between present life and former life, but on the tension between present life and future, glorified life' John W. Yates, *The Spirit and Creation in Paul* (WUNT 2.251; Tübingen: Mohr Siebeck, 2008), 152.

54. This repetition of the theme makes the contrast between sufferings and glory even stronger and closes the door to an instrumental-conditional reading of sufferings, which would see the latter somehow intrinsically related to glory: sufferings are relativized, not instrumentalized.

55. This comes out especially clearly in the quote of LXX Psalm 43.23 in Rom. 8.35: 'For your sake (ἕνεκεν σοῦ) we are counted as sheep of/for slaughter'. Note, though, that there are no human enemies in the impressive list preceding the quote: even the peril of unjust execution is simply referenced as 'the sword' (v. 35).

56. In martyrological texts suffering is a badge of honour, not a sign of divine rejection. For a clear comparison of these two patterns of texts, compare M. D. Mathews, 'Community Rule and Rom. 5.1-11: The Relationship between Justification and Suffering', in *Reading Romans in Context: Paul and Second Temple Judaism*, ed. B. Blackwell, J. K. Goodrich and J. Maston (Grand Rapids: Zondervan, 2015), 73–9.

57. There is some scholarly disagreement on whether the creation refers to non-human creation only or whether it includes human beings who are not believers. For the latter, compare S. Eastman, 'Whose Apocalypse? The Identity of the Sons of God in Romans 18.19', *JBL* 121, no. 2 (2002): 263–77. For the view that creation is the non-human world only compare Wolter, *Römerbrief*, 514, who approvingly quotes Dunn, *Romans* I, 471 as saying: 'Creation itself must be redeemed in order that redeemed man may have a fitting environment.'

58. Believers *are* part of creation, as convincingly argued by B. Gaventa Roberts, 'Neither Height nor Depth: Discerning the Cosmology of Romans', *Scottish Journal of Theology* 64, no. 3 (2011): 265–78 (276-7), even though they are a step ahead by the gift of the Spirit.

The reason for the groaning of creation is the futility (ματαιότης, v. 20) and the 'perishability' or decay (φθόρα, v.21) that creation has been subjected to.[59] Most exegetes think that the ὑπετάγη in v. 20 is a *passivum divinum*, where God is the implied subject. Quite a few see references to Gen. 3.14-19, where the earth shares in the curse and penalty that God pronounces following Adam and Eve's fall, a curse which includes the condition of decay and mortality.[60] And just as creation was caught up in the fall of the first humans, it will be caught up in the glory of the humans who are made new in the image of Christ (v.29).[61] Despite Adam's long shadow, the tone with which Paul speaks about 'death' has subtly changed now. Instead of depicting death as the awful wages dealt out by sin (Rom. 6.22) or characterizing the mortal bodies of the believers as worrying footholds for sin (8.10), mortality now appears more as a *tragic* reality. The choice of words is interesting; it suggests the possibility that Paul has a more ambiguous concept of death than he is usually credited with. What seems clear is that we have left the discourse where the royal powers of sin and death ruled together, capturing even God's good law and the most willing person with their lethal power.[62] The notion of 'suffering with Christ' is not rooted in this discourse but rather reflected upon under the signature of hope, which sees even mortality and suffering in the light of what is promised.

In sum, just as 'dying with Christ' marked out a sharp *separation* from the power of sin and was read as co-crucifixion, which indicates distance from the 'cosmos', so 'suffering with Christ' marks out a deep *solidarity* with the whole of creation.[63] Like creation, believers long for what is to be revealed, like creation they groan and sigh, unable even to find words for their prayer. It is notable that even the interceding Spirit does no more than amplify these wordless and painful groans.

---

59. The LXX uses ματαιότης to render Ecclesiastes' לבה, the vain chasing after the wind.

60. For example, Jewett, *Romans*, 212–13. Many scholars also draw attention to extra-biblical early Jewish texts, which emphasize that the earth is cursed for the sake of Adam. Compare, for example, LAB 37.3: 'And when the first-formed (Adam) was condemned to death, the earth was condemned to bring forth thorns and thistles.'

61. Compare Yates, *Spirit*, who sees the expression 'firstfruit' in v. 23 not just as applicable to the Spirit, but as shorthand for the renewing work of the Spirit, which is inaugurated in the renewal of the believers and the future raising of their bodies as the first token of the 'freedom from the bondage of decay' (v. 21) promised to all of creation.

62. We have already mentioned that ἁμαρτία/sin disappears after Rom. 8.10. The θάνατος, death, still makes an appearance in the list of powers at the end of the chapter (8.38), but is being used as part of a pair (death and life), which serves to denote the greatest possible range of reality.

63. Paul spells out the connection between co-crucifixion with Christ and crucifixion to the whole cosmos in Gal. 6.14: 'The world is crucified to me and I to the world.'

Ann Jervis suggests that 'Paul's mature consideration is that there is something of an identification of believers and nonbelievers precisely in their suffering'.[64] The believers' sufferings are not seen as instrumental, nor as bitter medicine for their own sanctification, nor as cruciform love which sets the cosmos right. These sufferings are borne with Christ and each other insofar as they are sufferings for the sake of the Gospel. But in a deeper and broader sense, they are borne as the consequences and markers of a tragic mortality, which is the lot of the whole of creation. Believers become the precentors and *cantores* of creation in its song of lament and longing, with the Spirit leading the way.

Conclusions

How, then, do 'dying with Christ' and 'suffering with Christ' relate to each other in Paul's discourse of Romans 6 and 8?

Paul uses 'dying with Christ' as a radical and dramatic inauguration into union with Christ, both his death and resurrection, but slants the phrase towards a 'once and for all' separation from sin and by implication death. The death to sin, because it is a death in Christ, simultaneously opens the life for God as the new space of being for believers. Paul acknowledges that this once-and-for-all inauguration must be appropriated cognitively and through ethical practice, even through 'killing' the deeds of the body.

'Suffering with Christ' in turn is part of the reality of 'being in Christ', which was inaugurated by 'dying with Christ to sin' but does not explicate 'dying to sin' in a continuous process of dying as suffering. It comes about in part as a suffering 'for the sake of God', which is inflicted by a world hostile to God. Read in this way, suffering is an unavoidable aspect of being in Christ while also living in 'this present evil age'. It recalls the reality of physical death and often enough leads to physical death. Paul does not know of a suffering which is a good suffering, seen, perhaps, as God's bitter but wholesome medicine against sin. On the contrary, Paul loosens the tight connection between sin and death in the second half of Romans 8. The futility and mortality of creation is presented as a tragic condition echoing the story of the fall in Genesis 3. Here mortality is not characterized as the personified power of death reigning together with sin: believers, though they have died to sin and death in their baptismal identification with Christ, are not released from groaning and suffering. If anything, the sphere of life they inhabit in Christ intensifies their suffering as they become painfully aware of the contrast between the futility and perishing of all creation, their own bodies included, and the promise of glory. There is nothing in their suffering, either the suffering from the targeted apocalyptic hostility or their suffering in solidarity with creation, which is good for something or redemptive. But the

---

64. L. Ann Jervis, *At the Heart of the Gospel: Suffering in the Earliest Christian Message* (Grand Rapids: Eerdmans, 2007), 77.

same hope of glory, the same foretaste of God's life, which increases their sorrow and sighing, also increases their confidence. On the one hand suffering is a painful reminder of the ongoing decay and futility of the created order. On the other hand, read as suffering together with Christ, it is the paradoxical token for glory: if we suffer with him we will be glorified with him. Paul thus disentangles suffering, the younger cousin of death, if you like, from its connection with sin. He quietly leaves behind the building blocks he himself had put together, which might have led all the way to a notion of mortification, of suffering as something useful in the battle against sin. Instead he starts a new approach, a new angle of contemplation of death and its harbinger, suffering. Seen from this angle, suffering is good for nothing, and it reduces even the heirs of glory to wordless groans. But because it expresses the union of the believers with Christ, it can be endured and focused in hope towards glory.

Chapter 2

GIVING THE SELF THROUGH DEATH: A CRUCIFIED CHRIST AS GIFT IN GALATIANS

Logan Williams

Anders Nygren's *Agape and Eros* initiated an unprecedented flurry of discussion and debate about the shape and content of Christian love.[1] Nygren's primary thesis in that widely influential work was that ἀγάπη and ἔρως represent two fundamentally opposed and antithetical configurations of love: whereas ἔρως – which refers to the Greek understanding of love stemming from the Platonic tradition – is acquisitive, self-righteous, egocentric and self-interested, ἀγάπη – which refers to the uniquely Christian idea of love – is spontaneous, unmotivated, indifferent to value, creative, universal and self-sacrificial.[2] According to Nygren, it is crucial that these two definitions and realizations of love remain wholly distinct, because any confusion between them results in serious theological dangers. Yet ever since Nygren's work gained such popularity and influence, critiques have multiplied from theologians and historians. Some have argued that Nygren's antithetical positioning of ἔρως and ἀγάπη was too sharp and led to numerous theological and practical problems,[3] and others have suggested that Graeco-Roman and Christian conceptions of love have real points of continuity and therefore cannot be played off one another in an absolute manner.[4] Despite these many (in my view) rather damaging theological and philological deconstructions of Nygren's thesis and his support thereof, one part of Nygren's thesis – that the Christian notion of love can be especially captured

---

1. Anders Nygren, *Agape and Eros*, trans. Philip S. Watson (Chicago: University of Chicago Press, 1982). For an overview of this work and its impact, see William Werpehowski, 'Anders Nygren's Agape and Eros', in *The Oxford Handbook of Theological Ethics*, ed. Gilbert Meilaender and William Werpehowski (Oxford: New York: Oxford University Press 2005), 433–48.
2. Nygren, *Agape and Eros*, 75–81, 175–81.
3. Notably John Burnaby, *Amor Dei: A Study of the Religion of St. Augustine; The Hulsean Lectures for 1938* (London: Hodder and Stoughton, 1938) and Gene Outka, *Agape: An Ethical Analysis* (Yale Publications in Religion; New Haven: Yale University Press, 1977).
4. See, for example, more recently Terence Irwin, 'Conceptions of Love, Greek and Christian', in *Love and Christian Ethics: Tradition, Theory, and Society*, ed. Frederick V. Simmons with Brian C. Sorrells (Washington DC: Georgetown University Press, 2016), 37–50.

by the notion of 'self-sacrifice' – still remains deeply influential.⁵ This view, of course, could be supported by appealing to scriptural texts: for example, in Paul's letters a number of texts could be read as portraying Christ's love to be essentially self-sacrificial. In Philippians Paul introduces Christ as being 'in the form of God' and states that he 'did not regard equality with God as something to be exploited' (Phil. 2.6).⁶ Rather, he 'emptied himself, taking the form of a slave, being born in human likeness. And being found in human form, he humbled himself and became obedient to the point of death – even death on a cross' (2.7-8). In one possible translation of 2 Cor. 8.9, Paul also claims that 'though [Jesus] was rich, yet for your sakes he became poor, so that by his poverty you might become rich'.⁷ And again, in Romans Paul writes that 'Christ did not please himself (ὁ Χριστὸς οὐχ ἑαυτῷ ἤρεσεν); but, as it is written, "The insults of those who insult you have fallen on me"' (Rom. 15.3). A plausible reading of these various Christological texts is that all three of them depict Christ as giving *up* something, either a possibility (Phil. 2.6-7; Rom. 15.3) or an actuality (2 Cor. 8.9): Christ could have pleased himself but instead gave up that possibility; he could have exploited his equality with God for his own gain but rather chose not to do so, and he was rich – and could have kept those riches to himself – but then gave up these riches to become impoverished in order to enrich others. On the basis of these texts, one could come to the conclusion that, in the words of Edmund Santurri, 'Christian love *just is* the agent's disposition to sacrifice the interests of the self for the sake of the neighbor'.⁸

---

5. Nygren is not the only one who has espoused this view (see, for example, the summary Reinhold Niebuhr in Outka, *Agape*, 7–54), but he is a good representative of it, and he deserves some (though not all) credit for the current popularity of this definition of love.

6. Unless noted otherwise, all biblical quotations are from the NRSV. I do not think that this is the best way to translate οὐχ ἁρπαγμὸν ἡγήσατο τὸ εἶναι ἴσα θεῷ (one problem with the NRSV is that the English phrase 'equality with God' would require the Greek to be τὸ εἶναι ἴσος θεῷ, instead of τὸ εἶναι ἴσα θεῷ). My intention is not to endorse the NRSV translation here but to provide an example of one translation which can form the basis of the view that Christ's action is self-sacrificial.

7. Again, I do not think the NRSV renders the Greek correctly; this translation is only possible if you take the participial phrase πλούσιος ὤν as concessive rather than causal. For a discussion of this issue, as well as an alternative translational proposal, see John M. G. Barclay, '"Because He was Rich He Became Poor": Translation: Exegesis, and Hermeneutics in the Reading of 2 Cor 8.9', in *Theologizing in the Corinthian Conflict: Studies in the Exegesis and Theology of 2 Corinthians*, ed. R. Bieringer et al. (Biblical Tools and Studies 16 (Leuven: Peeters, 2013)), 331–44.

8. Edmund N. Santurri, 'Agape as Self-Sacrifice: The Internalist View', in *Love and Christian Ethics*, 171–89, at 171, emphasis original. For an example of a Pauline scholar who argues for a similar view, see Michael Gorman, *Cruciformity: Paul's Narrative Spirituality of the Cross* (Grand Rapids: Eerdmans, 2001) and Michael Gorman, *Inhabiting the Cruciform God: Kenosis, Justification, and Theosis in Paul's Narrative Soteriology* (Grand Rapids: Eerdmans, 2009).

In this kind of reading, what makes the cross an act of love is that it both exemplifies Christ's complete disregard for his own interests and demonstrates his 'pure' regard for others.[9] As Nygren puts it, 'What, then, has the Cross of Christ to tell us about the nature and content of Agape-love? It testifies that it is a love that gives itself away, that sacrifices itself, even to the uttermost.'[10] To give this analysis a thicker description, for Nygren the degree that one loves another is directly proportionate to how much one is willing to diminish the self, limit the self, disregard one's interests or suffer for the sake of others. Put another way, *love essentially brings about, and is indicated by, self-subtraction for the benefit of another or others.*[11] Accordingly, it is rather telling that those who contend that love is essentially sacrifice regularly describe acts of love by taking the word 'self' and attaching a negative word or morpheme to it: 'self-abnegation', 'self-evacuation', 'selfless', 'self-denying', 'self-abandonment', 'self-surrender'. In this configuration, the cross represents just how far Christ is willing to 'give *up*' something actual or possible – whether his own interests, riches, status, life or potential self-actualizations – for the benefit of others, insofar as Jesus willingly diminishes, limits and subtracts from himself to the uttermost – that is, he limits himself to the point of death, non-existence and annihilation.

As will become clear in this chapter, I think that claiming (as Santurri does) that love 'just is' the sacrifice of one's own interests not only is based upon a misconstrual of certain texts but is also reductionistic, as it takes one aspect of love (self-limitation) and foregrounds it as the primary quality of love, to the

---

9. We must seriously question the assertion and assumption (which is pervasive in much of modern ethical theory) that the presence of any self-interest negates the 'purity' of other-regard or that all actions can and must be analysed as being either ultimately self-interested or other-regarding (as in, for example, H. Sidgwick, *The Methods of Ethics*, 7th edn (London: Macmillan, 1907), 498).

10. Nygren, *Agape and Eros*, 118. It is no surprise that many who espouse the view that love is self-sacrifice also demonize the concept of self-love (so Nygren, *Agape and Eros*, 101) or portray love as purely altruistic, with no view to one's own interests (so Santurri, 'Agape as Self-Sacrifice', 178: 'Kenotic love for Paul is altruistic all the way down. It is the other rather than the self that is ever in love's view'; see similarly e.g. Colin Grant, *Altruism and Christian Ethics*, New Studies in Christian Ethics (Cambridge: Cambridge University Press, 2005)). An absolute rejection of self-love probably betrays not only the influence of Luther (on which see Terence Irwin, 'Luther's Attack on Self-Love: The Failure of Pagan Virtue', *Journal of Medieval and Early Modern Studies* 42 (2012): 132–55) but also the eighteenth-century debates on human moral psychology, in which the possibility of the existence of real moral actions was tied to the possibility of a disinterested benefit of others (see Christian Maurer, *Self-Love, Egoism and the Selfish Hypothesis: Key Debates from Eighteenth-Century British Moral Philosophy* (Edinburgh: Edinburgh University Press, 2019).

11. The phrase 'self-subtraction' is not used by those who espouse this view, but by coining this term I am attempting to capture the force of 'self-sacrifice', 'selfless' and other similar terms.

(intentional or unintentional) exclusion of other integral aspects of love. Here I want to focus not on the Pauline texts mentioned above but rather on the language of self-giving in Galatians (δίδωμι ἑαυτόν in 1.4 and παραδίδωμι ἑαυτόν in 2.20),[12] regarding which many scholars have claimed – or rather in numerous cases have assumed – that it clearly refers to the self-sacrificial character of Christ death.[13] Since in Gal. 2.20 Paul speaks of 'the Son of God, who *loved* me and gave himself for me', this language can function as a basis to construct a theory of love as self-sacrifice and to affirm that Christ gives himself *away* in his death. A few scholars have suggested, however, that the language of self-giving refers not only to the death of Christ but also to Christ giving himself as gift,[14] and if this is correct, it would be profitable to look at what authors other than Paul have written about self-gifts in order to grasp what theological implications might be drawn from interpreting the death of Christ in connection with the bestowal of a self-gift. One such account of self-gifting is provided in Seneca's treatise *On Benefits* (*De Beneficiis*); here I will describe some elements of Seneca's treatise, present his account of self-gifting and finally suggest that interpreting the Christ event as a self-gift requires us to define love beyond self-sacrifice.

---

12. In the undisputed Pauline letters this kind of language only shows up in Galatians; other instances include Tit. 2.14 and Eph. 5.2, 25.

13. Michael Gorman uses 'self-giving' interchangeably with 'total self-abandonment', 'self-surrender' and 'kenosis', *Inhabiting the Cruciform God*, 21, cf. 32; Gorman, *Cruciformity*, 85, cf. 88, 92, 120; see also e.g. M. C. de Boer, *Galatians: A Commentary* (New Testament Library; Louisville: Westminster John Knox, 2011), 163; R. N. Longenecker, *Galatians* (WBC 41; Grand Rapids: Zondervan, 1990), 94; A. A. Das, *Galatians* (Concordia Commentary; St. Louis: Concordia, 2014), 273; J. D. G. Dunn, *The Epistle to the Galatians* (Black's New Testament Commentary; A&C Black, 1993), 147; J. L. Martyn, *Galatians: A New Translation with Introduction and Commentary* (AB 33A; New Haven: Yale University Press, 2004), 250; H. D. Betz, *Galatians: A Commentary on Paul's Letter to the Churches in Galatia* (Hermeneia; Minneapolis: Fortress, 1979), 125–6.

14. Gorman, *Cruciformity*, 84, 162; Barclay, *Paul and the Gift*, 1. This interpretation is supported by how, right after the statement that Christ 'gave himself', Paul states 'I do not reject *this* gift of God (οὐκ ἀθετῶ τὴν χάριν τοῦ θεοῦ)' (I take the article here as anaphoric). If this reading of the language is correct, then Paul's phrase 'gave himself' is a zeugma (see the explanation in V. Evans and M. Green, *Cognitive Linguistics: An Introduction* (Edinburgh: Edinburgh University Press, 2006), 288). A similar double-reference to death and the bestowal of a gift with the word παραδίδωμι is likely operative in Rom. 8.32 (so C. Eschner, *Gestorben und Hingegeben 'für' die Sünder: Die griechische Konzeption des Unheil abwendenden Sterbens und deren paulinische Aufnahme für die Deutung des Todes Jesu Christi* (WMANT 122; Göttingen: Neukirchener Verlag, 2010), 1: 453–7). I should note also that I consider the phrase 'gave himself' to refer not only to the death of Christ and the Christ giving himself as gift but also to the incarnation; my references to the death of Christ here are not meant to imply that this language only refers to that aspect of the Christ event.

One of the key theses in *De Beneficiis* is that gifts unleash the power of social creativity. Throughout his work Seneca repeatedly asserts that the practice of bestowing benefits finds its telos in creating and sustaining positive relationships,[15] binding fellow humans together and upholding the structure of society (*Ben.* 1.4.2; 1.15.2; 2.18.5; 6.41.2; cf. *Ira* 1.5.2-3.[16] Because gifts are, for Seneca, 'the glue that [holds] society together'[17] as well as the 'sine qua non of social stability',[18] an integral aspect of gift-giving is that, after an initial gift is given, each party continues the practice of giving, with gift leading to return-gift (and so on) in order to create and reinforce the connection between two persons or entities.[19] In other words, gift-giving intends to make ties with others, and these ties are strengthened and sustained by both parties' ongoing participation in a relationship of mutual reciprocity. Seneca's contention here does not amount to some wildly novel or divergent idea; he stands in the company of a longer tradition of philosophers for whom it was axiomatic that gift-giving aims at constructing relational bonds with others through a rhythm of gift and counter-gift (e.g. Xen. *Mem.* 1.2.7; 2.9.8; 3.11.11; Arist. *Eth. Nic.* V 5, 1133a1-2; Cic. *Off.* 1.2.200; Val. Max. 5.3. ext. 3-4). As one proponent of Aristotle's thought put it. 'the exchange and giving of a gift binds together the lives of men (χάριτος ἀμοιβὴ καὶ δόσις συνέχει τοὺς τῶν ἀνθρώπων βίους), some giving, others receiving, and others in turn reciprocating (τῶν μὲν διδόντων τῶν δὲ λαμβανόντων τῶν δ᾽ αὖ πάλιν ἀνταποδιδόντων)'.[20] Similarly,

---

15. I use 'relationship' instead of 'friendship' throughout my treatment of Seneca, following Griffin's caution that Seneca's treatise cannot accurately be considered only as a treatise on friendship ('*De Beneficiis* and Roman Society', *Journal of Roman Studies* 93 (2003): 92–113. Griffin's reading should be contrasted with Saller and Peter Leithart, who both suggest that *De Beneficiis* deals with the asymmetrical relationship of patronage (R. Saller, 'Status and Patronage', in *The Cambridge Ancient History, Volume 11: The High Empire, AD 70-192*, ed. A. K. Bowman, P. Garnsey and D. Rathbone, 2nd edn (Cambridge: Cambridge University Press, 2008), 817–54 at 838; P. J. Leithart, *Gratitude: An Intellectual History* (Waco: Baylor University Press, 2014), 48).

16. For a helpful introduction on these matters and to *De Benificiis* in general, see M. T. Griffin and B. Inwood, 'Translator's Introduction', in *On Benefits*, trans. M. T. Griffin and B. Inwood (The Complete Works of Lucius Annaeus Seneca; London: University of Chicago Press, 2011), 1–14.

17. Saller, 'Status and Patronage', 838.

18. Griffin, 'Introduction', 1.

19. On how Seneca expects gifts to be returned, see T. Engberg-Pederson, 'Gift-Giving and Friendship: Seneca and Paul in Romans 1-8 on the Logic of God's Χάρις and Its Human Response', *HTR* 101 (2008): 15–44 and Barclay, *Paul and the Gift*, 45–51.

20. M. Plezia (ed.), *Aristotelis Privatorum Scriptorum Fragmenta*, Bibliotheca Scriptorum Graecorum et Romanorum (Leipzig: BSB B.G. Teubner Verlagsgesellschaft, 1977), 31; cf. Arist. *Eth. Nic.* VIII 13, 1162b35-1163a1. For a further treatment of relationship between *De Beneficiis* and his philosophical predecessors and contemporaries, see Griffin, *Seneca on Society: A Guide to De Beneficiis* (Oxford: Oxford University Press, 2013), 15–24.

for Seneca, the hope that there would be a repeated cycle of benefit and return does not betray an ulterior 'selfish' motive but rather reflects the hope to initiate and deepen relational ties with others. Seneca's vision of gift-exchange therefore subordinates objects to people: we enjoy others *through* reciprocal giving (*Ben.* 1.6.1; 3.17.4).[21]

Because gift-giving aims at constructing relationships, we must, Seneca says, evaluate the quality of gifts not per se by what they contain but by how and why they are given. In Seneca's vocabulary, we should judge gifts not by their content but by the giver's *animus* – her spirit, attitude or intention with which she gives (1.5.2; 1.6.1-7.3; 2.1.2; 3.17.4; 5.3.3; 6.9.2-3; cf. Arist. *Rhet.* II 7, 1385a17-19).[22] This axiological criterion plays out in rather simple way: if one gives gifts eagerly, with lavish words of praise for the recipient, to indicate her hope to deepen the relationship between the recipient (*Ben.* 2.3.1), then a giver has honourable *animus*; but if one gives begrudgingly and reluctantly (2.1.2), with pride (2.4.1; 2.13.2) or the intent to harm another (6.8.2), then the giver exhibits a dishonourable *animus*.

As a supporting argument for this point, Seneca recounts a story about Aeschines, a poor man who, in the near absence of possessions, gives himself as gift to his teacher, Socrates:

> Everyone used to offer Socrates gifts, each according to his own resources. Aeschines, who was poor and a student of Socrates, said, 'I cannot find anything worthy of you which I could give you; it is only in this respect that I feel poor. And so I give you the only thing I have: myself (*Itaque dono tibit, quod unum habeo, me ipsum*). I only ask that you appreciate my gift, such as it is, and reflect that although other people have given you a great deal, they have kept back more for themselves.' Socrates replied, 'Of course you have given me a great gift – unless, that is, you set a low value on yourself. So I will be sure to return you to yourself in better condition than I received you.' With this gift, Aeschines outdid Alcibiades, whose intentions matched his wealth, and the generous gifts of all the wealthy young men.

---

21. We could contrast this kind of exchange relationship with Aristotle's notion of a 'utility-friendship' (φίλοι διὰ τὸ χρήσιμον). In that kind of relationship, contact between two parties occurs solely for the purpose of acquiring a particular object, and in the event that each party in a utility friendship receives the desired object, the relationship serves no further purpose and is thus severed (*Eth. Nic.* VIII 3, 1156a10-12). This form of exchange is distinct from Seneca's ideal gift-relationship (and Aristotle's ideal of friendship based on virtue), which is oriented towards people, not objects. This does not mean that exchange is excluded altogether in relationships but rather that exchange must be contextualized within and subordinated as a means to reinforcing relationships.

22. On the function of *animus* in *De Beneficiis*, see B. Inwood, 'Politics and Paradox in Seneca's *De Beneficiis*', in *Reading Seneca: Stoic Philosophy at Rome* (Oxford: Clarendon, 2005), 65–93, especially 86–92.

> Do you see how a well-intentioned donor (*animus*) can discover the raw material for generosity, even amidst straitened circumstances? In my opinion, Aeschines was saying, 'Fortune, your desire to make me poor has been ineffectual. Despite you, I will send this man a worthy gift; since I cannot give it from your resources, I will give it from my own (*de meo dabo*).' And there is no reason for you to conclude that Aeschines was undervaluing himself. He was willing to offer himself as payment for himself. This talented young man found a way to give Socrates to himself (*quemadmodum Socraten sibi daret*). You should not consider the magnitude of each gift, but the quality of the giver.[23]

Overcoming the apparently inhibiting circumstances of his poverty, Aeschines presents an ideal gift with his virtuous *animus* by giving directly 'from himself' (*de meo*). The contrast between Aeschines and the other pupils is not merely their economic status; the deeper and more fundamental contrast is that, whereas the other students gave 'according to [their] own resources', Aeschines did not pull from his surplus but gave to Socrates his sole possession as one who is poor – his very own self. In desiring to give to Socrates so much, he found the most precious item to give (himself) without which he would have been unable to give anything at all.

Reflecting Seneca's insistence that gift-giving intends to establish a two-way mutual relationship, Aeschines' self-gift is interpreted as a paradigmatic expression of the circularity of beneficence. In response to Aeschines' self-gift, Socrates seeks to sustain some ongoing mutuality between them and promises to give a counter-gift to Aeschines: 'I will return you to yourself in better condition than I received you.' But this is a distinctive form of reciprocity not seen elsewhere in Seneca's treatise. Aeschines's extension of his own self to Socrates is curiously interpreted as 'a way to give Socrates to himself'. Seneca usually suggests that we should not offer counter-gifts as an immediate response to an initial gift: there must be an appropriate degree of time which passes before one can return. By contrast, here Seneca signals that Aeschines, by giving his own self to Socrates, also receives Socrates's own self in that same moment, such that in this single event Socrates also both receives and is given to Aeschines. In this sense, Aechines's self-gift enacts a coincidence of gift and counter-gift, an event in which Aeschines simultaneously gives himself and receives another. Thus, Aeschines's self-gift does not do away with reciprocity but presses into the dynamic of mutuality that Seneca contends should be operative in all instances of gift-giving.

It is crucial to recognize what we have not seen in this account. There is neither any implication nor any suggestion that Aeschines's life or well-being is jeopardized when he gives himself as gift. This is not just an insignificant coincidence; there is, I think, a particular logic that undergirds the absence of death, self-sacrifice or self-jeopardization in this story about self-gifting. One apparent difference between self-gifts and other kinds of gifts is that, whereas normal gifts operate

---

23. *Ben.* 1.8.1-9.1. Translations from Griffin and Inwood (trans.), *On Benefits*.

according to a tripartite structure which includes a giver, a gift and a recipient, self-gifts function according to a bipartite structure which includes a recipient and a giver who is *identical* to the gift. In other words, in a tripartite structure of giving, there are three functions (gift, giver, recipient) which are fulfilled by two distinct persons and a distinct object; in a bipartite structure of giving, there are still three functions, but these roles are fulfilled by only *two* persons, with one person functioning both as giver and gift. In a tripartite structure of gift-giving, one can presumably die in the act of gift-giving, since the object bestowed would be *external* to the self and thus can be possessed by another without the presence of the giver. Put another way, death can be the means by which one gives some*thing*. But in a bipartite structure, one's own death cannot be the means by which one gives the self, because the self *is* itself the content of the gift. To die in the act of giving the self would therefore nullify the gift-event, since in such an instance the material of the gift would be destroyed in the act of giving.

This point is well illustrated by one of Seneca's sections in *De Beneficiis*. Seneca spends a good deal of time arguing, against the apparent opinion of others, that slaves can in fact give benefits to their masters (3.18.1-29.1). Seneca imagines two situations: one in which a slave dies to save his master's life and another in which a slave does not give his master's secrets over to his enemies even in the face of bribes, threats or torture, but then dies for his loyalty to his master. After presenting these hypothetical situations, Seneca asks rhetorically, 'Will you deny that he has conferred a benefit on his master, just because he is a slave?' (3.19.2). Seneca considers it obvious that everyone will affirm that the slave has indeed bestowed a gift on the master. But what in Seneca's mind is the *content* of the benefit bestowed by the slave in these examples? When the slave dies for the master, does he give his own life to the master? When Seneca writes that, to remain loyal to his master in the face of death, the slave willingly *impendisse spiritum*, Griffin and Inwood translate this phrase to mean that the slave 'has given his life', which implies that, when the slave dies for his master's benefit, the content of the gift is the slave's own life (and thus potentially a self-gift). But *impendisse spiritum* is better translated as 'has expended his life'. (Using 'give' as a translation of *impendo* in a treatise on gift-giving is deeply misleading, since *impendo* never means 'to give something as gift'.) What is more, Seneca goes on to claim that, when a slave dies to save his master's life, what the slave has given as gift to the master is, in fact, *the master's own life*. This is clear when Seneca contrasts examples of slaves who benefit their masters, writing that 'one slave gave his master life; another gave him death. One saved his master from perishing, and if that is not enough, saved him by perishing. One helped his master to die; another tricked him out of dying (*Dedit aliquis domino suo vitam, dedit mortem, servavit periturum et, hoc si parumest, pereundo servavit; alius mortem domini adiuvit, alius decepit*).'[24] When a slave saves his master's life, the slave is giving the master's life to the master. Thus the slave, when he dies to save another, does not give his own self or life as gift to anyone; here we rather see a tripartite structure of giving, in which a gift external to

---

24. Sen. *Ben.* 3.23.1.

the self (the master's own life) can be given through the death of the giver (the slave) to a particular recipient (the master). But how would it be coherent for the slave to give the gift of his own self, if the self is destroyed in the process of giving it and the slave then does not enter into relationship with the master? Instead, for Seneca, one can die in order to give something *other* than the self to someone, but one cannot, by dying, give oneself as the content of the gift. To use a more contemporary example, it would not count as a gift to present a set of china to another if, while in the act of handing it over, one threw the china on the ground and smashed it into pieces. Thus, whereas in a tripartite structure one can die to give an object external to the self to another, in a bipartite structure of self-giving – in which gift and giver are identical – dying in order to give the self as gift would contradict the gift itself. Destruction of the self makes the self-gift impossible.

We can now turn back to Galatians. If it is the case that the language of self-giving in Gal. 1.4 and 2.20 refers both to the bestowal of a self-gift and the death of Christ, then we run into a bit a problem. Presumably, Christ could 'give himself' into death in order to give something external to himself to believers; but, if 'gave himself' in 1.4 and 2.20 also includes reference to gift-giving, then Christ just *is* the content of the gift. (It is not, as Derrida would say, a 'gift of death'; it is the self-gift of the one who died.[25]) But how is this not a complete contradiction? If Christ destroys himself in the act of giving, he cannot be the content of the divine gift. But the opening divine announcement of Galatians, that God is 'the one who raised him (Jesus Christ) from the dead' (1.1), permits Paul to declare the possibility of something that would otherwise be a sheer impossibility: someone has given himself as gift through death. The only possible way that this self-gift can be real – and thus the only way in which the language of self-giving in Gal. 1.4 and 2.20 can refer both to death and the giving of a self-gift – is if Christ retains his identity and existence through his entry into death. In short, Paul can say Christ both dies and gives himself as gift only if he presupposes resurrection.

As we saw with Seneca, the bestowal of the self as gift functions like all other gifts: to initiate or reinforce a relationship of mutuality. It seems that Paul agrees, since the references to Christ's self-giving in Galatians are set next to statements about ongoing mutuality. Christ's self-giving in 1.4 is followed by the claim that Paul is a 'slave of Christ' (1.10), and the phrase 'he loved me and gave himself for me' follows the claim that Paul has 'died to the law' in order that he might 'live to God' (2.19). If Paul thinks, like Seneca, that the bestowal of the self-gift is oriented towards supporting or creating a mutual relationship in which Christ both gives himself and receives another into relationship, then the intention and hope for relational mutuality between Christ and believers is *internal* to the language of self-giving in Gal. 1.4 and 2.20.[26]

---

25. J. Derrida, *The Gift of Death* (Chicago: University of Chicago Press, 1995).

26. This does not mean that 'gave himself' directly refers to these realities; rather, it is simply that these other aspects of Paul's thought are a necessary reality for the language to make any sense.

What does this mean for defining love? None of this is necessarily implies that for Paul Christ's love does not involve any form of self-limitation or self-sacrifice per se. Indeed, a text like Rom. 15.3 indicates that Christ's action in the Gospel can be understood in contrast to some other form of self-pleasing behaviour. But Paul's portrayal of the Christ event as a self-gift suggests that there is something more to the phrase 'loved me and gave himself for me' than just self-subtraction, self-limitation or self-negation. The language of self-giving is just not adequately captured if understood to mean that Christ gives himself *away*, subtracting from himself to the point of annihilation in order to benefit others.[27] Rather, because Christ's self must continue through death in order to be the content of the gift, the cross is only 'self-sacrifice' in a limited and qualified sense. Any definition of love which utilizes 'gave himself' as evidence must speak beyond the concepts of self-negation or self-subtraction and should point out that Paul's language of self-giving in Galatians can only be appropriately described in light of the intention to create a relationship of mutual fellowship beyond his death. The phrase 'gave himself' signals not that Christ gives himself *away* in death but that through his death he gives himself *into* relationship; Christ does not die in order to give just something to others, but someone – himself – and thus he dies *for* others so that, on the other side of death, he would exist *with* others. In this sense, the content of the love of Christ is not entirely 'selfless' in opposition to any kind of 'acquisitiveness', as Nygren would hold. The point of Christ's self-giving is not just to benefit believers per se but to benefit them by existing with them – and this hope for mutuality and reception is internal to love itself. Thus, to hold or to imply that love is essentially about self-subtraction – or that the degree of love is determined by how much one is willing to limit, diminish or annihilate oneself for another – will end up radically imbalanced; more straightforwardly, the view that love is identical to self-sacrifice takes one legitimate aspect of love – the limitation of possible realizations of the self – as exhaustive of the definition of love, and by positing this one aspect of love as its sole definition, this view is bound to misconstrue the love of Christ. As John Burnaby so helpfully summarized decades ago, 'The love which endures, which offers itself [or gives itself] to the unloving, is always the servant of its own high purpose – not to rest till the sundered fellowship is restored, till rejection is changed to response. Calvary is for the sake of Pentecost.'[28]

---

27. As Barth says in CD IV/1, 185: 'God gives himself, but he does not give himself away'; cf. Asle Eikrem, *God as Sacrificial Love: A Systematic Exploration of a Controversial Notion* (T&T Clark Studies in Systematic Theology; London: Bloomsbury T&T Clark, 2018), 127.

28. Burnaby, *Amor Dei*, 307.

Chapter 3

GREGORY OF NYSSA ON PAIN, PLEASURE AND THE GOOD: AN EARLY CHRISTIAN PERSPECTIVE ON REDEMPTIVE SUFFERING

Siiri Toiviainen Rø

Introduction

Early Christian literature abounds with accounts of saintly suffering. Stories about the heroic struggles of martyrs and feats of asceticism displayed by other holy women and men may lead modern readers to conclude that ancient Christians thought that pain was good. But attitudes towards pain and suffering were not straightforward. Despite the popularity of martyr accounts and stories about living ascetics, many early Christian thinkers would have been uneasy with the idea that pain was good in an unqualified sense. L. Stephanie Cobb has recently suggested that even stories about martyrs 'do not reflect the meaningfulness of pain', but are completely disinterested in it. Instead of regarding pain as redeeming, these stories highlight the martyrs' complete disregard of pain and 'construct a death without pain'.[1]

In this chapter, I suggest that there are more nuanced ways of assessing the value of pain in early Christian literature than simply affirming the unconditional goodness of suffering or negating its importance altogether. Pain, we shall see, is often understood as an instrumental good. I will argue, furthermore, that fruitful perspectives on the redemptive relevance of pain can be opened if we first understand the role that early Christian writers assigned to pleasure (ἡδονή) when thinking about the fall and about sin. My aim is to show that the ability to endure pain is presented as a clear signal that a Christian has overcome the mistaken notion that pleasure is the good, which once prompted humanity's fall, and understood that the true good lies beyond one's present perceptible surroundings.[2]

---

1. L. Stephanie Cobb, *Divine Deliverance: Pain and Painlessness in Early Christian Martyr Texts* (Oakland: University of California Press, 2016), 12–13, 23.

2. This article is partly adapted from my doctoral thesis. See Siiri Toiviainen, *'The Instigator of All Vicious Actions': Pleasure, Sin, and the Good Life in the Works of Gregory of Nyssa* (Durham: Durham University, 2017), 230–42.

Taking as my guide Gregory of Nyssa, the fourth-century Cappadocian bishop and one of the early Christian authors Cobb discusses in her work, I will examine three texts from different genres to show how the mistaken idea that pleasure is the good – that is, the problem of hedonism – underpins his understanding of spiritually beneficial pain not only in doctrinal reflections but also in texts intended for popular audiences. While my focus will be on bodily pain (derivatives of ἄλγος, sometimes πόνος), I will also touch on the emotion of distress (λύπη); in fact, the distinction between bodily sensation and mental distress is vital for understanding early Christian accounts of pain.

Pleasure, pain and the good

In order to understand in what sense pain can and cannot be considered 'good', it is necessary to outline briefly Gregory of Nyssa's conception of the purpose of the Christian life and possible obstacles that may prevent its fulfilment. Like most ancient authors, Gregory builds his thinking on the good life around the notion of the final good that humans ought to pursue above other goals and for its own sake.[3] To discuss the notion of 'goodness', Gregory employs two key terms, τὸ ἀγαθόν and τὸ κάλον.[4] The former means 'good' in a general sense, while the latter, notoriously difficult to translate, refers especially to the attractive aspect of goodness as an object of love and desire. Thus, it is often translated as 'beauty', though it can also denote the good in a broad moral sense without an emphasis on its attractive quality.

For Gregory, the true good and the source of all goods is God, in whose goodness humans are invited to participate. Practically, this participation entails the development of virtues – positive inner dispositions that restore the soul to its likeness with the divine.[5] Subscribing to a widely held principle of ancient ethics, Gregory argues that virtue alone suffices for the good life: the true good is always available to all people, and thus virtues, such as wisdom or justice, can be cultivated regardless of one's physical circumstances. Wealth and poverty, good fortune and adversity are equally suited to serve as a training ground for the good life since it depends solely on one's deliberately chosen inner attitude.[6] From this perspective, bodily pain makes little difference to the Christian life.

---

3. A *locus classicus* of the ancient definition of the final good can be found in Aristotle, *Nicomachean Ethics* 1.2.1094a19-23. See also Julia Annas, *The Morality of Happiness* (New York: Oxford University Press, 1993), 30–4.

4. For these terms in Gregory, see Ilaria Ramelli, 'Good/Beauty', in *The Brill Dictionary of Gregory of Nyssa*, ed. Lucas Francisco Mateo-Seco and Giulio Maspero; trans. Seth Cherney; Supplements to Vigiliae Christianae 99 (Leiden: Brill, 2010), 356–63.

5. See, for example, *De beatitudinibus* 1, Gregorii Nysseni Opera VII/2.

6. See, for example, ch. 4 of Gregory's *On Virginity*.

In Gregory's view, however, human beings are remarkably bad at distinguishing the true good from those things which merely appear good to the senses. Instead of pursuing the likeness of the intelligible and invisible God by cultivating virtues, humans yield to the irrational but instant appeal of sensual pleasure and label it as the good. As I have argued, this dynamic forms the core of Gregory's hamartiology and is an early Christian adaptation of the widespread ancient opposition to hedonism, the notion of pleasure as the final good.[7] The hamartiological significance of pleasure is illustrated by the primary role it plays in Gregory's interpretation of the fall.[8] In several works, Gregory presents a reading of Genesis 3 in which the first humans exchange the perfect good, in which they have been made participants, for the sensual pleasure provided by the tree of the knowledge of good and evil.[9] The devil prepares a 'bait' (δέλεαρ) by covering the fruit with a 'fair appearance and pleasure' (εὐχροίᾳ τινὶ καὶ ἡδονῇ) in order to create a false impression of goodness and lead the guileless humans to sin and death.[10]

Gregory's *Catechetical Oration* – a doctrinal work written as a manual for catechists – makes it plain that false ideas about pain go hand in hand with the problem of seeking pleasure as the good. Here, Gregory probes the origin of evil to refute the 'Manichaean' view that God himself is the creator of evil. He argues that this erroneous conception essentially boils down to a hedonistic evaluation of the world: those who in their definition of the good (ἀγαθόν) 'look to the pleasure of bodily enjoyment' (τὸ ἡδὺ τῆς σωματικῆς ἀπολαύσεως) will inevitably come to the conclusion that pain, its opposite, must be evil. Thus, when such people observe 'some painful sensation' (ἀλγεινήν τινα αἴσθησιν) that arises from the inherent mutability of the body, they will conclude that God as the creator of the body is the origin of evil.[11] Since they seek to distinguish good and evil by the senses (τῇ αἰσθήσει τὸ καλὸν καὶ τὸ κακὸν διακρινόντων), they fail to understand that the true good lies beyond sense perception and that evil is nothing more than alienation from the true good (ἡ τοῦ ἀληθινοῦ ἀγαθοῦ ἀλλοτρίωσις), brought about by an act of human will through pleasure (διά τινος ἡδονῆς).[12] Gregory likens these heretical hedonists to irrational animals who lack the ability to move beyond sense perceptions and

---

7. This is my overarching argument in Toiviainen, '*The Instigator of All Vicious Actions*'.

8. See ibid., 107–49.

9. *De opificio hominis* 19-20; *Oratio catechetica*, GNO 3/4, 56.19-57.3; *In Canticum canticorum* 12, GNO 6, 350.

10. *Op. Hom.* 20, Patrologia Graeca 44, 200a, cf. Plato, *Tim.* 69d; *Op. Hom.* 20, PG 44, 197b.

11. *Or. Cat.*, GNO 3/4, 27.16–28.1. Translations of *Or. Cat.* are from J. H. Srawley, *The Catechetical Oration of St. Gregory of Nyssa* (London: Society for Promoting Christian Knowledge, 1917).

12. Ibid., 29.13-6; 34.22-4.

who thus judge the good and its opposite based on pains and pleasures (πόνοις δὲ καὶ ἡδοναῖς).[13]

To summarize, humans have a tendency to yield to their irrational drives and misjudge pleasurable sensations as good and desirable and painful sensations as bad and undesirable. But the opposite evaluation is also false: it is not true that pleasure is unequivocally evil and pain good. As mere sensations, both arise spontaneously from the fluctuations of the material body rather than from a deliberate choice of the mind – and thus both are amoral. It is only the judgement of the mind, which judges the sensation as good or evil and decides whether it should be pursued or avoided, that invests it with moral significance.

But what criteria should be applied when making these judgements? In line with the teleological character of ancient ethics, Gregory locates the criterion in the final good: pleasures and pains that are directly prompted by this good or chosen rationally in order to attain it become 'good' in a derivative sense. As regards pain, no text addresses the topic more extensively than *Homily 8 on the Beatitudes*, in which Gregory expounds on the blessings of persecution.

Blessed persecution

Written most likely during the early years of Gregory's episcopate, *Homilies on the Beatitudes* form a progressive account of the spiritual life, each blessing taking the believer towards a greater likeness of her divine archetype. The coherent sequence of the homilies suggests that the work is an edited exegetical commentary rather than a collection of 'ordinary' homilies preached in front of a congregation.[14] In their Greek form, the Beatitudes (Matt. 5.3-10) revolve around the adjective μακάριος ('blessed', 'happy'). In early Christian literature, the corresponding noun μακαριότης is typically understood as a synonym of the more famous word εὐδαιμονία which stands for the supreme state of happiness and well-being that forms the end goal of the human life in ancient ethics. For Gregory, 'the blessed (μακαριστόν) is the divine itself' from whom humans as the image of God derive

---

13. Ibid., 34.25–35.3.

14. On the differences between homilies preached on martyr feasts and homilies on more learned theological and scriptural topics, see Johan Leemans, 'General Introduction', in *'Let Us Die That We May Live': Greek Homilies on Christian Martyrs from Asia Minor, Palestine and Syria (c. AD 350–AD 450)*, ed. Johan Leemans, Wendy Mayer, Pauline Allen and Boudewijn Dehandschutter (London: Routledge, 2003), viii. See also Johan Leemans, 'Gregory of Nyssa', in *'Let Us Die That We May Live'*, 79–80, for a classification of Gregory's works in which *Beat.* is identified as a collection of homilies rewritten into an exegetical tract and thus distinguished from ordinary homilies.

their blessedness.[15] The Beatitudes, then, speak of the ultimate goal of the human life, the restoration of the likeness of God.[16]

While several of the Beatitudes refer to special blessings that accompany states of lack and lowliness, it is especially the second and the eighth that proclaim blessings on individuals in states of outright suffering: mourning and persecution. The two homilies dedicated to these proclamations address different aspects of suffering. The homily on mourning (*Beat.* 3) focuses on spiritually productive uses of the *emotion of grief* (λύπη, here also πένθος). At the core of the emotion of λύπη is a judgement that something good has been lost or something bad is at hand.[17] If λύπη is correctly ordered, it arises from separation from that which is truly good, not from that which merely seems so. Thus, the good use of λύπη entails mourning the loss of the original blessed state of humanity and the soul's present separation from God.[18]

Since Gregory's notion of spiritual mourning has been extensively discussed in scholarship, I will focus my analysis on the blessing of persecution (*Beat.* 8).[19] The purpose of *Beat.* 8 is to explain how *external adversity* can be turned into a source of blessing. Here, Gregory describes situations that appear painful to the senses but do not warrant an emotional response of λύπη since the true good is not lost but, on the contrary, gained through these struggles. It is important to note that Gregory states at the very beginning that the eighth Beatitude has to do with the undoing of the consequences of sin: it promises 'the restoration to the heavens of those who once fell into bondage, but were then called back again from bondage to a kingdom'.[20] While much of the homily is spent on discussing the exemplary suffering of the martyrs, the notion of persecution appears to involve various forms of bodily pain, deprivation and separation from people and things.

By employing agonistic language typical of ancient accounts of martyrdom, Gregory describes the persecuted as athletes who run away from evil, towards their goal in God.[21] The blessing, simply put, lies in the way in which the chase by evil becomes the reason for attaining the good (τὸ ἀγαθόν), which Gregory again

---

15. For this terminology see Friedhelm Mann, 'Zur Wortgruppe μακαρ – in *De beatitudinibus*, in den übrigen Werken Gregors von Nyssa und im *Lexicon Gregorianum*', in *Gregory of Nyssa, Homilies on the Beatitudes: An English Version with Commentary and Supporting Studies. Proceedings of the Eighth International Colloquium on Gregory of Nyssa (Paderborn, 14–18 September 1998)*, ed. Hubertus R. Drobner and Albert Viciano (Leiden: Brill, 2000), 345–9. All translations of *Beat.* are from Stuart George Hall, 'Gregory of Nyssa, On the Beatitudes', in *Gregory of Nyssa, Homilies on the Beatitudes*, 23–90.

16. On the general meaning of the Beatitudes, *Beat.* 1, GNO 7/2, 79.26–81.7.

17. *Beat.* 3, GNO 7/2, 102.15–103.15; cf. *SVF* 1.211.

18. *Beat.* 3, GNO 7/2, 103.27–107.2.

19. See especially J. Warren Smith, 'Macrina, Tamer of Horses and Healer of Souls: Grief and the Therapy of Hope in Gregory of Nyssa's De Anima et Resurrectione', *Journal of Theological Studies* 52, no. 1 (2001): 37–60.

20. *Beat.* 8, GNO 7/2, 161.23–162.2.

21. Ibid., 164.8.

defines as 'the Lord himself, towards whom the pursued person runs'. The 'truly blessed', then, is the person who 'uses his enemy as a help towards the good'.[22] In other words, the struggle of the persecuted gains ethical value when persecution is deliberately endured for the sake of the final good; the good aim yields good pain.

One of Gregory's key points in this homily is that the value of suffering should not be judged externally by sensation but from the perspective of the final, invisible goal of the Christian life. While the 'outward and openly visible form of the persecution ... may seem to the senses (τῇ αἰσθήσει) painful (ἀλγεινόν), the final end (σκοπός) of what is being done surpasses every blessedness', Gregory writes.[23] The words of the Beatitude, promising the kingdom of heaven to the persecuted, serve as a reminder of this intangible reality. The blessing hidden in adversity is not available to sensation but is grasped with the virtue of hope (ἐλπίς), which is able to envision a reality presently unavailable to the senses and thus helps to 'overthrow the immediate sensations of pain' (τὴν πρόσκαιρον τῶν ἀλγεινῶν αἴσθησιν).[24]

According to Gregory, the ability to evaluate present pain from an eschatological perspective belongs only to those who cling to the promise of Christ since it runs counter to the tendencies of the fallen human being. The abundance of sensory pain (πολὺ κατὰ τὴν αἴσθησιν τὸ ἀλγεινόν) inflicted by persecutors 'makes it difficult for the more carnally minded to believe the hope of the kingdom held out to them through those pains'.[25] Gregory notes that without Christ's help it may, in fact, be 'totally impossible to prize the invisible good above the visible sweet things of this life' (τῶν κατὰ τὴν ζωὴν ταύτην ἡδέων τὸ μὴ φαινόμενον ἀγαθὸν προτιμῆσαι τῶν φαινομένων). He attributes the problem to the bond which the bodily sensations create with the 'sweets (ἡδέα) of life' to which the soul is 'fastened as if by a nail', finding it difficult to detach itself.[26] This kind of soul is easily threatened by the persecutor since, holding on to pleasure as the good, it fears the potential pain caused by the loss of its material attachments. Here, Gregory does not allude only to pain as a physical sensation but speaks to any form of loss of perceived goods and so comes close to the definition of λύπη.[27] In short, the life that seems pleasing to the senses can be turned into an instrument of pain in the hands of the persecutor who manipulates the human love of pleasure to push the persecuted person off her spiritual course.

The exemplarity of martyrs, then, lies in the way they are able to shatter the bonds of this world, shake off worldly pleasures (τὰς κοσμικὰς ἡδονάς) and run swiftly towards their goal, keeping their eyes fixed on the prize instead of what

---

22. Ibid., 164.11-5.
23. Ibid., 164.21-3.
24. Ibid., 165.16-7. Similar ideas regarding the virtuous endurance of pain and the hope of the future life occur in many early Christian texts on martyrdom, such as Origen's *Exhortatio ad martyrium*.
25. *Beat.* 8, GNO 7/2, 165.11-4.
26. Ibid., 166.7-29. The metaphor of 'nail' (ἧλος) is a Platonic commonplace frequently cited by patristic authors. Compare Plato, *Phaedo* 83c–d.
27. For the definition of λύπη, see the beginning of this section.

has been left behind. By keeping their focus on the final good, martyrs are able to confront physical pain, persecution and other difficulties without succumbing to the emotion of distress that arises from the notion that pain is evil and should be avoided. A martyr 'does not cast his eye backwards to the pleasure left behind (τὸ κατόπιν ἡδύ), but goes for the intended good (τὸ προκείμενον ἀγαθόν); he does not feel anguish over the loss of earthly things, but rejoices at gaining the heavenly'. He will understand that torture paves the way to joy (χαρά) that is greater than the earthly pleasure he must now leave behind.[28]

Crucially, then, awareness of the blessedness that awaits in the life to come relativizes the pleasures and pains of this life: sensual pleasures are proved insignificant in comparison, while pain is regarded as a small price to pay for the everlasting joy. This altered evaluation and transformation of pain is highlighted earlier in the homily as Gregory describes the pains of Stephen who, consoled by the hope embedded in the Beatitude, 'rejoices (χαίρει) as he is encircled and stoned, and as if they were gentle dewdrops (δρόσον ἡδεῖαν) gladly accepts on his body rain upon rain of stones'.[29] For Gregory, the account of Stephen's martyrdom shows that pain is not only to be endured; to the rightly disposed, it will be transformed into – or at least accompanied by – a higher pleasure which anticipates the future joy. What at first appears painful to the senses is reordered eschatologically into a pleasurable experience since it paves the way to the final blessedness in the kingdom of heaven.

However, even if Gregory's martyrs 'overthrow' pain with hope and even transform it into pleasure, the fact that martyrs must grapple with pain and not some other external factor has special redemptive relevance. For Gregory, the endurance of pain for the true good is a powerful instrument of salvation because it breaks the pernicious association between pleasure and the good which underpins all sin. The motif of undoing the effects of the fall becomes explicit as Gregory remarks: 'Since it was by pleasure that sin came in (δι' ἡδονῆς εἰσῆλθεν ἡ ἁμαρτία), it will surely be expelled by its opposite.' Pain, he says, acts like a bitter medicine that cures the effects of pleasure since 'one who is in pain cannot enjoy pleasure' (οὐκ ἔστι γὰρ ἡσθῆναι τὸν ἀλγυνόμενον).[30]

The martyr who does not shrink from pain is able to break away from sin because he understands that what appeals to the senses is neither truly good nor eternally enjoyable. This redemptive relevance becomes even more obvious in Gregory's *Homilies on the Forty Martyrs of Sebaste* to which I shall now turn.

Martyrs as the antithesis of Adam and Eve

While the problem of pleasure as a false good was fundamentally a learned concern which Gregory treated much like other highly educated Graeco-Roman authors,

---

28. *Beat.* 8, GNO 7/2, 167.10-5.
29. Ibid., 165.18-20.
30. Ibid., 167.24-5.

it provided a crucial interpretive key also when he was preaching about pain in a popular context. Indeed, scholars have shown that the Cappadocians embedded a multitude of ethical and doctrinal ideas into their homilies on the martyrs in order to leverage the popularity of martyr piety for pedagogical purposes.[31] The text at hand is Gregory's *Homily* 1b *on the Forty Martyrs of Sebaste*, preached on the annual feast of these popular martyred soldiers. According to Cobb's assessment of this homily, Gregory presents an account of martyrdom that 'concedes the experience of pain but rejects its importance'.[32] In what follows, I hope to show that reading the homily against what we already know about the link between pleasure and sin can help us see that the pain of the martyrs does, for Gregory, hold redemptive significance.

Gregory's homilies 1a and 1b on the martyrs of Sebaste form a whole delivered on the same occasion over two days. The two homilies give an impression of unpolished authenticity since the first is interrupted by the noise from the bustling crowd that has gathered to celebrate the feast of the martyrs.[33] These feasts were frequently as much about enjoyment as they were about suffering since they provided occasions for merry communal gatherings, at times much to the annoyance of church leaders.[34] However Gregory, who is known for his life-long affinity to the cult of martyrs, does not seek to suppress the audience's booming enthusiasm, even as it reportedly disrupted his own preaching. When he picks up the sermon in *Homily* 1b, he welcomes the noise of the day before as 'wholeheartedly wished and sweet (ἡδύς) to us' and acknowledges that a martyr story should bring pleasure (ἡδίους) to its hearers. In the homily that follows, Gregory seeks not to extirpate but to harness and elevate the high festive mood for the purposes of Christian teaching. This is accomplished through the rhetorical technique of *ekphrasis*, a vivid and detailed description that allows the audience to witness the martyrs' struggle as if it were happening in front of their eyes.[35] By

---

31. See especially Johan Leemans, 'Schoolrooms for Our Souls: The Cult of Martyrs: Homilies and Visual Representations as a Locus for Religious Education in Late Antiquity', *Paedagogica Historica* 36, no. 1 (2000). Leemans (Ibid., 122–3) expresses some reservations about the efficacy of this method. See also Vasiliki M. Limberis, *Architects of Piety: The Cappadocian Fathers and the Cult of the Martyrs* (Oxford: Oxford University Press, 2011), 10.

32. Cobb, *Divine Deliverance*, 120.

33. Leemans, 'Gregory of Nyssa', 92–3.

34. Leemans, 'Schoolrooms for Our Souls', 118–19.

35. *Mart.* 1b, GNO 10/1, 145.15, 146.6-8. All translations of *Mart.* are from Johan Leemans, 'First Homily on the Forty Martyrs of Sebaste (Ia and Ib)', in *Let Us Die That We May Live*, 98–107. On *ekphrasis* in early Christian martyr accounts, see Cobb, *Divine Deliverance*, 3–11, esp. p. 8 for Gregory's use of *ekphrasis* in his *Homily on the Forty Martyrs of Sebaste*; Johan Leemans, 'Style and Meaning in Gregory of Nyssa's Panegyrics on Martyrs', *Ephemerides Theologicae Lovanienses* 81, no. 1 (2005): 126–8; Limberis, *Architects of Piety*, 53–96.

narrating the story in a way that directs the inner gaze of his hearers, Gregory tells his audience not only what to look at but how to look and respond to it. Thus, in the homily Gregory does not only emphasize that the Christian life entails a shift of perception and an accompanying re-evaluation of pain and pleasure but also aims to elicit this very transformation in his hearers.[36]

Gregory creates this effect by highlighting the beauty of the martyrs' outward sufferings. He recounts how, shackled together, the martyrs carry their chain like an adornment.[37] Crucially, the martyrs' chains and their impending torture seem 'elegant and sweet' only to Christians who understand its hidden nature and aim. They create a sight that is beautiful to 'those who [want] to behold beauty', such as the angels and other heavenly powers – but hateful to demons and their followers.[38] The ambiguity of beauty that hides from those who are not aware of the deeper reality beyond appearances, but reveals itself to spiritually sound beings, shows that perception depends on one's inner condition.

From the holy onlookers who are able to perceive true beauty, Gregory turns to the analogous example of the martyrs who demonstrate a correct understanding of the true good and order their pains and pleasures accordingly. Here, the link between virtuous suffering and the undoing of the effects of the fall is even more pronounced than in *Homily 8 on the Beatitudes*. Gregory presents the martyrs' combat as round two in a wrestling contest in which the first round consisted of Adam's failed match with the serpent: 'At the time, man didn't withstand one attack of the Evil One, which happened by offering him an attractive bait (διά τινος εὐχροίας καὶ δελεάσματος); rather, at once the Devil assaulted him and man was overturned by the Fall.'[39] The allusion to the fall accomplished through an attractive bait introduces the paradigmatic example of Gregory's critique of pleasure as the false good.[40] And it is this very hedonist error that the martyrs set right in their steadfast endurance and detachment from worldly delights:

> What is more wretched than the fruit of the tree? What is meaner than the tree itself? Its fruit, while looking attractive because of its colour and sweetness of taste (εὐχροίᾳ τινὶ καὶ ἡδονῇ γεύσεως[41]), caused men to dishonour the grace of Paradise.
>
> To these, the greatest of contestants, however, not even the sun appeared sweet (οὐδὲ αὐτὸς ὁ ἥλιος ἐφάνη γλυκύς): they voluntarily estranged themselves from

---

36. Limberis, *Architects of Piety*.
37. *Mart.* 1b, GNO 10/1, 148.10-5.
38. Ibid., 148.26–149.2.
39. Ibid., 150.14-16.
40. See my discussion in section 'Pleasure, pain and the good'.
41. The phrase is virtually identical to the one in Gregory's account of pleasure and the fall in *De hominis opificio*, which I have cited above.

it, so that they should not apostatise from the true light. What does Scripture say about Eve? (for I am led beyond what is due to attack their ancestors). It says: 'She saw that it was attractive to see and good to taste' (ἀρεστὸν τοῖς ὀφθαλμοῖς καὶ ὡραῖον εἰς γεῦσιν) (Gen 3:6). Then they exchanged Paradise for the attractiveness of these things. But to the martyrs the visible things also carried with them the sweetness of temptation (τούτοις δὲ ἄρα καταγεύσεως ἡδονὴν τὰ ὁρώμενα ἦν): heaven, the sun, the earth, people, one's country, mothers, brothers, friends, relatives, comrades. What is sweeter to observe (ὀφθῆναι γλυκύτερον) than these things? What is more valuable than coming to enjoy these? … But for them, all this was hateful, all this was strange. Only one thing was good (μόνον ἀγαθόν): Christ. They renounced everything in order to gain him.[42]

Here, Gregory presents the martyrs as the antithesis of Adam and Eve. They set right their ancestors' failure by adopting an opposite course of action: whereas Eve exchanges Paradise for the attractive fruit that symbolizes sensual pleasures and worldly delights, the martyrs demonstrate their complete detachment from worldly goods, wary even of the everyday pleasures offered by natural surroundings and family relationships. While here Gregory does not explicitly elaborate on the notion of pleasure as the false good, the idea is present when he highlights the martyrs' act of renunciation and notes that for them 'only one thing was good: Christ'.

Conclusion

By exploring works from three different genres – a manual for Christian teaching, an exegetical commentary and a homily preached on the feast of martyrs – we have seen that reading theoretical reflections on the ethical value of pain along with popularized depictions of suffering can help us attain a more nuanced understanding of the value of pain in early Christian writings. I have sought to demonstrate, first of all, that Gregory of Nyssa neither glorifies nor rejects the theological importance of suffering, but views pain as an instrumental good. Second, I have argued that the redemptive relevance of pain can be grasped more fully if we first understand the fundamental role that pleasure plays in bringing about sin: pleasure, which distracts humans from the true good, is remedied when pain is borne for the sake of the good. This is exemplified by the figure of the martyr whose ability to bear pain signals that he has overcome the tendency to seek pleasure and, more broadly, to determine the good on the basis of what appears good to the senses. Finally, the martyrs' joyful suffering shows that with the acceptance of pain for the sake of the good comes also a renewed understanding of what is truly enjoyable. Only by setting aside immediate bodily sensations and adopting the hopeful perspective of eschatological fulfilment can the Christian evaluate the true value of her pains and pleasures.

---

42. *In XL Martyres* 1b, GNO 10/1, 151.13–152.3. Trans. Leemans, 103.

Chapter 4

GREGORY OF NAZIANZUS ON THE ROLE OF SATAN IN HUMAN SUFFERING

Gabrielle Thomas

What difference does it make if theologians, as Robert Jenson puts it, 'take the devil with theological seriousness', within a Christian vision of human suffering?[1] Is it possible that an account of suffering which incorporates powers of opposition ensures that suffering is not sacralized? What is at stake in this kind of enquiry?

I will explore these questions in conversation with Gregory of Nazianzus (circa AD 329–89), one of the so-called 'Cappadocians' and a leading theologian in fourth-century debates. Alongside his well-known work on Christology and the Trinity, Gregory reflects frequently on his own suffering and diminishment, especially in his poetry.[2]

His preoccupation with suffering is rooted, to a great extent, in his experience as archbishop of Constantinople during the Second Ecumenical Council in AD 381.[3] Gregory worked hard to achieve a particular objective through the debates; namely, the Council should recognize explicitly the Holy Spirit as consubstantial with the Father and the Son in the Niceno-Constantinopolitan creed. After lengthy and acrimonious discussions, Gregory did not achieve the outcome for which he longed, and subsequently resigned from his role as archbishop with no small degree of bitterness. In the poem aptly entitled, 'Complaint Concerning His

---

1. Robert W. Jenson, 'Evil as Person', in *Theology as Revisionary Metaphysics: Essays on God and Creation*, ed. Stephen John Wright (Eugene: Wipf and Stock, 2014), 136–45, 136.

2. Much of the poetry is not yet translated into English. For the Greek edition see volume 37 of J. P. Migne, ed., *Patrologia Graeca* [= Patrologiae cursus completus: Series graeca], 162 vols (Paris, 1857–1886).

3. John A. McGuckin explores Gregory's sufferings during the Council of Constantinople in *St. Gregory of Nazianzus: An Intellectual Biography* (New York: St. Vladimir's Seminary Press, 2001), 311–69. For an insightful discussion on Gregory as an autobiographer see Andrew O. P. Hofer, *Christ in the Life and Teaching of Gregory of Nazianzus* (Oxford: Oxford University Press, 2013), Ch. 2.

Own Calamities', he reflects, somewhat self-pityingly, on his failure. He concludes, 'My fame lies in my sufferings.'[4]

An interesting dynamic is at play in Gregory's theological reflection on suffering. On some occasions, Gregory calls out to God and asks why God has afflicted him with various kinds of trials and tribulations. On other occasions, Gregory attributes his suffering to powers of opposition. This suggests that he believes there is more than one way of contextualizing suffering.

The way in which Gregory locates 'the devil' in suffering, I will argue, creates a space in which to construe suffering negatively or – though he would not use the terminology himself – as simply meaningless. In short, Gregory's theologizing about the role of 'the devil' contributes to a view of suffering as a complex mystery, and one which is not necessarily sacralized.[5]

Gregory's vision of hostile powers

Gregory weaves his views on powers of opposition into all kinds of theological work, ranging from the incarnation, soteriology, creation, baptism, through to suffering. However, this aspect of his thought has made little impact on modern scholarship. This is, in part, due to the effects of the Enlightenment rendering discussion of hostile powers an embarrassment to Christian theology.[6]

We should recall that those living in the fourth century held a radically different world view which Catholic philosopher, Charles Taylor, describes as 'enchanted'.[7] By this, he means that the reality of 'spirits, demons and moral forces' was readily accepted.[8] Moreover, the inhabitants of this 'enchanted world' believed themselves

---

4. Poem 2.1.19 (Patralogia Graeca 37, 1271–9, 29); *Gregory of Nazianzus, Autobiographical Poems*, translated and edited by Carolinne White (Cambridge: Cambridge University Press, 1996), 157.

5. Nazianzen also depicts suffering, on one occasion, as aiding spiritual formation. He arrives at this view through a discussion of how God creates the human person, arguing that God limits the human by creating her as a unified mixture of 'spirit and flesh'. Suffering, he argues, which occurs because of these limitations, can serve to educate a person out of any aspirations of grandeur and can guard against pride; see *Oration* 38.11, *St. Gregory of Nazianzus, Festal Orations*, trans. Nonna Verna Harrison (Crestwood: St. Vladimir's Seminary Press, 2008), 68.

6. On this, see Emil Brunner, *The Christian Doctrine of Creation and Redemption: Dogmatics* Vol. II, translated by Olive Wyon, D.D. (London: Lutterworth Press, 1952), 135.

7. 'Enchantment is an antonym to Weber's application of "disenchantment" as a means of describing our modern condition'; Charles Taylor, *A Secular Age* (Cambridge: Harvard University Press, 2007), 446.

8. Taylor, *A Secular Age*, 29.

to be 'open and porous and vulnerable to a world of spirits and powers'.[9] As we shall see, when Gregory writes on hostile powers, he depicts himself as vulnerable to them. He does not treat the devil or demons as rhetorical constructs. Rather, they constitute a genuine threat to the human person.[10] Having said this, it is important to note that while his world view takes seriously the spiritual realm, Gregory does not envisage a world in which powers of opposition are, in any way, equal to God.

Locating himself within the *privatio boni* tradition, later developed in the West by Augustine, Gregory writes, 'Believe that no aspect of evil has either substance or royalty, or is without beginning, or has a substantial nature by itself, or comes from God.'[11] It is widely recognized that *creatio ex nihilo* is the foundation for Gregory's beliefs about the existence of hostile powers, in which he presents the devil as a creature who does not pose a serious threat to God.[12] The devil and his host of demons cannot be considered evil in themselves because they began their existence as part of God's good creation. As Morwenna Ludlow has argued, these evil spirits perform evil actions and possess an evil will, but neither the devil nor his army can be understood as evil according to their nature.[13] Consequently, Gregory attributes to evil spirits a 'diminishing' existence in which they exist by nourishing themselves, somewhat parasitically, on the hearts of human persons.[14]

The titles which Gregory attributes to the devil are many and varied. Many of them are listed in the poem 'Aversion of the Evil One and Invocation of Christ': Thief, Serpent, Fire, Belial, Vice, Death, Dragon, Beast, Night, Ambusher, Rage, Chaos, Slanderer and Murderer.[15] Elsewhere, Gregory also speaks of the devil as 'Envy', 'the Evil One', 'Adversary', 'Tempter' and 'the Enemy'. These epithets derive from scripture and their frequent use by fourth-century theologians marks the prevalence of the devil and demons in early Christian thought. The work of Evagrius Ponticus demonstrates this. He was Gregory's protégé, serving as a

---

9. Ibid., 27.

10. Dayna Kalleres concurs that Gregory's devil is 'real'; 'Demons and Divine Illumination: A Consideration of Eight Prayers by Gregory of Nazianzus', *Vigilae Christianae* 61, no. 2 (2007): 157–88 (186).

11. *Oration* 40.45 (SC 358, 304). Translations are my own, unless stated otherwise. I have used the critically edited *Sources Chrétiennes* series where possible, indicated by 'SC'. Where no critical edition exists, I have used Jacques-Paul Migne, *Patrologia cursus completus, series Graeca*, Vols. 35–8 (Paris, 1857–1862).

12. For an exploration of this see Gabrielle Thomas, *The Image of God in the Theology of Gregory of Nazianzus* (Cambridge: Cambridge University Press, forthcoming 2019), Ch. 4.

13. Morwenna Ludlow, 'Demons, Evil and Liminality in Cappadocian Theology', *Journal of Early Christian Studies* 20, no. 2 (2012): 179–211.

14. For extensive discussion of this see Thomas, *The Image of God*, Ch. 4.

15. Poem 2.1.55 (PG 37, 1399–401).

deacon in Constantinople. Influenced by Gregory, Evagrius went on to devise a comprehensive demonology and method of combat for over 500 kinds of battles between demons and human persons.[16]

Following the early Christian tradition, Gregory identifies the devil with the fallen angel Lucifer, the serpent in the Garden of Eden, the Satan in the book of Job and the dragon in the Revelation of St John, using the titles interchangeably.[17] According to this tradition of interpretation, Lucifer does not work alone after he has been banished from heaven but gathers together an army of rebel angels to work towards the destruction of humankind. Gregory refers to these rebel angels as 'demons', drawing on Origen's advanced demonology for his description of their ontology and purpose.[18]

The fall

By identifying the devil with the serpent in the Garden of Eden, Gregory locates the fall as the first occasion upon which the devil is associated with human suffering. Death interrupts human existence through the fall, and suffering ensues. It is important to note that for Gregory, sin and suffering are inextricably linked. They each represent ways in which the devil keeps the human person enslaved and oppressed. A remedy is needed; this is the incarnation, life, death and resurrection of Christ:

> If we had remained the very thing which we were and kept the commandment, we would have become that which we were not, coming towards the tree of life, after the tree of knowledge. And what would we have become? Immortal and consorts with God. But since death came into the world through the envy of the Evil One, and filched the human person through trickery, God has come to suffer as we suffer, by becoming human.[19]

---

16. David Brakke suggests that it is probable that Evagrius 'learned from Gregory about the danger of demonic thoughts, and the possibility of refuting them verbally with powerful words'; *Talking Back: A Monastic Handbook for Combating Demons* (Minnesota: Cistercian Publications, 2009), 19.

17. For an excellent overview of the tradition, see Jeffrey B. Russell, *Satan: The Early Christian Tradition* (New York: Cornell University Press, 1987).

18. Poem 1.1.7 (PG 37, 444, 74). For a translation of the poem which describes the fall of Lucifer see Peter Gilbert, *On God and Man: The Theological Poetry of St. Gregory of Nazianzus* (Crestwood: St. Vladimir's Seminary Press, 2001), 57–61. Origen's principal discussion of demons is found in *Against Celsus* 5.5.

19. *Oration* 44.4 (PG 36, 612A-B.) For a complete translation of *Oration* 44, see Brian Daley, *Gregory of Nazianzus* (London: Taylor & Francis, 2006), 155–61.

Building on the work of theologians such as Athanasius, Gregory teaches that human persons are created with the potential to become gods through *theosis*.[20] This is developed from an interpretation of Gen. 1:26-28, which speaks of the human person as 'the image of God'. The devil is envious of this 'image', which results in a severe enmity directed towards humankind. The first 'image of God' is tempted and won over by the 'envious murderer's wrestlings', which leads to the bite of fruit from the forbidden tree.[21] The outcome of this is the banishment of Adam and Eve from the Garden of Eden.

While he argues that Adam and Eve were tricked into eating from the tree of knowledge due to 'the malice of the evil one', Gregory recognizes human responsibility for sin.[22] He assumes repeatedly his own responsibility for the sin in the world as one who has eaten the fruit from the forbidden tree in paradise.[23] In identifying with this initial consumption, Gregory sits in the tradition of the Eastern fathers whereby he displays an awareness of historical events, but tends 'more to collapse history and read past events as present'.[24] Thus, he reads himself, and every human person, into the account of the fall.[25]

For the most part, after the fall, human persons lapse into an existence of continual struggle with powers of opposition, which Gregory describes as a 'vexatious life'.[26] He makes explicit to his readers that it is not positive, in any sense, to share the earth with these evil spirits, who are constantly interfering in human affairs.

Existence on earth alongside powers of opposition

Gregory does not aim to provide a cohesive explanation for the problem of evil through his theologizing on the relationship between human suffering and powers of opposition. He is consistent in his recognition of God's omnipotence and benevolence in the face of evil. He stipulates that Christ could have 'done away with the devil' through his death on the cross and resurrection if this had been what

---

20. Poem 1.1.8 (PG 37, 452, 74–5).
21. Poem 1.1.8 (PG 37, 455, 112); Gilbert, *On God and Man*, 67.
22. Oration 38.12 (SC 358, 128).
23. *Oration* 19.14 (PG 35, 1060C-D); see Donald F. Winslow, *The Dynamics of Salvation: A Study in Gregory of Nazianzus* (Cambridge: Philadelphia Patristic Foundation, 1979), 69.
24. Andrew Louth, 'The Fathers on Genesis', in *The Book of Genesis: Composition, Reception, and Interpretation*, ed. Craig A. Evans, Joel N. Lohr and David L. Petersen (Leiden: Brill, 2012), 561–78, 574.
25. Richard J. Clifford, 'The Hebrew Scriptures and the Theology of Creation', *Theological Studies* 46, no. 3 (1985): 507–23.
26. Poem 1.1.8 (PG 37, 455, 118).

Christ 'had in mind'.²⁷ In a short section of his poem entitled 'Concerning Spiritual Beings', Gregory offers three possible reasons why demonic activity persists. He reassures his readers that Christ did not allow the devil to go unpunished, but instead

> gave him dreadful strife on either side, so as to have a dreadful
> shame also in this, that he must fight his own subordinates,
> and so that strugglers for virtue should have eternal glory,
> like gold, refined in the furnaces of life:
> or perhaps, so that afterwards the stubborn one should render
> punishments.²⁸

Elsewhere, in his work, as we shall see shortly, Gregory does not present his own experience of 'wrestling with the devil' as a means of winning 'eternal glory' but rather as a miserable aspect of human existence. Gregory's use of 'perhaps' is significant, since it suggests that he is aware his explanation is unsatisfactory and that it does not incorporate the breadth of evil as it is experienced on earth. This might be why in a further oration, despite having defended Christ's decision to allow the devil to continue to exist, Gregory bewails the continued presence of the devil: 'Would that evil be destroyed utterly, both the first seed of evil and the Evil One, who sowed the weeds in us while we were sleeping.'²⁹ His lament highlights the tension around human suffering in the Christian tradition.

Christ, the devil and human suffering

Having surveyed Gregory's views on powers of opposition, I will move on to explore how he describes the devil's involvement in certain kinds of suffering. The result is that suffering is construed as destructive.

We will begin by considering how Gregory weaves the devil into his account of Christ's response to human suffering. One particular example of this is the way in which Gregory utilizes *kenosis*. While *kenosis* was not in general a widely discussed theme in the fourth century, Brian Matz has demonstrated that Gregory either cites or alludes to Phil. 2:6-7, the well-known verses which speak of Christ's *kenosis*, on forty-four occasions.³⁰ Matz builds on seminal work by Donald Winslow, who has argued that Gregory brings *kenosis* into soteriological focus to the same extent as theologians, such as, Irenaeus and Athanasius, achieved through the incarnation.

---

27. Poem 1.1.7 (PG 37, 445, 83).
28. Poem 1.1.7 (PG 37, 445–6); translation by Gilbert, *On God and Man*, 60–1.
29. Oration 19.14 (PG 35, 1060C).
30. Brian J. Matz, 'Philippians 2:7 as Pastoral Example in Gregory Nazianzen's Oration 12', *Greek Orthodox Theological Review* 49, no. 3–4 (2004): 270–90, 282.

Matz writes, 'Unlike other Greek patristic writers who focused on the incarnation as the soteriological apex, Gregory put the *kenosis* of Christ on an equal plane. Rather than lowering Christ, the *kenosis* elevated humanity.'[31] While one needs to be a little careful about the contrast that seems to be implied here between *kenosis* and incarnation here, Matz's observation is important for two reasons. Firstly, the observation is important to our discussion because it highlights how Gregory treats *kenosis* as a Christological and soteriological concept. In keeping with the early Christian tradition he does not relate it, in any way, to trinitarian doctrine: Gregory envisages Christ's *kenosis* as temporary, not as an eternal property of God.[32] Even temporarily, furthermore, the Son's divinity, for Gregory, is not diminished through the incarnation.[33]

Secondly, Gregory interprets Phil. 2:6-7 against the backdrop of the well-known 'exchange formula' described first by Irenaeus.[34] Gregory writes, 'Let us become like Christ, since Christ became like us. Let us become gods for his sake, since he became human for our sakes.'[35] The 'exchange', in this instance, is the *theosis* of the human person. However, human persons have an enemy whose aim is both to prevent their *theosis* and to destroy them completely:

> Christ, on seeing as great a heavenly share as he placed in the mortal body
> being devoured by heart-gnawing evil
> and the crooked dragon (the devil) ruling over mortals,
> in order that he might raise his portion
> he did not send towards the disease other forms of help,
> (for a little cure is of no use to great sufferings). But having emptied
> (*kenōsas*) his glory,
> the heavenly and the eternal Image of heaven,
> assumed flesh in the holy womb of an unwed woman.[36]

The above-mentioned lines follow a long section in which Gregory describes how the people of God are caught up in patterns of sin. His rationale for this is that the devil is ruling over humankind and that demons are parasitically 'gnawing on hearts' of human persons. Through his description, Gregory locates the devil's involvement in human suffering in such a way as to prevent the valourizing of suffering. For, as far as he is concerned, when powers

---

31. Ibid., 281; Winslow, *The Dynamics of Salvation*, 95–6.

32. Ibid.

33. John Behr, *The Mystery of Christ: Life in Death* (Crestwood: St. Vladimir's Seminary Press, 2006), 35.

34. *Against Heresies* (Book 5, Preface); also see Athanasius, *On the Incarnation*, 54.

35. *Oration* 1.5 (SC 247, 78).

36. Poem 1.2.1 (PG 37, 533, 139–47). For an alternative translation, see Gilbert, *On God and Man*, 93–4.

of opposition are connected to suffering, the suffering itself is deemed as unconstructive, serving no positive end. Thus, a 'cure' is the only appropriate response to this kind of suffering, which, in itself, has no value. Gregory argues that there is only one way to defeat the devil and his accompanying demons, and for human persons to be healed from their cycles of sin: this is through Christ's *kenosis*, life, death and resurrection.

Gregory weaves the devil not only into his thought about *kenosis* and the incarnation but also into his understanding of the cross, although he does not elucidate this systematically. He believes that the principal purposes of Christ's death on the cross are 'to triumph over the serpent … and heal Adam and restore the fallen image of God'.[37] Christ's death on the cross 'conquers the tyrant by force' and leads the human race back to God.[38] In his discussions of this, Gregory draws on a theme prevalent in Irenaeus's work on atonement.[39] This is brought to the fore in the work of Gustaf Aulén, who identified the theme as 'Christus Victor'. Aulén writes, 'The work of Christ is first and foremost a victory over the powers which hold mankind in bondage: sin, death, and the devil.'[40] Gregory's vision of the atonement is more nuanced than Aulén's observation suggests. He does not envisage Christ's death on the cross solely in light of victory over the devil, but also draws in terms of ransom and sacrifice.[41] However, as with his writing on *kenosis*, Gregory weaves the devil into his thought on the cross, revealing a key theme in his theology; namely, if human suffering involves powers of opposition, then Christians should focus upon victory over these, rather than supposing glory follows the suffering.[42]

Gregory's views on Christ's victory over hostile powers become clearer when we turn to his prayers. Oppression by the devil is not an abstract issue, but relates to the spiritual life of the believer. Gregory's belief that Christ has beaten the powers of opposition leads him to pray that he would experience effectually the victory Christ has won for human persons.

---

37. *Oration* 24.4 (SC 284, 46). Gregory refers to the human person created according to the image of God.

38. *Oration* 45.22; translation by Harrison, *Festal Orations*, 182.

39. *Against Heresies* 3.18.7; Hendrickus Berkhof, *Christ and the Powers* (Scottdale: Herald, 1962), 31.

40. Gustaf Aulén, *Christus Victor: An Historical Study of the Three Main Types of the Idea of Atonement*, trans. A.G. Herbert (London: SPCK, 1931), 20.

41. *Oration* 45.22 (PG 36, 653B).

42. Aulén's 'Christus Victor' was a hugely influential recovery of early Christian ideas on atonement. That said, it has been critiqued for its lack of attention to the important theme of sacrifice and for the way in which dualism appears to be a necessary feature. See, for example, Hans Boersma, *Violence, Hospitality, and the Cross: Reappropriating the Atonement Tradition* (Grand Rapids: Baker Academic, 2004), 181–201.

Victory over powers of opposition

You have come, o Evil-doer, I recognize your thoughts.
You have come, in order that you might deprive me of the light and beloved life
Ever since first you cast Adam from paradise,
A creation of God, and with evil you ambushed a wise command,
And provided bitter food to a sweet life;
How am I to flee from you? What remedy shall I find for my sufferings?[43]

The above poem, entitled 'Against the Evil One', is one of no fewer than fifteen poems and prayers concerned with the way in which powers of opposition effect suffering, in some way. In these poems, Gregory invariably asks for Christ's help and deliverance from the evil spirits.[44] To understand the kind of harm these powers of opposition cause, let us turn to one of the many poems entitled 'Lament':

The image is being destroyed, what word will rescue?
The image is being destroyed, gift of excellent God.
The image is being assaulted, I am burning, O Envy, Envy,
with others' words and deceits.[45]
Spring of evil, do not flow forth. Let my heart not be empty.
Therefore, if you, tongue, do not receive the abusive one,
Therefore, if you, hand, do not receive what is beneath you,
Perhaps our image will remain uncorrupted.[46]

Firstly, note that 'the image' is a form of shorthand Gregory uses to describe the human person as she is created according to the image of God, following Gen. 1:26-28. When he depicts human persons as such, it is to draw attention to the way that they are becoming divine and to remind his readers that human persons are godlike precisely because they are created according to the image of God. Gregory's use of this description also recalls the devil because the devil's envy of the divine image is a concern which he raises across the texts. In the previous poem, Gregory describes the devil as a 'human slayer'. He declares that the devil is as interested now in the destruction of human life as he was in paradise. Once

---

43. Poem 2.1.54 (PG 37, 1397–9). Translation by Kalleres, 'Demons and Divine Illumination', 162–3.
44. Only eight of these poems are published in English currently and may be found at the beginning of Kalleres's article. See also (PG 37, 1394–430).
45. A word on the translation: Gregory applies *kenoō* to describe the effects upon the divine image, which I have translated as 'destroy' because the expression arrives after a sequence in which Gregory speaks about the devil longing to kill each human person. Following Phil 2:7, *kenoō* is commonly translated as 'empty', but there is nothing in the text to indicate here that Gregory has Christ's *kenosis* in mind.
46. Poem 2.1.61 (PG 37, 1404–5).

again, Gregory's response to this kind of suffering is to reach for resistance and victory and to lament the effects of powers of opposition.

Let us turn now to our final extract which concerns a different kind of suffering, namely disease. In a poem entitled, 'On Illness' Gregory describes his own experience of being unwell.[47] He provides no details of his condition, other than to refer to his suffering as a 'disease'. Gregory's response is to seek Christ's healing, because he believes that if there are remedies to be found, these come from Christ, who is the 'source of everything'. After ten lines of petitioning Christ, he laments,

> I am in the pits of destruction, my Christ, what then, shall I do?
> While you are a just judge, you are also gentle.
> How does this profit you? Are we cut off, alone?
> Having chopped me up, Satan hurled me – he hurled me!
> Why are these things happening, Christ? I am ashamed before evil men.
> I have been worn out, by time, by illness, by the wickedness of friends.
> I have been set up as a target for all, and I have been struck ...
> Let the Envious One be brought to a standstill, let him be brought to a standstill soon.
> But surely you do not wish this? I come towards you, give your hand.[48]

Rather than rationalizing how his suffering fits within the will of God, Gregory's belief in demonic activity provides him with a means of interpreting his experience as that which has no explanation and is futile. It is not within his control to end his own suffering nor is he responsible for all the suffering that befalls him. His response to suffering is that Christ could not possibly think it is 'good' and therefore it must be connected to Satan, in some way. Thus, it must be beaten. If it cannot be beaten, then lament is the only response which remains, and to pray fervently to God for deliverance.

Conclusion

Where does this leave us? One could say that Gregory's approach to suffering is like a rug which has been woven with myriad bright colours to form an intricate pattern. If one were to pull out a brightly coloured thread, there would be a strong possibility of losing the pattern. In the same way, if we were to try and take 'the devil' out of Gregory's theologizing, we would lose the key thread of Christ's victory over evil powers, which runs through his soteriology and theological anthropology, and so profoundly shapes his approach to human suffering.

---

47. Elsewhere, Gregory speaks of those with leprosy as being more Christ-like (*Oration* 14). He does not indicate that he believes all illness to be demonically activated, rather certain illnesses, although he does not explain which these are.

48. Poem 2.1.89 (PG 37, 1442–5).

I began by asking 'what difference would it make if theologians were to "take the devil with theological seriousness", within a Christian vision of human suffering?' While we have considered only very briefly Gregory's approach, we have seen that the devil plays an important role in his view of suffering. It is a role in which the devil is not, in any sense, on an equal footing with God. The devil is a creature, after all, albeit radically distorted. However, it is precisely this distortion which means that the devil's activity cannot bring about meaning and value in human existence. Thus, when powers of opposition are involved, suffering has no glory or valour. It is not sacralized.

Through the inclusion of hostile powers, when speaking about human suffering, Gregory provides an account which takes seriously the reality of the degradation of human identity through suffering. His belief that the devil is often involved with suffering means that he is able to depict suffering as that which serves negative ends or as simply meaningless. He does not ascribe worth, praise or value to powers of opposition for their involvement in human suffering, rather with an opposite stance that Gregory 'gives the devil his due'.

Chapter 5

SUFFERING, DERELICTION AND AFFLICTION IN CHRISTIAN MYSTICISM

Bernard McGinn

If you endure and do right and suffer for it, you have God's approval.
For to this you have been called, because Christ also suffered for you,
leaving you an example, so that you should follow in his steps.

(1 Pet. 2.21)

In Christian history the theology of suffering rests on two New Testament pillars. The first is the witness in the Gospels and Acts that Christ himself had to 'suffer many things' (*polla pathein*) in order to redeem humanity (Mt. 16.21; Mk. 8.31 and 9.12; Lk. 17.25), as foretold by the scriptures (Lk. 24.26 and 46; Acts 3.18, 17.3, 26.23). An addendum to the Gospel message about the necessity of Christ's suffering is found in the teaching of the Epistle to the Hebrews about Christ being 'tested' by what he suffered (Heb. 2.18), and even that 'he learned obedience through what he suffered; and having been made perfect, he became the source of eternal salvation for all who obey him (Heb. 5.8)'. The second pillar of the Christian view of suffering is the insistence, both in the Pauline corpus and in 1 Peter, that the believer is called upon to suffer with Christ. As Paul put it in Rom. 8.17, we are children and 'heirs of God and joint heirs with Christ – if, in fact, we suffer with him so that we may also be glorified with him'. Thus, the sufferings of Christ abound in us, as also his consolations (2 Cor. 1.5). The privilege of believing in Christ entails suffering for him, according to Phil. 1.29. If we share in his sufferings by becoming like him in death, like him, we will attain resurrection from the dead (Phil. 3.10), that is, as Paul says in Col. 1.24, 'In my flesh I am completing what is lacking in Christ's afflictions for the sake of his body, that is, the church' (see also 2 Thess. 3.5).

This message has never been absent from Christian history, however uncomfortable some historical manifestations of it make us feel today. In modern times it has been strongly endorsed by Pope John Paul II in an address delivered in 1984 in commemoration of the appearance of the Blessed Virgin at Lourdes. Commenting on Paul, the Pope said, 'The joy comes from the discovery of the meaning of suffering. ... What we express with the word "suffering" seems to be particularly *essential to the nature of Man*. ... Suffering seems to belong to

Man's transcendence. Christianity ... is not a system into which we have to fit the awkward fact of pain. ... In a sense it creates, rather than solves, the problem of pain.'[1] Suffering inevitably calls up the language of pain, as we can see from John Paul's statement, but it is worth remembering that while suffering and pain often go together, they are not the same. Pain is a physiological sensation related to some injury to the body, one that involves complex neurological issues. Suffering is an emotional reaction to some situation, often connected to bodily pain, but it can also be related to events, like the death of a loved one, that do not entail physical injury.[2] The sufferings of Jesus referred to in the New Testament embraced both physical pain and mental anguish.

The Gospels depict Jesus 'suffering, or undergoing, many things' during his preaching years. The difficulties of his wandering life, the threats and opposition he encountered, all involved mental suffering and probably some measure of physical pain, but the preacher from Galilee specifically noted that his was not a life of severe asceticism in the manner of John the Baptist (Lk. 7.33-34). It is the events surrounding Jesus's death on the cross that the Pauline and Petrine texts have in mind when they talk about filling up Christ's sufferings. The scenario of the passion begins with the account of Jesus in the Garden of Gethsemane on the night preceding his crucifixion, when he announced, 'I am deeply grieved, even to the point of death' (Mt. 26.38), and prayed to his Father to let the cup of his sufferings pass from him, if at all possible (Mt. 26.39-46; see Mk. 14.32-42, Lk. 22.39-46). Luke heightens Jesus's inner turmoil by recounting that his sweat became like drops of blood (Lk. 22.44).[3] Christ's inner sufferings were increased by the physical pain involved in his arrest, trial and scourging during the night and next morning. They culminated in the horrific act of his public crucifixion. Matthew and Mark record that, while on the cross, Jesus cried out with a loud voice, '"Eli, Eli, lema sabachtani?", that is, "My God, my God, why have you forsaken me?"' (Mt. 27.46; Mk. 15.34; see Ps. 22.1). I mention these familiar details here, because the model of completing the sufferings of the crucified Christ was always tied to the passion narrative. The mental anguish of Christ in Gethsemane and his cry of alienation and estrangement from the Father while on the cross were particularly important for the strand in Christian thinking, especially mystical thinking, that holds that Christ's mental sufferings were even worse than the physical pain he underwent.[4]

---

1. The address is cited in Patrick D. Wall and Mervyn Jones, *Defeating Pain: The War against a Silent Epidemic* (New York: Plenum Press, 1991), 150–1.

2. On the distinction, Ariel Glucklich, *Sacred Pain: Hurting the Body for the Sake of the Soul* (Oxford: Oxford University Press, 2001), 11. The first three chapters in Glucklich's book present a theory of pain and explore its neurological and psychological dimensions.

3. Luke 22.43-44 is missing in some manuscripts and may be a later addition.

4. This theme is found in many authors. For an extended treatment, see Camilla Battista da Varano, *The Mental Sufferings of Christ in His Passion*, a popular work written in 1488 and often printed. There is a brief account in Bernard McGinn, *The Varieties of Vernacular Mysticism 1350–1550* (New York: Crossroad, 2012), 310–11.

An important result of the medicalization of pain beginning in the second half of the nineteenth century is that it is often difficult for modern people to understand the role of pain and suffering throughout most of recorded history. Pain was a fact of life, not an aberrant condition to be overcome by medical intervention. This is what makes Pope John Paul's statement startling to some. The fact that Christians often suffered pain inflicted by others, as, for example, in the case of the martyrs, and, even more so, that Christians inflicted pain on themselves through severe ascetic practices appears to many today as bizarre, perhaps a species of masochism. Nonetheless, as Ariel Glucklich has pointed out in *Sacred Pain*, many religions have viewed pain as an important, even necessary, step in the religious progress of the person. It is not so much the suffering caused by the pain, but the attitude towards the suffering that is central. 'Metaphorically', according to Glucklich, 'pain creates an embodied "absence" and makes way for a new and greater "presence"'.[5]

There are many attitudes to pain and suffering in Christian history. Here, I will focus on one strand of primarily mental suffering that has had a long trajectory in the story of Christian mysticism, that is, the sense of being abandoned by God – the dereliction, estrangement and forsakenness of which so many mystics have spoken. It is a paradox, of course, that those most devoted to finding God have often experienced, sometimes for great lengths of time, abandonment by God. In other cases, God has been present to them, but as a torturer, a source of affliction, not as the loving God. Like Jesus on the cross, these mystics feel compelled to cry out, 'My God, my God, why have you forsaken me?' Mystical dereliction and affliction, as I am calling it, involves a wide range of terms and images, but two modalities seem predominant. The first is the sense of immense loss and alienation, the pain of estrangement that comes from being abandoned by God. The second is the feeling of dread and terror in the face of the presence of God, who appears as Judge or as the *mysterium tremendum*. In some mystics one side prevails over the other; in others, both forms are present.[6]

There is little evidence for mystical dereliction in the first five Christian centuries, perhaps because the early views of the passion and cross did not emphasize Christ's physical or mental sufferings, but rather the triumph over sin and death effected by the entire paschal mystery. The cross that most often appears in early Christian public art, such as the mosaics of the great basilicas, is the triumphant *crux gemmata*, shining with the gold and jewels figuring the splendour

---

5. Glucklich, *Sacred Pain*, 207.

6. I have touched on some aspects of this tradition in Bernard McGinn, 'The Hidden God in Luther and Some Mystics', in *Silence and the Word. Negative Theology and Incarnation*, ed. Oliver Davies and Denys Turner (Cambridge: Cambridge University Press, 2002), 94–114; and 'Three Forms of Negativity in Christian Mysticism', in *Knowing the Unknowable. Science and Religion on God and the Universe*, ed. John Bowker (London: I.B. Tauris, 2009), 99–121. I shall use some materials from these chapters, but the present piece goes further. A number of articles on suffering in mysticism can be found in Bernd Jaspert, ed., *Leiden und Weisheit in der Mystik* (Paderborn: Bonifatius Verlag, 1992).

of heaven.[7] The first figure who advances a mysticism in which the theme of fear and affliction is strong is Pope Gregory the Great (AD 590–604), who can be seen as a kind of hinge between Christian antiquity and the early Middle Ages. Despite his aristocratic background and successful career in the Roman church, Gregory suffered much, both through ill-health and the desperate situation of sixth-century Rome harassed by barbarian foes. Thus, he felt a particular sympathy for the figure of the suffering Job and composed his longest work, the massive *Moralia in Iob (Moral Interpretation of Job)*, to reveal the moral and mystical message of the book. For Gregory, like most patristic exegetes, Job and his sufferings were not so important in themselves, but as a type for the sufferings of Christ. As he put it in Book 23 of the *Moralia*: 'Holy Job is the one who more truly is a type of the Mediator insofar as he prophesied his Passion, not only in words, but also in suffering. Because he depended on the suffering of the Redeemer in his own words and deeds, he is sometimes quickly drawn to a bodily signification.'[8]

Gregory's biblical mysticism features many explorations of the necessity of holding opposed polarities in tension during life in this fallen world: light and darkness, silence and sound, joy and fear and, above all, the tension between the inner and the outer. Jean Leclercq once said that Gregory's thinking is characterized by a 'law of alternation' between one and the other side of such polarities.[9] Contemplative ascent to God, for Gregory, involves both joy and fear, elevation and terror, because the overwhelming majesty of God goes beyond all human categories. Job 4:13 contains an account of Eliphaz's seeing God 'in the horror of a vision by night' (*in horrore visionis nocturnae* Vg). Gregory explains this 'fear of hidden contemplation' (*pavor occultae contemplationis*) by noting that the higher the soul is drawn towards God, 'the incircumscribable Light', the more it is conscious of its sins and imperfections and therefore is filled with terror.[10] There is a direct correlation between the height of the soul's contemplation and the intensity of its fear. 'The human soul is lifted high by the engine of its contemplation so that the more it gazes on things higher than itself the more it is filled with terror.'[11] This is not to say that contemplative experience does not also contain joy and loving desire, but the dialectical character of Gregory's thinking insists on

---

7. Robin M. Jensen, *The Cross: History, Art, and Controversy* (Cambridge: Harvard, 2017), Ch. 5. This is not to say that there were no portrayals of the crucifix, that is, the image of Christ's body on the cross, although these did not emphasize physical suffering in the way that so many later crucifixes did (see Jensen, Ch. 4).

8. *Moralia in Iob* 23.1.2, as found in Marc Adriaen, ed., *S. Gregorii Magni. Moralia in Iob Libri XVII-XXXV* (Turnhout: Brepols, 1979. Corpus Christianorum 143B), 1145.79-82 (my trans.).

9. Jean Leclercq, in Jean Leclercq, François Vandenbroucke and Louis Bouyer, *The Spirituality of the Middle Ages* (New York: The Seabury Press, 1982), 28.

10. See *Moralia in Iob* 5.30.53 (Corpus Christianorum 143), 254-55 (my trans.).

11. *Moralia in Iob* 5.31.55 (Corpus Christianorum 143), 258.80-82 (my trans.). See also *Moralia* 10.8.13-9.15, and the exegesis of Job 33:15 in *Moralia* 23.20.37-21.43.

a kind of coincidence of opposites in contemplation, one in which the fear that induces humility is at least as important as the delight of experiencing God that might, nonetheless, lead to pride. God does not abandon the contemplative in Gregory's view, but his presence brings a special form of fear and suffering.

Although Gregory was widely read by medieval monks, I have not found examples of monastic writers who picked up on this theme in his thought. From the thirteenth century on, however, in the era of what I have called 'The New Mysticism',[12] we find a strong wave of a mysticism of dereliction, that is, a consciousness of God that often implies terror, but that also emphasizes the suffering and affliction that comes when God abandons the soul, leaving the human lover of God in a situation that resembles hell, the place of ultimate loss and estrangement. This is evident in the case of both female and male mystics from diverse linguistic worlds and religious backgrounds.[13] Two premier thirteenth-century representatives are the German beguine Mechthild of Magdeburg (ca. 1208–80), and the Italian third-order Franciscan, Angela of Foligno (ca. 1250–1310).

Mechthild's *Das fliessende Licht der Gotheit* (Flowing Light of the Godhead) is a collection of seven books of chapters in many genres gradually put together in her lifetime as a beguine and also during her last years as a Cistercian nun.[14] It does not survive in its original Low German, but only in subsequent Latin and High German translations. Though not very popular in the Middle Ages, in recent years the *Flowing Light* has emerged as one of the most studied medieval mystical texts, for both its linguistic virtuosity and its challenging theology.[15] There is no simple way to describe Mechthild's notion of the path to union with God, but in terms of our theme, it is clear that the journey involves not only experiences of erotic delight in God but also times of 'painful estrangement' (*gotesvremedunge*) and 'rejection' (*verworfenheit*). Mechthild describes these with startling directness. In some late texts, she sketches a threefold itinerary to God that seems to place the state of rejection and suffering in the highest place. For example, in *Flowing Light* 6.20 she says, 'God bestowed on me the favour that is written down in this book in a threefold manner. First of all with great tenderness; then, with high

---

12. On the 'New Mysticism', see Bernard McGinn, *The Flowering of Mysticism: Men and Women in the New Mysticism – 1200–1350* (New York: Crossroad, 1998).

13. For a survey of the role of suffering in medieval German mysticism, Alois M. Haas, '"Trage Leiden geduldiglich"'. Die Einstellung der deutschen Mystik zum Leiden', in *Gott Leiden. Gott Lieben. Zur volkssprachlichen Mystik im Mittelalter*, Haas (Frankfort-am-Main: Insel Verlag, 1989), 127–52.

14. Hans Neumann, ed., *Mechthild von Magdeburg. Das fliessende Licht der Gottheit*, 2 vols (Munich: Artemis, 1990–3) (hereafter FL). There is a translation by Frank Tobin, *Mechthild of Magdeburg: The Flowing Light of the Godhead* (New York: Paulist Press, 1998).

15. There is an extensive literature; two English summaries are McGinn, *The Flowering of Mysticism*, 222–44 and Sara S. Poor, *Mechthild of Magdeburg and Her Book* (Philadelphia: University of Pennsylvania, 2004).

intimacy; now with intense suffering. I much prefer to remain in this [last] state than in the other two.'[16]

Here, Mechthild may be reflecting her situation as a sick and blind old woman, but it is equally possible that she is summarizing the powerful experiences of being rejected by God that are recorded in the earlier books. Mechthild often speaks of soaring up into God, but there are contrasting passages in which she 'sinks down' into pain and suffering, and even into hell. An example is found in Book 4.12, where God allows her to fall down to the state of the souls in Purgatory, and even of those in hell. Mechthild, nonetheless, welcomes the loss of all consolation with the prayer: 'O, leave me, dear Lord, and let me sink further for your honour.' Sinking ever deeper, she says: 'After this came constant estrangement from God and enveloped the soul so completely that the blessed soul said, "Welcome, very blessed Estrangement. ... But, Lord, you should take delight from me and let me have estrangement from you."' Mechthild recognizes that God is with her even in this estrangement, although 'her body sweated and writhed in painful cramping' during the experience. She overhears a conversation between Christ and Lady Pain in which Jesus reminds Pain that, although she is the devil's servant, she was his closest garment while he was on earth.[17] So with Mechthild, Christ the Redeemer suffering on the cross has become the exemplar of painful affliction, including estrangement from God.[18] Mechthild comes to identify more and more with the kenotic and compassionate Christ on the cross, as we see in the poem found in *Flowing Light* 3.10 where the beguine's 'loving soul' (*minnende sele*) lives out the events of Christ's passion in her daily life and practices.[19]

Angela of Foligno was a generation younger than Mechthild and came from a different spiritual tradition, that of the third-order Franciscans, laymen and women who sought to imitate St Francis, the perfect model of the crucified Christ. Angela was not lettered, but her account of her spiritual journey, the *Memorial*, was taken down by a friendly friar, who, however, found it hard to understand her, as the text with its thirty stages (*passus*) remains to this day.[20] Angela's encounter with Christ centred on the cross, as did those of so many medieval women mystics. What is special about her version of passion mysticism is how she goes beyond the state of sharing in Christ's physical sufferings to explore the realm of dereliction and

---

16. FL 6.20 (ed., 1:229-30; my trans.). See also FL 7.3.

17. FL 4.12 (ed., 1:124-25; trans. Tobin, 154-55).

18. Mechthild speaks of the necessity of suffering in the mystical life in a number of places; for example, FL 1.2, 1.35, 4.5 and 5.4. On Mechthild and suffering, Margot Schmidt, '"Frau Pein, Ihe Seid mein nächstes Kleid." Zur Leidenmystik im "Fliessende Licht der Gotheit" der Mechthild von Magdeburg', in *Die Dunkle Nacht der Sinne. Leiderfahrung und christlicher Mystik*, ed. Gotthard Fuchs, et al. (Düsseldorf: Patmos, 1989), 63–107.

19. FL 3.10; see also FL 7.18, 7.21, and 7.27.

20. On Angela of Foligno, McGinn, *Flowering of Mysticism*, 142–51. The edition used here is Ludger Thier and Abele Calufetti, eds, *Il libro della Beata Angela da Foligno* (Rome: Editiones Collegii S. Bonaventurae, 1985).

despair in the face of the God who hides himself and torments the soul who seeks him. Still, the stage of suffering and estrangement is not final with Angela, since it occupies the sixth place among the seven final supplementary steps recorded by the friar.²¹ After enjoying erotic union with Christ in stage five, in stage six God allows Angela to suffer demonic assaults both in soul and in body that bring her to the edge of despair. In a telling image she says, 'She found herself incapable of finding any other comparison than that of a man hanged by the neck who, with his hands tied behind his back and his eyes blindfolded, remains dangling on the gallows and yet lives, with no help, no support, no remedy, swinging in the empty air.'²² At that point she turns the tables on Christ, crying out, 'My son, my son, do not abandon me!' This is an experience of damnation: 'I see myself as damned, but I am in no way preoccupied with this damnation; rather, what concerns me and grieves me most is having offended my Creator.'²³

It would be a mistake to suppose that the mysticism of dereliction was restricted to women mystics. Angela's contemporary, the poet-mystic and Spiritual Franciscan Jacopone da Todi (ca. 1236–1306), is a case in point. Two male mystics from the fourteenth century can provide evidence for just how widespread this form of mysticism became in the later Middle Ages. The Dominican John Tauler (1300–61), although deeply influenced by Meister Eckhart, differed from his master in many ways, not least by his extensive teaching on the sufferings endured by those whom God seemingly had abandoned, conditions that he described by using terms like 'lostness' (*verlossenheit*), 'distress' (*getrenge*) and the evocative metaphor of 'night work' (*arbeit der nachte*).²⁴ The imitation of the passion was central for the Dominican preacher, but he did not revel in bloody imitation of Christ's physical sufferings, such as we find in his contemporary Henry Suso. Rather, Tauler insisted that the essence of imitating Christ rests in total 'releasement' (*gelossenheit*), a surrendering of the will closely tied to experiencing the desolation that Christ endured on the cross. Sermon 39, for example, distinguishes three stages in the mystical path. The first is that of the milk of spiritual sweetness, which prepares the devout soul for the stronger food of the second stage. In stage two, Tauler says,

---

21. On the relation of the sixth and the seventh supplemental *passus*, which he describes as 'Due Passi "Gemelli"', see Massimo Vedova, *Esperienza e dottrina. Il 'Memoriale' di Angela da Foligno* (Rome: Istituto Storico dei Cappuccini, 2009), 299–346.

22. *Memoriale*, Ch. VIII (ed., 338). The translation is that of Paul Lachance, *Angela of Foligno. Complete Works* (New York: Paulist Press, 1993), 197.

23. *Memoriale* Ch. VIII (ed., 338–44; trans. Lachance, 198, 200) for these passages.

24. For Tauler's sermons it is necessary to use the old edition of Ferdinand Vetter, *Die Predigten Taulers* (Weidmann: Berlin, 1908. Reprint 1968). For a general study of Tauler, Bernard McGinn, *The Harvest of Mysticism in Medieval Germany, 1300–1500* (New York: Crossroad, 2007), Ch. 6 (240–96). On Tauler's view of affliction, Alois M. Haas, '"Die Arbeit der Nacht". Mystische Leiderfahrung nach Johannes Tauler', in *Die Dunkle Nacht der Sinne*, 9–40.

> A person is led along a very wild path, totally dark and foreign. On this road God takes away from him everything he ever gave him. The person is left so much alone that he knows nothing of God, and he comes into such distress that he is not sure if he was ever right, or if he ever had a God or not, or even whether he really exists or not.²⁵

This state is spoken of as a state of 'poverty of spirit', when in a strange way God withdraws himself from the soul, leaving it in 'painful deprivation of spirit' (*qwelender beroubunge des geistes*). The third stage is the union of the created spirit with 'the self-existent (*istigen*) Spirit of God'. In Sermon 37 Tauler looks to Christ as the example of the dereliction of love. 'This is love', he says, 'that a person is ever on fire in seeking and in lacking, and in the feeling of being abandoned. One remains in constant torment, but content to be tormented. In this torment a person is melted and consumed by the fire of desire; yet is in equal contentment.' He concludes, 'This is love. It is not what you imagine it to be.'²⁶ Tauler's Christocentrism and reliance on faith were welcomed by Luther, as was his emphasis on the suffering and terror endured by the believer whom the hidden God abandoned to hell. As the reformer once put it, 'By living, yet more by dying and being damned, you become a theologian, not by understanding, reading, and teaching.'²⁷ This is what Luther once called 'fleeing to God against God'.²⁸

Less well known than Tauler, and far less educated than the learned friar, was Jan van Leeuwen (ca. 1310–78), a lay brother known as 'the good cook' at the Augustinian monastery of Groenendaal outside Brussels, the house of the most famous Flemish mystic, Jan van Ruusbroec (1291–1381).²⁹ The good cook was very influenced by Ruusbroec,³⁰ but his several mystical treatises in Middle Netherlandish display some features and themes not found in his master. Jan van Leeuwen worked out an original, if somewhat confusing, mystical itinerary in his treatise *What Pertains to a Person Poor in Spirit*.³¹ Of more interest to us is

---

25. Tauler, Sermon 39 (ed., 161; my trans.). The extended description of the three stages are found in the Vetter edition at 159-62.

26. Tauler, Sermon 37 (ed., 143; my trans.).

27. Martin Luther, *Operationes in Psalmos*, in *D. Martin Luther Werke. Kritische Gesamtausgabe* (Weimar: Böhlau, 1883. Abbreviated WA), WA 3:163 (my trans.).

28. WA 3:204. On the theme of the hidden God in Luther, Brian A. Gerrish, '"To the Unknown God": Luther and Calvin on the Hiddenness of God', *Journal of Religion* 53 (1973): 263–92.

29. For an introduction to Jan van Leeuwen, see McGinn, *The Varieties of Vernacular Mysticism*, 71–6.

30. Ruusbroec himself has a role for abandonment and desolation, if more restricted than that of his disciple Jan van Leeuwen; see Léonce Reypens, 'La "nuit de l'esprit" chez Ruusbroec', *Études Carmelitaines* 23 (1938): 75–81.

31. There is a translation of this treatise by Marcel Cock in Rik Van Nieuwenhove, Robert Faesen and Helen Rolfson, eds, *Late Medieval Mysticism of the Low Countries* (New York: Paulist Press, 2008), 36–46.

the dominance of mystical dereliction in both his vernacular work *On the Ten Commandments,* as well as in the Latin excerpts from this found in the account of his life written by the Groenendaal hagiographer, Johannes Pomerius.[32] Pomerius says that on a certain night God manifested himself to Jan, first in an experience of loving union, and then with 'seven torments not so much wondrous as unbearable to any person from a natural point of view, and almost unbelievable to someone who did not experience them – punishments he bore altogether at the same instant' (*Vita 'Boni Coqui'* Ch. XI). The account of the seven 'hellish torments' (*angustiae infernales*) that follows features trials such as interior desolation, loss of hope in God and a sense of total sinfulness (Chs XII-XIV). The seventh torment is by far the worst and provides us with a remarkable image of the 'hellish pain' of mystical dereliction. Jan describes being trapped in hell in the following lengthy and fascinating text:

> It was as if the ground we walk on became so many thousands of dense and deep pieces as there are blades of grass on earth, drops of water in the sea, or grains of sand on the seashore. When that happened, it was as if the earth ... divided itself from top to bottom so that the person was placed in the middle with both body and soul, and then the earth fastened that person with its weight from every side, pressing towards the centre, squeezing and contracting with its force. This would certainly be an intolerable torment, if the person were compelled to always live there in the middle of the earth, at every moment longing to die due to the insupportable violence of the pressure.[33]

The wave of mystical affliction did not cease in the fourteenth century, since there is ample evidence for its importance in the fifteenth and sixteenth centuries. Among the many possible witnesses, I will consider two fifteenth-century female mystics: Alijt Bake (1415–55) from the Low Countries and the Italian Camilla Battista da Varano (1458–1524). In the sixteenth century the Carmelite mystics Teresa of Avila and John of the Cross provide important examples, Teresa in passing, but John in a systematic way through his rich exploration of the 'Dark Night' (*noche oscura*).

Alijt Bake was born in Utrecht from a wealthy family. In 1440 she entered the Galilee convent at Ghent, a house of the Augustinian nuns of the Windesheim congregation associated with the *devotio moderna*.[34] Although she encountered opposition in the beginning, Alijt later served as prioress of the house for ten years.

---

32. Johannes Pomerius, *De origine Monasterii Viridisvallis et de gestis patrum et fratrum,* in *Analecta Bollandiana* 4 (1885), where Book 3 contains the *Vita 'Boni Coqui'* (309–22). There is no modern edition of the vernacular treatise *On the Ten Commandments*.

33. *Vita 'Boni Coqui',* Ch. XIV (ed., 317; my trans.).

34. On Alijt Bake, Wybren Scheepsma, *Medieval Religious Women in the Low Countries: The 'Modern Devotion', the Canonesses of Windesheim and Their Writings* (Rochester: Boydell Press, 2004), 197–226; and McGinn, *The Varieties of Vernacular Mysticism,* 116–23.

Unlike most of the Devout, she had a strong calling to an inner mystical life, which she saw as confirmed by two visions, one on Christmas, 1440, the other on the Vigil of the Ascension in 1441. Well read in mystical literature, she composed a spiritual autobiography, *My Beginning and Progress* (ca. 1451), as well as several mystical treatises, the most important being *The Four Ways of the Cross* (ca. 1445–6).[35] This treatise is one of the most powerful witnesses to late medieval passion mysticism, despite its lack of clarity in some places. The fundamental message is about attaining transforming union with God by 'co-suffering' (*medelijden*) with Christ on the cross according to the threefold pattern of *laten-liden-minnen* ('letting go-suffering-loving'). The first three ways of the cross are treated fairly briefly, while the fourth way takes up two-thirds of the treatise.

The fourth way (nn. 27-63) is a detailed account of the path of darkness, abandonment, dereliction and annihilation following the model of Christ's passion. Alijt says this way is not like the first three, 'because all that is exercised in them must be left behind, because this way does not lead upward in exercises of enlightening and of tasting and of enjoying, but downward in letting go, and suffering and purer love'. The person must become nothing by dying with Christ, so that 'she is thereby brought into great darkness and desolation and dryness and into as great a poverty and misery as she once was rich'.[36] The letting go and suffering of the fourth way are described in strong terms (nn. 30-32), but, unlike some other mystics, Alijt says that God does not totally abandon the soul, but continues to whisper within the depths of the soul in 'a voice without words, born of God into the spirit of a person, but giving witness, awakening and renewing desire, speaking beyond any reason' (n. 37). God may provide brief moments of union during this fourth way, but Alijt insists that the soul must not desire to know, or to feel, or to taste divine delights, but must continue 'the letting go and suffering where love is exercised most highly and nobly in everything a person might do' (n. 42). Towards the end of the account Alijt emphasizes that this way is the truest imitation of Christ, following the footsteps where 'he stood in that night when he had begun to suffer his bitter Passion for our sakes' (n. 54). Hence it is necessary to begin with Gethsemane, to suffer and die with Christ, in order to gain resurrection as 'a saving harvest for holy church' (n. 63).

Camilla Battista da Varano was a Franciscan nun who composed her spiritual autobiography, the *Spiritual Life (Vita spirituale)*, about 1491.[37] The work has two

---

35. The text was edited by Bernard Spaapen, 'Middeleeuwse passiemystiek II: De vier kruiswegen van Alijt Bake', *Ons geestelike Erf* 40 (1966): 18–64. There is an English translation by John Van Engen, in *Late Medieval Mysticism in the Low Countries*, 176–202.

36. *The Four Ways*, nn. 27–8 (trans. Van Engen, 136).

37. For a brief account of Camilla, McGinn, *The Varieties of Vernacular Mysticism*, 306–11. Camilla's writings have been edited by Giacomo Boccanera, *Beata Camilla da Varano, Le opere spirituale* (Iesi: Scuola Tipografica Francescana, 1958). There is a French translation with extensive notes by Bernard Forthomme, *Camilla da Varano. Histoire de mon bonheur malheureux* (Paris: Les Éditions Franciscaines, 2009).

main parts: Chapters III–XI tell the story of her life in the world (ca. 1466–81) and Chapters XII–XIX recount her first decade in the convent (1481–91). This section treats the many mystical graces she received, but concludes in Chapters XVII–XIX with an account of her hellish state of mystical dereliction, what she calls *mia infelicissima felicità* ('my most unhappy happiness').[38] These trials, which she describes as 'her great battle against Satan', began in October 1488 as a part of her 'holy desire to enter the inner places of the desert, that is, the most secret sufferings of the heart of Jesus'.[39] Although Camilla uses erotic images from the Song of Songs to illustrate her encounters with Jesus, the predominant note of these years was of divine love as the source of pain and suffering. The tears she shed for Christ crucified were merged with the sea of her own inner suffering with Christ. She describes herself as

> introduced into the most secret bedchamber of the myrrh-soaked heart of Jesus, the one and true most envenomed sea that cannot be navigated by any intellect … [where] I would have often been submerged and drowned in that sea, if the powerful hand of God had not aided me, because I was much less able to support such bitterness than the sweetness of divine love. I would say: 'No more, no more, my Lord. I am drowning because this sea has no bottom or end.'

In such an experience Battista says that God's essence no longer seems like the paradise of joy, but 'like a cruel hell' (*uno crudele inferno*).[40] The paradoxes of divine love (How can the soul ever love God enough?) that are explored in the final chapters of the *Spiritual Life* lead Camilla to cast herself at the feet of the Redeemer and to express her wish, following St Paul (Rom. 9.5) even to be damned, if that should be the will of God.

Experiences of desolation and dereliction do not have a constitutive role in the mystical path of Teresa of Avila (1515–82), as presented first in her *Life* (1562–5) and then in *The Interior Castle* (1577). Nonetheless, the *Life* does recount several harrowing experiences that God sent her as part of the purgation necessary on the way to union. Three such passages are found in the *Life*. The first in *Life* Chapter 20.9-16 (ca. 1565) was a painful experience of extreme desolation, like being set down in a desert without any other creatures. Here the soul receives no consolation and feels that it is crucified, but its desire for heaven so increases that it loses sense awareness and becomes rigid. Despite many comparisons, Teresa has trouble describing this form of solitude and suffering (20.13-16). God seems far away, she says, but he is

---

38. On dereliction in Camilla, Pietro Luzi, 'L'infelicissima felicità dell'esperienza di Dio', in *Del timore ad amore. L'itinerario spirituale della Beata Camilla Battista da Varano*, ed. Luzi (Assisi: Edizioni Porziuncula, 2009), 81–112.

39. *Vita Spirituale*, Ch. XII (ed., 38; my trans.): '… uno santo desiderio di intrare ad interiora deserti, coiè alle secretissime pene del core de Iesu'.

40. *Vita spirituale* Ch. XII (ed., 39–40; my trans.).

actually communicating 'his grandeurs in the most strange manner thinkable' (20.9), and he tells Teresa that she should esteem this gift more than all others because of its effectiveness in purifying the soul (20.16). The second and third experiences recounted by the Carmelite deal with the sense of being consigned to hell. In *Life* Chapter 30.11-14 she speaks of how God allowed the devil to torture her with an internal sense of being completely in the dark and suffering the fires of hell. She says, 'In my opinion, the experience is a kind of copy of hell … for the soul burns within itself without knowing who started the fire, or where it comes from, of how to flee from it, or what to put it out with' (30.12). The final event, which probably happened around 1560, was a brief experience of being trapped in hell that terrified Teresa for years afterwards. She says that she felt a 'constriction, suffocation and affliction' that made it seem like the soul was tearing itself apart. She goes on, 'I felt myself burning and crumbling; and I repeat [that] the worst was that interior fire and despair' (Ch. 32.2). The fire was accompanied by a feeling of suffocation, of being placed 'in a kind of hole made in a wall'. 'Those walls', she goes on to say, 'which were terrifying to see, closed in on themselves and suffocated everything. There was no light, but all was enveloped in the blackest darkness' (32.3). Nonetheless, Teresa says that this experience was one of the greatest gifts God gave her because it helped her lose her fear of all earthly tribulations.[41]

John of the Cross (1546–91), Teresa's friend and collaborator in the Carmelite reform, is probably the best-known proponent of the necessity of inner stripping and suffering on the path to union with God, what the friar memorably called the 'Dark Night' (*noche oscura*).[42] John underwent great physical suffering at the hands of his Carmelite brethren during his imprisonment in Toledo (December 1577–August 1578) – a period that he compared to the three days that Jonah spent in the belly of the whale (Jon. 2:1-2). Nevertheless, John later testified that the Lord had given him great consolations during these difficult days, and the poem on which his account of the dark night is based is not one of the poems he wrote in prison.[43] His imprisonment was a decisive event in John's life. He had been known as a gifted spiritual director before his ordeal; after it, he emerged as also a great poet and writer. As John began to share his poems and spiritual counsel with the Carmelite nuns and friars, he received requests to explain his teaching about ascending Mount Carmel to attain union with God (he drew a sketch of

---

41. *Life* Ch. 32.5. These passages are cited from the translation of the *Life* found in *The Collected Works of St. Teresa of Avila*, translated by Kieran Kavanaugh and Otilio Rodriguez, vol. 1 (Washington DC: ICS Publications, 1976), 32–286.

42. Some of what follows is based on Ch. 4, 'John of the Cross: Night, Flame, and Union', in Bernard McGinn, *Mysticism in the Golden Age of Spain, 1500–1650* (New York: Crossroad, 2017), 230–335.

43. The poem 'En una noche oscura' appears to have been written in late 1578 after his escape from prison.

the ascent possibly as early as 1580).⁴⁴ During the period ca. 1581–5 he composed two versions of commentaries on two of his poems: *The Spiritual Canticle* on the 'Cantico espiritual' he had begun while in jail and *The Ascent of Mount Carmel* on the poem 'En una noche oscura'. The *Ascent* treatise explaining the 'Noche oscura' poem enshrines John's teaching on the 'night of sense' and 'night of spirit' (he never actually used the phrase 'dark night of the soul').⁴⁵

The Ascent of Mount Carmel and *The Dark Night* are really two parts of the same work. The book is structured according to the basic anthropological division of the sense and spirit aspects of the human person.⁴⁶ Both sense and spirit must be purged of all human attachments in order to attain God, John says, and in two ways: actively, when a person cooperates with grace, and passively, when God alone is at work.⁴⁷ Thus, there are four nights altogether. The whole process is called a 'night' (*noche*) for three reasons: first, the denial of the senses is like a night; second, the road that must be taken is the night of faith; and third, the goal is God, who is 'a dark night to the soul in this life' (*Ascent*, Book 1, Chapter 2.1). The practice of the four nights goes far beyond ordinary asceticism.⁴⁸ It involves negative language

---

44. John's four major works: *The Ascent of Mount Carmel*, *The Dark Night*, *The Spiritual Canticle* and *The Living Flame of Love*, all make use of the traditional three stage path to union of the purgative way, the illuminative way and the unitive way, but in an original fashion.

45. John's works are available in Crisógono de Jesús, Matias del Niño Jesús and Lucinio del SS. Sacramento, eds, *Vida y Obras de San Juan de la Cruz*, 5th edn (Madrid: Biblioteca de Autores Cristianos, 1964). The translation used will be that of Kieran Kavanagh and Otilio Rodriguez, *The Collected Works of Saint John of the Cross* (Washington DC: ICS Publications, 1991).

46. For a sketch of John's anthropology, McGinn, *Mysticism in the Golden Age of Spain*, 253–61.

47. John bases the necessity for absolute purgation on the Aristotelian principle that two contraries cannot exist in the same subject, that is, in order for God to fully enter into the person, all imperfections must be cast out; see McGinn, *Mysticism in the Golden Age of Spain*, 269.

48. Everyone who has written on John has studied the four nights. Along with the sketch in McGinn, *Mysticism in the Golden Age of Spain*, 269–85, see Constance Fitzgerald, 'Impasse and Dark Night', in *Living with the Apocalypse*, ed. Tilden Edwards (San Francisco: Harper & Row, 1984), 93–116; Hein Bloomestijn, 'The Dark Night in John of the Cross: The Transformational Process', *Studies in Spirituality* 10 (2000): 228–41; Keith Egan, 'Contemplation in the "Spiritual Canticle": The Program of the Dark Night: Education for Beauty', in *Carmel and Contemplation: Transforming Human Consciousness. Carmelite Studies 8*, ed. Kevin Culligan and Regis Jordan (Washington DC: ICS Publications, 2000), 241–66; and Edward Howells, 'Is Darkness a Psychological or Theological Category in the Thought of John of the Cross?' in *The Renewal of Mystical Theology: Essays in Memory of John N. Jones (1964–2012)*, ed. Bernard McGinn (New York: Crossroad-Herder, 2017), 140–61.

about God, the negation of all desire, and even the negation of affliction wherein God subjects the soul to severe inner suffering. John uses the language of mystical dereliction (e.g. *Dark Night* Book 2, Chapters 5 to 8), but God never really abandons the soul. Rather, God remains present, but veiled under the dark burning action of faith, hope and charity as these three theological gifts purify the soul of all its false appetites, attachments and intellectual apprehensions.[49] This rigorous purgative process is founded in John's conviction that in order to overcome the sensory and spiritual barriers to attaining God we must become subject to the dialectic of *todo – nada*, 'everything or nothing'. As he put it at the outset of his treatment of the nights: 'To reach satisfaction in all/desire satisfaction in nothing. To come to possess all/desire the possession of nothing. To arrive at being all/desire to be nothing.'[50] The renunciation of desire, not excessive mortification, is the key to John's dark night.

The 'active night of the senses', or ascetic disciplining of the appetites, takes up Book 1 of the *Ascent*. Books 2 and 3 treat the active purging of the intellective power in the spirit through the dark path of faith and the purgation of the memory by hope and the purgation of the will by charity. John insists on the Christological nature of the purifying process – 'supreme nakedness and emptiness of spirit' is the truest following of Jesus who died fully annihilated on the cross, crying out 'My God, my God, why have you forsaken me?' (*Ascent* Book 2, Chapter 7. 11). John did not finish his account of the active night before he turned to the passive nights of sense and spirit in the two books of *The Dark Night*. The passive night of the senses, which deals with overcoming the imperfections that disturb even advanced souls, is common to many according to John, while the passive night of the spirit treated in Book 2 is experienced by only a few (*Dark Night* Book 1, Chapter 8. 1). It is here that John makes his deeply felt and systematic contribution to the theme of mystical affliction. The passive night of the spirit involves a 'dark contemplation' (*contemplación oscura*) that is felt as inner suffering, even torture, a dry emptiness in which God is seen as the agent of pain and in which the soul becomes so numbed by suffering as to be incapable of action.

Some modern investigators have compared John's analysis of the inner dismantling of the old self to modern depressive states. The verbal analogies are sometimes telling, although for John the dark night of the spirit, while sounding like the personal disintegration of depression, is actually aimed at a new integration, the reunification of the true self attained in mystical union.[51] In Book 2 of the *Dark Night* God is totally in control and does whatever is necessary to

---

49. Much of John's language about the sensory appetites is so negative that many have dismissed him as totally rejecting human nature, forgetting the important distinction he makes in *Ascent* Book 1, Ch. 11, between the neutral 'natural appetites' and the disordered 'voluntary appetites'.

50. *Ascent*, Book 1, Ch. 13. 11 (trans. Kavanaugh and Rodriguez, 150).

51. See Denys Turner, 'Chapter 10. John of the Cross: The Dark Nights and Depression', in *The Darkness of God*, ed. Turner (Cambridge: Cambridge University Press, 1995), 226–51.

5. Suffering, Dereliction and Affliction in Christian Mysticism

bring the purifying process to its transformative conclusion. As John puts it, 'He leaves the intellect in darkness, the will in aridity, the memory in emptiness, and the affections in supreme affliction, bitterness, and anguish by depriving the soul of the feeding and satisfaction it had previously obtained from spiritual blessings.'[52] Chapters 5 through 9 of Book 2 return again and again to the language of 'suffering and torment' (*pena y tormento*) in ways reminiscent of the earlier mystics we have examined. John says 'persons feel so unclean and wretched that it seems God is against them and they are against God' (Book 2, Chapter 5. 5), and 'sometimes this experience is so vivid that it seems to the soul that it sees hell and perdition open before it' (2, 6. 6). Although souls in this state continue to love God, 'they are unable to believe that God loves them' (2, 7. 7). But the goal is not suffering for the sake of suffering. After the intellect, memory and will have been fully cleansed by the 'substantial darkness' (*tinieblas sustanciales*) felt in the soul's very substance, the now purified soul is 'ready to feel the sublime and marvellous touches of divine love' (2, 9. 3).

It would be fruitful to pursue the theme of mystical affliction into the Great Age of French mysticism of the seventeenth century, where there is a multitude of witnesses, such as the personal narrative of the Ursuline nun, Marie de l'Incarnation (1599–1672),[53] and the teaching of Francis de Sales (1567–1622) on tribulation and the love of total surrender in his *Treatise on the Love of God*.[54] Lest we think that mystical dereliction is only a thing of the past, however, I will close with brief accounts of two modern women mystics whose lives and teaching involve profound inner suffering and the sense of being abandoned by God. The Carmelite nun Thérèse of Lisieux (1873–97), now known through her true writings instead of the versions doctored to advance her canonization, is a powerful witness to an inner dereliction caused by her temptations against faith during the last days of her physical suffering through advanced tuberculosis (1896–7). In her autobiographical *Story of a Soul* she speaks of how she found it impossible to believe there were people without faith until Jesus sent her into a cloud of lack of faith. 'He permitted my soul to be invaded by the thickest darkness', she says, 'and that the thought of heaven, up until then so sweet to me, be no longer anything but the cause of struggle and torment'. Travelling through this dark tunnel was not a passing experience, but continued almost down to her death. She could not adequately describe the darkness that obscured her soul, saying that she did not want 'to write about it any longer; I fear I might blaspheme; I fear even that I have

---

52. *Dark Night*, Book 2, Ch. 3. 3 (ed., 570; trans. Kavanaugh and Rodriguez, 399).

53. The writings of Marie are now available in English: *Marie of the Incarnation: Selected Writings*, ed. Irene Mahoney (New York: Paulist Press, 1989). Marie describes her hellish torments in her 'Twelfth State of Prayer' (141–7).

54. Francis's analysis of mystical dereliction, while not as extensive as that of John of the Cross, has considerable profundity. This is especially evident in Book IX of the *Treatise on the Love of God*, Chs 2, 3, 5, 11, 12 and 13. It is also found in *Treatise* Book VI, Ch. 14, and in a number of his letters, such as those exchanged with Jane de Chantal.

already said too much.' Nevertheless, Thérèse asks Jesus, 'Is there a joy greater than that of suffering out of love for you?'[55]

The final example is that of Mother Teresa of Calcutta (1910–97), a mystic of our own times. It was not until the publication of the posthumous 'private writings' of the 'Saint of Calcutta' that awareness of her long years of mystical dereliction became public knowledge.[56] The nature of this prolonged 'Dark Night', and even the status of the documents testifying to it, has provoked much discussion and cannot be addressed here. Nevertheless, the expressions of pain and suffering found in many of the letters she sent to her clerical advisors and confessors will by now be familiar. Here is just one example from a letter of 3 September 1959:

> They say people in hell suffer eternal pain because of the loss of God – they would go through all that suffering if they had just a little hope of possessing God. – In my soul I feel just that pain of terrible loss – of God not wanting me – of God not being God – of God not really existing. ... In my heart there is no faith – no love – no trust – there is so much pain, the pain of not being wanted.[57]

Conclusion

The prophet Malachi says that 'God is a refining fire' (Mal. 3:2-3). The Old Testament prophets were aware of this purgative aspect of God and spoke of the fear and distress that encountering the God of fire induced in those who came close to him. The theme of mystical affliction and dereliction in the history of Christian mysticism builds on this, but took a new direction centred on Christ's passion and death. For Christian mystics, it was not just because God is so radically other from humans as the *mysterium tremendum* that meeting God involves suffering and affliction, and sometimes even a sense of God's withdrawal, leaving his lovers abandoned and derelict in what seem like hell. The Christian mystics who suffered the pain of the loss of God took solace in the sense that they were being invited to fulfil what Jesus himself had experienced on the cross when he cried out, 'My God, my God, why have you forsaken me?' Affliction and dereliction therefore are not peripheral to Christian mysticism, but are part of its core.

---

55. Excerpted from *Thérèse of Lisieux. Story of a Soul*, trans. John Clark (Washington DC: ICS Publications, 1975), 211–14.

56. *Mother Teresa: Come Be My Light. The Private Writings of the 'Saint of Calcutta'*, edited and with a commentary by Brian Kolodiejchuk (New York: Doubleday, 2007). The relation between these published materials and the manuscript sources remains under consideration.

57. *Come Be My Light*, 192–3. References to dark faith and dereliction abound in this collection; see, for example, 149–77, 186–94, 209–12, 222–32, 245–50, 272–82.

Chapter 6

PROTEST THEISM, AQUINAS AND SUFFERING

Rik Van Nieuwenhove

Introduction

In Albert Camus's novel *The Plague* (1947), the protagonist, Dr Rieux, faces an onslaught of meaningless suffering caused by a sudden outburst of the plague in the Algerian town of Oran. In this context he challenges the religious world view, expressed by the Jesuit priest Fr. Paneloux, who encourages him to accept or even love what we cannot understand. Having witnessed the agony and cruel death of a child Rieux retorts that he refuses to love a scheme of things in which children are put to torture. In an earlier essay, *The Myth of Sisyphus* (1942), Camus had outlined in a more philosophical vein the modern attitude towards meaninglessness and absurdity. Our only sensible response is revolt. Indeed, it is this very revolt that can generate meaning in our lives. Camus is trenchant: we should refuse to be reconciled; we should refuse to hope. It is little wonder that Camus chooses Sisyphus as the symbol of the modern person: Sisyphus had defied the gods by refusing to return to Hades out of sheer love for this world. As a result, the gods condemn him to push a bolder endlessly up a hill, from which it rolls down again, in a never-ending cycle of absurdity and defiance. It is in his defiance that Sisyphus finds meaning. Sisyphus rejects hope; he lives without consolations, without illusions. There is to be no reconciliation.[1]

There is undoubtedly a certain freshness, honesty and integrity about Camus's proposal. His essay genuinely captures the spirit of a post-Christian age. Critical questions can nonetheless be raised: If the gods do not exist, what is the point of revolt, which, according to Camus, 'gives life its value'?[2] Can it not be argued, however, that this very revolt also implicitly affirms the existence of God? Revolt can only be a source of meaning if there is somebody to revolt against. It involves persons. We do not *revolt* against natural disasters or afflictions. We may grieve over their disastrous impact, and we try to *remedy* them or fight them, but

---

1. A. Camus, *The Myth of Sisyphus* (Harmondsworth: Penguin Books, 1975), 54–62; *The Plague* (Harmondsworth: Penguin Books, 1960). See Rik Van Nieuwenhove, 'Albert Camus, Simone Weil and the Absurd', *Irish Theological Quarterly* 70 (2005): 343–54.

2. Camus, *The Myth of Sisyphus*, 54.

attempting to do so is not the sole prerogative of the post-religious. Christians do so as well, and no less.

There is perhaps a certain intellectual fittingness that Camus draws on literary examples from antiquity (such as Sisyphus or Oedipus) to describe the modern condition. Christianity had explicitly rejected the notion of Fate, which shaped the ancient outlook on suffering.[3] Christians, on the other hand, traditionally detected the providential hand of God in all things, including afflictions. In a post-Christian world this view appears to have become indefensible, if not incomprehensible altogether, and this not just in the eyes of those who reject the Christian faith. Indeed, the eloquent critique by Camus and others does not merely express the attitude of the non-religious, modern person towards suffering. Significantly, several Christian theologians in the twentieth (and twenty-first) century have adopted similar views and have espoused a kind of protest theism. They refuse to see any links between suffering and the broader Christian narrative of salvation. Suffering simply happens, and it is theologically deeply problematic, if not pathological, to valorize it or to claim that it is somehow desired by God.

From a historical perspective these views may seem surprising, given the centrality the cross occupies in both the New Testament and ensuing tradition. The cross, however, also falls under this critique and is likewise being emptied of the saving meaning it traditionally had. According to Edward Schillebeeckx, for instance, we have been saved 'despite the Cross'.[4] In his view, to argue that the cross is somehow an integral part of God's saving plan – that God wills it to do away with sin – evokes the spectre of a cruel, vindictive God who subjects his mercy to his justice. These preliminary remarks sketch the context against which I would like to re-engage with the soteriology of Thomas Aquinas.

When we talk about evil, we usually distinguish between moral evil, or sin, and natural evil – a distinction inspired by St Augustine's *De Libero Arbitrio* (Bk I, 1 and Bk III, 9). A strict distinction between these two kinds of evil is, of course, not possible (as the present-day ecological crisis vividly reminds us). Aquinas usually calls the two kinds of evil *malum poenae* (which is affliction, or evil suffered) and *malum culpae* (which is evil done, or sin).[5] In what follows I will mainly focus on the issue of natural evil, and particularly those kinds of afflictions we cannot

---

3. See E. Gilson's chapter 'The Middle Ages and Nature' from *The Spirit of Mediaeval Philosophy* (South Bend: University of Notre Dame Press, 1991), 364–82.

4. Edward Schillebeeckx, *Christ: The Christian Experience in the Modern World* (London: T&T Clark: 2018), 717–24.

5. See Thomas Aquinas, *Summa Theologiae* [*ST*] I, q. 49, a. 2 and q. 48, a. 5; in *ST* I, q. 19, a. 9 he writes that God 'in no way wills the evil of sin ... the evil of natural defect, or of punishment, he does will, by willing the good to which such evils are attached'. All quotations and translations from the *ST* and *Summa contra Gentiles* are taken from www.dhspriory.org/thomas

remedy. I will give first a general philosophical account; secondly, I will offer a more 'Christian-existential' response.

Philosophical considerations

When Aquinas offers a range of theoretical insights to account for the existence of evil his main concern is to show that the presence of evil does not contradict Christian faith in providence.[6] This is, as he sees it, the main purpose of the book of Job on which he wrote a commentary in 1261–5. As he writes in the prologue to that work (which coincided with the redaction of Book III of the *Summa contra Gentiles*, which also deals with providence), 'The affliction of just men is what seems particularly to impugn divine providence in human affairs. ... That the just are afflicted without cause seems to undermine totally the foundation of providence.'[7]

Providence extends beyond care for human beings. God's primary object of care is the order of the universe, rather than simply humankind per se: among created things, what God cares for most is the order of the universe 'because the good order of the universe best reflects the divine goodness, which is the ultimate end of the divine will'.[8] In an age of ecological crisis, this sobering insight, profoundly anti-modernist, may perhaps find a renewed resonance. At any rate, this perspective enables Aquinas to argue that divine providence, concerned as it is with a more universal order, can allow instances of particular evil.

One of the implications of Aquinas's characteristically positive appraisal of creation is, ironically, the view that goodness is the cause of evil. This applies primarily to natural evil, which God desires indirectly for the sake of the good of the universe, as we will see. There is also a connection between sin (*malum culpae*) and goodness – obviously not in the sense that it is desired, even indirectly, by God, but rather in terms of human teleology. Because Aquinas believes that every agent acts for the sake of goodness, we pursue evil only indirectly. To use his

---

6. Aquinas was, of course, familiar with the question, 'If God is omniscient, omnipotent, and all-good, then why is there evil?' The atheist critique questions the plausibility of the very existence of God considering suffering and evil. For Aquinas, as a Dominican writing in the aftermath of the Cathar heresy that partly inspired the founding of the Order to which he belonged, the issue is subtly different: Given the unquestionable acceptance of God's existence, how can we give a plausible, non-dualist account of suffering and evil? See for instance *Summa contra Gentiles* III, 71, 12: 'By these considerations, the occasion of erring is also taken away from the Manicheans who maintained two agent principles, good and evil, as though evil could have no place under the providence of a good God.'

7. *Commentary on the Book of Job*, Prologue. I use the translation by B.Th. Becket Mullady in *The Works of St Thomas Aquinas*, vol. 32 (Wyoming: The Aquinas Institute, 2016), 8.

8. *Summa contra Gentiles* III, 64.10.

stock example, the adulterer commits sin, of course, but he pursues, not the evil of adultery per se, but the sexual pleasure which accompanies it; and pleasure is something good.[9]

Natural evil also finds its source in goodness. Aquinas has the theological courage to argue that God is, at least indirectly, the cause of natural evil.[10] This may seem to erode his robust defence of divine providence but, as I suggested, the opposite is the case: Aquinas's standpoint simply follows from his rejection of metaphysical dualism: because evil is not on the same metaphysical level as goodness, Aquinas must argue that natural evil finds its ultimate source in God. Modern theologians who argue that (natural) evil 'just happens' would, I suspect, in Aquinas's view be veering towards a dualist world view, in which God's providence and goodness is no longer the all-encompassing principle.

Even if natural evil finds its origin in God, God cannot be said to be directly responsible for it. Aquinas explains this by appealing to the traditional notion that evil is *privatio boni*, the absence of goodness. This too has a surprising implication: because everything that God has made is good, evil (as the privation of goodness) can itself be a pointer towards goodness – the goodness that should be there but is absent. When Aquinas discusses the popular objection that the existence of evil precludes belief in a good, omnipotent God ('If God exists, whence comes evil?') he writes, 'But it could be argued to the contrary: "If evil exists, God exists." For there would be no evil if the order of good were taken away, since its privation is evil. But this order would not exist if there were no God.'[11]

Our philosophical diet is more phenomenological than metaphysical. We can perhaps translate Aquinas's provoking statement in terms of what Edward Schillebeeckx called 'negative contrast experiences'.[12] Whenever we cry out, in the face of suffering, 'This is not how it should be!' our very revolt implicitly affirms the overall goodness of the world. This acknowledgement, therefore, in turn, implies that revolt or moral indignation cannot have the *final* word from a Christian point of view. Our revolt or indignation only makes sense

---

9. Such a positive metaphysical outlook has, incidentally, an interesting implication from a theological point of view, for it makes accounting for malice, in which we pursue evil for the sake of evil, extremely difficult, if not impossible. Aquinas grapples with the topic of malice in detail in *De Malo* q. 3, a. 12.

10. *ST* I, q. 49, a. 2: 'The evil which consists in the corruption of some things is reduced to God as the cause. And this appears as regards both natural things and voluntary things. ... Now, the order of the universe requires ... that there should be some things that can, and do sometimes, fail. And thus God, by causing in things the good of the order of the universe, consequently and as it were by accident, causes the corruption of things. ... And so God is the author of the evil which is penalty, but not of the evil which is fault ... .' See also *ST* I, q. 19, a. 9.

11. *Summa contra Gentiles* III, 71. 10

12. See Kathleen McManus, 'Suffering in the Theology of Edward Schillebeeckx', *Theological Studies* 60 (1999): 476–91.

in light of an implicit affirmation of the thesis that goodness overrides evil in this world.

Given the negative nature of evil (as absence of goodness) we cannot fathom its mystery. Because evil finds its indirect origin in God, the mystery of evil is a reflection of God's own mystery. In the twentieth century Karl Rahner has explicitly argued this point: in our suffering we encounter the mystery of God in a concrete, existential way. Aquinas does not phrase it in a manner as explicit as this. In *ST* I, q. 25, however, he does consider the question whether God could have made our universe better than it is. He initially responds by saying that this is impossible, for it then would no longer be our universe. When pushed on the issue he does concede that 'God could make other things, or add something to the present creation; and then there would be another and better universe'.[13] Thus, insofar as Aquinas is concerned, we do not live in the best of all possible worlds. And he offers no explanation as to why this is the case. For Aquinas, too, the mystery of evil points indirectly to the mystery of God.

A Christian-existential response

On a more existential-religious level it is perhaps just as well that we cannot ultimately account for suffering in the world. The reason is that a rationally coherent insight into how good and evil are being dished out to us would destroy the gratuity of the loving relationship between humanity and God. In other words, in a world in which the just always and invariably receive their rewards, and the not-so-good theirs, we would almost inevitably fall into the temptation of instrumentalizing our relationship with God. This is a key theme in the book of Job, in which Satan claims that Job's devotion to God is calculated: Job's devotion to God is not for nothing (cf. Job 1:9). As Aquinas writes, commenting on this passage:

> So it is clear that the good things which we do are not referred to earthly prosperity as a reward; otherwise it would not be a perverse intention if someone were to serve God because of temporal prosperity. The contrary is likewise true. Temporal adversity is not the proper punishment for sins, and this question will be the theme dealt with in the entire book.[14]

This is an important insight: the absurdity and seemingly randomness of afflictions keep us from instrumentalizing our relationship with God. This theme would be developed in greater detail by some of mystics, including Aquinas's later fellow-Dominican, Meister Eckhart, who encouraged us to live and to love God 'without a why', and not for the benefits that might accrue from it.

---

13. *ST* I, q. 25, a. 6 ad 3.
14. *On Job*, Ch. 1, lect. 2 (p. 20 in Mullady's edition).

These considerations still do not get to the heart of the matter for they lack a Christocentric dimension. The notion that suffering can be a way of becoming more Christ-like, as it is a participation in his passion, only makes sense if we accept that the passion of Christ is redemptive or salvific in the first place. As hinted at earlier, some twentieth-century theologians have questioned the saving significance of Christ's passion, and others have even gone so far as claiming that Aquinas himself contributed to a vindictive, penal notion of salvation. Probably echoing Gustave Aulen's study *Christus Victor* (published first in 1931), Gerald O'Collins, for instance, argued that Aquinas's soteriology contributed to the development of 'a monstrous version of redemption: Christ as the penal substitute propitiating the divine anger'.[15] Although he does not name Aquinas explicitly Edward Schillebeeckx writes in a similar vein:

> Many existing theories of our redemption through Jesus Christ deprive Jesus, his message and career of their subversive power, and even worse, sacralise violence to be a reality within God. God is said to call for a bloody sacrifice which stills or calms his sense of justice.[16]

Schillebeeckx concludes therefore that we have been saved 'despite the Cross'.[17] Christ's execution is the result of the machinations of evil which simply happen to crush an innocent man whose life exemplified a deep solidarity with the outcasts and the downtrodden.

There appear to be two issues. First, there is the notion that Christ's passion is said to appease the demands of divine justice, placating the divine anger. This evokes the spectre of an angry deity who subjects his mercy to the demands of retributive justice. Even if we do not subscribe to such a problematic notion of a vindictive god, a second issue remains: Should we attribute any saving meaning at all to Christ's suffering?

I will start by considering the issue of justice and mercy. In this context it is useful to consider Aquinas's observations on Psalm 50. It is one of the great penitential psalms of the canon, prayed on Ash Wednesday, and it commences by imploring God's mercy: 'Have mercy on me, O God, according to thy great mercy (*Miserere mei, Deus, secundum magnam misericordiam*), and according to the multitude of thy tender mercies blot out my iniquity.' Mercy (*misericordia*), so Aquinas claims in the *ST* I, q. 21, a. 3, 'is especially attributed to God'. Of course, mercy involves, strictly speaking, an affect or emotion: when we take pity we are sorrowful or sad at heart, as the etymology of the Latin word suggests (*miserum cor*). In that sense, namely as an emotion, we cannot attribute sorrow to God, and

---

15. Gerald O'Collins, *Christology: A Biblical, Historical and Systematic Study of Jesus* (Oxford: Oxford University Press, 1995), 207.
16. Edward Schillebeeckx, *Church: The Human Story of God* (London: SCM, 1990), 190.
17. Schillebeeckx, *Christ*, 717–24.

only in a metaphorical sense. So how, then, can Aquinas attribute mercy to God in the *proper* sense? He writes,

> A person is said to be merciful (*misericors*), as being, so to speak, sorrowful at heart (*miserum cor*); being affected with sorrow at the misery of another as though it were his own. Hence it follows that he endeavours to dispel the misery of this other, as if it were his; and this is the effect of mercy. To sorrow, therefore, over the misery of others belongs not to God; but it does most properly belong to him to dispel that misery.[18]

Hence, God can be said to be merciful insofar as he is concerned with removing our misery. Seen in this light, the Incarnation itself is an act of mercy, as Aquinas reminds us in his *Commentary on Psalm 50*. The fact that Aquinas singles out mercy as one of the central attributes of God allows us to question the claim that Aquinas contributed to a vindictive notion of God.[19] A brief consideration as to how divine mercy relates to justice (in *ST* I, q. 21) will strengthen this argument. Aquinas discusses an objection that states that God's mercy appears to clash with his justice: 'God cannot remit what appertains to his justice.' In his reply Aquinas makes an important observation:

> God acts mercifully, not indeed by going against his justice, but by doing something more than justice; thus a man who pays another two hundred denarii, though owing him only one hundred, does nothing against justice, but acts liberally or mercifully. The case is the same with one who pardons an offence committed against him, for in remitting it he may be said to bestow a gift. ... Hence it is clear that mercy does not destroy justice, but in a sense is the fullness thereof.[20]

These comments remind us of the fact that a different kind of justice operates among friends than among people who are not on friendly terms. The reference to the parable of the workers in the vineyard (Matthew 20) is no coincidence. In that story, God bestows an equal reward on all workers, even though some started labouring much later than others. This may clash with our natural sense of justice; it is, however, simply an illustration of God's superabundant generosity.

All acts of divine justice are predicated upon God's prior generosity, goodness and mercy, if only because there is no proportion between God and creatures. Divine justice is squarely founded upon divine mercy from whom we have received

---

18. *ST* I, q. 21, a. 3.
19. O'Collins, *Christology*, 207; Brandon Peterson, 'Paving the Way? Penalty and Atonement in Aquinas's Soteriology', *International Journal of Systematic Theology* 15, no. 3 (2013): 265–83.
20. *ST* I, q. 21, a. 3 ad 2.

everything in the first place, including our very existence.[21] Furthermore, the utter indebtedness of the creature to God who is sovereign over all explains why every sin is ultimately a sin against God. As David confesses in Ps 50:4 *Tibi soli peccavi*: 'Against Thou alone I have sinned.' Thus, when we commit sin we are not necessarily hurting other people nor are we only damaging ourselves. We infringe upon the good order of creation that God established. In sinning we may be committing injustices and inflicting deep hurt on our fellow-human beings; but ultimately, and more profoundly, it destroys our relationship with God. As creatures we stand in a relationship of radical dependency on God. In sinning, then, we deny this relationship of dependency; we turn away from God and set ourselves up as 'auto-nomous' beings, that is, beings who are a law unto themselves and who, in the words of Evelyn Waugh in *Brideshead Revisited*, 'set up a rival good to God'.

The fact that every sin is a sin against God has, of course, a positive implication. For if every sin is against God, it is also from God that we can ultimately obtain forgiveness and be healed. This is no mere theory; there is life-giving consolation in this. There are many instances in which the victims of the ravages of sin cannot or will not forgive the perpetrators their crimes. In those circumstances the guilty can turn to God who is willing to forgive and bring healing through Christ.

It is no coincidence that I speak of healing here. Time and again Aquinas characterizes sin in terms of a sickness of the soul.[22] This too is revealing, for it once again illustrates that vindictiveness is alien to Aquinas's notion of God. A judge may punish; a doctor, however, heals. Sin is a sickness of the soul in need of healing. In mortally sinning we forfeit our loving orientation towards God, and we end up in a shadow existence.[23] Grave sin is like a dark cloud which casts its shadow over the soul, blocking the light of charity or love for God. It is from this shadow existence that we can be redeemed by inscribing our lives into that of Christ.

Aquinas does not subscribe to a forensic theory of salvation. Reconciliation with God therefore requires a process of transformation that will reorient our lives towards the light of God. Now, Aquinas (and the tradition before him)

---

21. *ST* I, q. 21, a. 4:

> Now the work of divine justice always presupposes the work of mercy; and is founded thereupon. For nothing is due to creatures, except for something pre-existing in them, or foreknown. Again, if this is due to a creature, it must be due on account of something that precedes. And since we cannot go on to infinity, we must come to something that depends only on the goodness of the divine will – which is the ultimate end. ... So in every work of God, viewed at its primary source, there appears mercy. In all that follows, the power of mercy remains, and works indeed with even greater force; as the influence of the first cause is more intense than that of second causes.

22. See R. Van Nieuwenhove, 'Bearing the marks of Christ's Passion: Aquinas's Soteriology', in *The Theology of Thomas Aquinas*, ed. R. Van Nieuwenhove and J. Wawrykow (South Bend: University of Notre Dame, 2005), 277–302, especially 282–7.

23. *ST* I-II, q. 86, a. 1 ad 3.

accepts that suffering may offer an occasion for disciplining our at times unruly desires. Penitential practices (including Lenten ones) are predicated on this. This espousal of penance Aquinas calls *poena satisfactoria*, sometimes (mis)translated as 'satisfactory punishment' rather than as 'satisfactory affliction or pain'.[24] It is exactly the terminology of 'satisfactory punishment [affliction]' that has wrong-footed some scholars and has led them to claim that Aquinas paves the way for a penal interpretation of Christ's saving work.[25] More particularly, they argue that by introducing the notion of *poena satisfactoria* Aquinas muddled the clear distinction Anselm had maintained between punishment (*poena*) and making satisfaction, thereby anticipating a (supposedly Calvinist) notion of penal substitution. This claim seems misguided to me. First, *poena* can indeed be translated as punishment, but it can also simply mean affliction or pain. Hence, it does not necessarily have a penal connotation. More importantly, by introducing *poena satisfactoria* Aquinas actually lessens the penal aspects of traditional soteriology rather than reinforcing it. In order to see this we need to remember that the distinction between *malum poenae* (evil suffered) and *malum culpae* (the evil of sin; moral evil) is derived from Augustine's *On Free Choice* 3.9,[26] and that according to Augustine, *all* afflictions or *poenae* (sickness, death ...) are punishments for sin from God, including original sin. Insofar as Aquinas accepts this he qualifies the penal aspect: some afflictions may acquire a satisfactory dimension if we freely espouse them.[27] Aquinas generally uses the word *poena* to refer to anything that goes against our will. Insofar, however, as we freely espouse it, it loses the strong penal dimension. Hence he writes,

> Now when punishment [affliction] (*poena*) is satisfactory, it loses somewhat of the nature of punishment [affliction] (*de ratione poenae*): for the nature of punishment is to be against the will; and although satisfactory punishment, absolutely speaking, is against the will, nevertheless in this particular case and for this particular purpose, it is voluntary. Consequently, it is voluntary simply, but involuntary in a certain respect.[28]

24. See for instance *ST* I-II, q. 87, a. 7. In the response Aquinas also mentions *medicinas poenales* – and it does not make sense to translate this as 'medicinal punishments'. A doctor who prescribes 'bitter potions to his patients that he may restore them to health' (which is how Aquinas illustrates *medicinas poenales*) does not inflict punishment, nor is he acting in a vindictive manner.

25. See Peterson, 'Paving the Way ...'.

26. Bonaventure writes in II *Sent*. d. 35, a. 1, q. 2 (quoting Augustine, *De Lib. Arbitr.* 3. 9): 'Malum culpae est affectio voluntaria, malum vero poenae est affectio involuntaria.' Modern editions of Augustine's texts have: 'Non enim peccatum et supplicium peccati naturae sunt quaedam, sed adfectiones naturarum, illa voluntaria, ista poenalis.'

27. In *De Malo* q. 5, a. 4 & 5 he qualifies the Augustinian legacy by arguing that natural afflictions are merely 'concomitant punishments' for original sin rather than direct punishments, and he affirms that there is a natural dimension to death and other ills given our corporeal nature.

28. *ST* I-II, q. 87, a. 6.

Nobody enjoys doing penance but we still freely embrace it. In one sense it is in accordance with our will; in another sense it goes against it. Hence, if we are willing to do penance the stain of sin is removed – we begin to dwell back in the light of God's grace.[29] It should be reiterated that language of making satisfaction is an integral part of penance for Aquinas. We engage in penance, not because it is demanded from us by a vindictive God to placate him but because we ourselves freely desire to do so in order to restore the broken relationship with God. When we have gravely hurt or offended somebody we will want 'to make it up to that person', as colloquial English has it, even if the person herself does not demand such a manifestation of sorrow and repentance. Penance transforms us and restores the relationship. Similarly, it does not change God who has no need of inflicting punishments to satisfy his alleged wrath.

The personalist and penitential (as distinct from penal) aspect of Aquinas's soteriology is further illustrated by his adoption of the theme of 'making satisfaction'. From his earliest theological synthesis Aquinas describes making satisfaction in terms of restoring a relationship (*restitutio amicitiae*) with God through penance.[30] He draws on two sources to develop his theology of making satisfaction: the first one is from a work that Aquinas attributes to Augustine although it is actually by Gennadius of Marseilles (d. 496); the second is by Anselm of Canterbury.[31] According to Gennadius's definition, satisfaction is penance, whereby the causes of sin are being removed, and we are strengthened against their enticements in the future.[32] In short, Aquinas characterizes satisfaction as a medicine which heals past sins and preserves us from future ones.[33]

---

29. We must still engage in actual 'satisfactory punishment' to heal our soul and to restore the equality of justice (cf. *ST* I-II, q. 87, a. 6, ad 3). It is because of his very sorrow over his sin that David wants to make satisfaction (*ST* I-II, q. 87, a. 6 ad 2: 'The virtuous man does not deserve punishment [affliction] simply, but he may deserve it as satisfactory: because his very virtue demands that he should do satisfaction for his offenses against God or man').

30. IV *Sent*. d. 15, q. 1, a. 3 sol. 1. I have used the English translation by Beth Mortensen et al. in *Saint Thomas Aquinas: Commentary on the Sentences, Book IV, Distinctions 14–25* (Wyoming: Aquinas Institute, 2017).

31. IV *Sent*. d. 15, q. 1, a. 1, qc. 3, obj. 1 & 5.

32. According to Anselm's definition, satisfaction refers to paying the honour due to God. Aquinas harmonizes the two definitions by understanding Anselm's one as referring to past offences, and Gennadius's one to preserving us from future faults. We pay due honour to God when we remove the offence, which Aquinas understands in terms of a restoration of friendship. See IV *Sent*. d. 15, q. 1, a. 3 sol. 1: 'The removal of an offense is the restoration of friendship; and so if there is something that blocks the restoring of friendship, satisfaction cannot even exist between men.'

33. IV *Sent*. d. 15, q. 1, a. 3 qc. 1, Sed contra 2.

Aquinas's discussion of the theme of 'sacrifice' illustrates the same point. Consider Aquinas's comments on Ps. 50.18-19:

If you had desired sacrifice, I would indeed have given it;
With burnt offerings you will not be delighted.
A sacrifice to God is an afflicted spirit;
A contrite and humbled heart (*cor contritum et humiliatum*)
O God, you will not despise.

God takes no delight in burnt offerings; what God desires is a humble and contrite heart. Humility is a virtue that reminds us of our createdness, of the fact that we have been made from earth (*humus*) and to earth we will return. It is a virtue that governs the way we relate to God rather than to other people.

When Aquinas comments on these verses he quotes Augustine's *De Civ. Dei*, Bk X, where Augustine had argued that it would be foolish to assume that God needs our sacrifices. Augustine is insistent that sacrifices do not change God; they transform us. It is we ourselves, not God, who benefit from the worship that is offered to God. The purpose of past and present offerings is that 'we may cleave to God and seek the good of our neighbour for the same end. Thus the visible sacrifice is the sacrament, the sacred sign, of the invisible sacrifice.' He concludes that in offering our sacrifices 'we shall be aware that visible sacrifice must be offered only to him, to whom we ourselves ought to be an invisible sacrifice in our hearts'.[34] The visible sacrifice in all its multifarious expressions (e.g. liturgical, moral-practical, ascetical) is the manifestation of the invisible sacrifice, which is a radical centring of our heart and mind on God, a theocentric focus in everything we do. Ultimately, sacrifice refers to a gift of self to God, establishing a communion with God and our fellow-human beings. This self-gift derives its meaning and value from the self-gift of Christ.

Following Augustine, Aquinas argues that an external sacrifice symbolizes an internal spiritual sacrifice, whereby the soul offers itself up to God.[35] We can offer external things (our possessions), bodily goods (fasting, martyrdom) and goods of the soul (e.g. devotion, prayer).[36] These external sacrifices manifest an internal gift of self through devotion to God. Now Augustine's dictum that the external sacrifice is the sacrament, or sacred sign of the internal sacrifice also applies to Christ's sacrifice. This means that Christ's sufferings *as such* are not pleasing to God but rather the love and obedience they exemplify.

This is the reason why Christ's saving work is a source of merit: merit should not be primarily understood in terms of a reward for a deed you perform. In

---

34. Augustine, *De Civ. Dei*, X, 19 translated by H. Bettenson as *St Augustine: The City of God* (Harmondsworth: Penguin Books, 1996).

35. *ST* II-II, q. 85, a. 2. Every virtuous act assumes the character of sacrifice through being done in order that we might cling to God in holy fellowship (*ST* II-II, q. 85, a. 3 ad 1).

36. *ST* II-II, q. 85, a. 3 ad 12.

Aquinas's understanding, merit depends mainly on the love or charity with which you perform the praiseworthy act: charity is the root of merit. Our acts are meritorious insofar as they are founded upon charity or love for God. The primary reason why somebody gives something freely – the way God bestows his gifts – is friendship. Therefore, it is our friendship or love for God (charity) that creates the context in which we can receive merit from God.[37] This is of central importance in understanding Aquinas's notion that through suffering we can become Christ-like, itself inspired by Col. 1.24 (where the author writes that he rejoices in his suffering, and has to supplement in his flesh the suffering of Christ for the sake of the Church) and other Pauline writings. The possibility to regard our afflictions as a means of entering into the passion of Christ is predicated on an intimate loving union between Christ as Head and the members of his body, the Church. This intimate union works both ways: Christ identifies with our suffering in radical solidarity, and we can see our own sufferings as a participation in Christ's. Thus, suffering itself can become a kind of communion with Christ. As Michael Dodds has argued, this radical union surpasses mere compassion.[38] When we see others suffer we feel, hopefully, a profound sympathy; but when these others are actually another self, or part of ourselves (such as our children) their suffering is almost literally ours. Through charity or friendship between God and humanity, a most intimate solidarity in suffering is established between Christ and his followers.

Christ's passion, then, is meritorious because it manifests his perfect love for God, which can then be shared with the faithful who are members of the one body, of which Christ is the Head.[39] Aquinas therefore emphasizes the intimate union between Christ and his members. This emphasis excludes a substitutionary notion of salvation. If there is a corporate dimension to Adam's Fall, so there is – even more – a collective dimension to the merits of Christ that are being shared:

> Grace was bestowed upon Christ, not only as an individual, but inasmuch as he is the Head of the Church, so that it might overflow into his members; and therefore Christ's works are referred to himself and to his members in the same way as the works of any other man in a state of grace are referred to himself.[40]

But even if we accept that Christ restores the relationship and friendship between sinful humanity and God we are still left with the question, Is it not deeply problematic to attribute saving efficacy to the death of an innocent man? Can God truly be said to have wanted the suffering of his Son? At one level Aquinas would agree that God does not want innocent people to perish; and he is quite in

---

37. See IV *Sent.*, d. 15, q. 1, a. 3 qc. 4.
38. M. Dodds, 'Thomas Aquinas, Human Suffering, and the Unchanging God of Love', *Theological Studies* 52 (1991): 330.
39. *Comm. John* no. 1976; *ST* III, q. 48. a. 1.
40. *ST* III, q. 48, a. 1.

agreement to call the execution of Christ the gravest of sins.[41] Here Aquinas and some of the contemporary theologians I mentioned are at one. But Aquinas can, if you like, 'situate' the horrible crime of the Son's execution in a broader perspective of divine providence. Schillebeeckx and other theologians cannot. For them the death of Christ was simply the result of Christ's theocentric mission which evoked, perhaps predictably, deadly resistance from worldly and even religious authorities.

Now it is correct to say that the Gospels attribute the passion of Christ to the intrigues of this-worldly powers; but they *also* suggest that the Father gives up his Son on our behalf, and that there was a sense in which Christ had to die.[42] In Lk. 24.26 the resurrected Christ himself admonishes his disciples on the way to Emmaus: 'Ought not Christ to have suffered these things, and so enter into his glory?' Similarly, in the Gospel of John we find repeated assertions that the Son 'must' suffer on the cross, which is his moment of glorification. 'Such is the command I received from my Father …' Christ says in Jn 10.18 (quoted in III, q. 47, a. 2 ad 1), while in Phil. 2.8 we read that Christ was 'obedient (to his Father) even unto death' (quoted in Sed Contra of III, q. 47, a. 2). And in the Gospel of Mark we find a hurried rush towards the cross. In describing the cross merely in terms of this-worldly abhorrence of the purity of Christ, Schillebeeckx and others therefore have to ignore some considerable scriptural evidence that suggests that these evil machinations do not fall outside of the remit of divine providence. Aquinas can do justice to both elements: that is, he can not only affirm that the passion of Christ was a most heinous crime but *also* assert that it does not fall outside the scope of the divine plan. The reason he can make these two seemingly contradictory assertions is that he operates with a more sophisticated notion as to how divine causality and creaturely activity relate to one another.

In Aquinas's view divine causality and creaturely activity do not operate on the same level and are, therefore, not in competition with one another. God causes at a transcendental level, so to speak: God is the condition of possibility of creaturely activity. This creaturely activity can occur necessarily or in a contingent manner, but in either case it is subject to divine providence.

This is not a new insight. Scholars have long since recognized that we cannot make sense of Aquinas's Five Ways unless we understand them as pointing towards a vertical or transcendental notion of divine causality. In other words, when Aquinas considers arguments from motion, causality, contingency and necessity and so forth, he is not claiming that God is a first cause operating on the same level as creaturely causality (as in a Deist understanding). Rather, he is suggesting that the existence of the world as we know it cannot be explained in purely inner-worldly terms. Attempting to explain the ultimate cause of the world in scientific or philosophical terms is merely question-begging, for these scientific laws are obviously part of the *explanandum*. In short, the very existence of the world – why

---

41. *ST* III, q. 47, a. 4.

42. As Hans Urs von Balthasar observed in *Mysterium Paschale* (Edinburgh: T&T Clark, 1990), 89ff.

there is anything at all rather than nothing – constitutes a philosophical question that requires a theological answer, namely God as the transcendental cause of all created beings and activity.

Given this broader understanding of divine causality it is not incoherent for Aquinas to claim that the passion of Christ was the result of profoundly evil opposition to his mission *and* also wanted by God as the chosen means of salvation. Given the end – namely the salvation of humankind – it was 'necessary' that Christ suffer for our sake. This 'necessity' is not stringent; it is rather a case of being more 'fitting' (*convenienter*), for without it the end cannot be attained in a most suitable manner. Hypothetically, God could have chosen a different way of redeeming humankind.[43] The death Christ suffered on the cross, however, manifested the radical nature of Christ's love for, and solidarity with, humankind in a supreme manner.

It is required, however, that we avail of the salvation that Christ effected. If Christ is the doctor who prepared the medicine necessary for our salvation we still need to take it by partaking in the sacraments, such as baptism, penance and Eucharist. In *ST* III, q. 73, a. 4 Aquinas considers three different names for the sacrament of the Eucharist or the Last Supper. When one considers it from the perspective of the past, it can be called a *sacrifice* as it commemorates and re-enacts our Lord's passion; in relation to the present it refers to union with Christ and the other faithful, which is why it is called *communion*. Quoting John of Damascus he writes that through the sacrament we communicate with Christ, partaking of his flesh and Godhead, and thereby we commune with Christ and one another. Finally, with regard to the future it is called *Eucharist* or good grace as we receive God's grace and indeed Christ himself who is filled with grace. The whole sacramental economy converges on the Eucharist: the sacrifices of the Hebrew people prefigured, and the Eucharist commemorates and re-enacts, the sacrifice of Christ. Indeed, as Aquinas writes, 'the Eucharist is the perfect sacrament of our Lord's passion, containing Christ crucified'.[44]

The sacraments are the material extension, so to speak, of the Incarnation. Given the fact that we are corporeal beings, drawn towards material things (for better or for worse), and given the fact that we acquire knowledge of the intelligible or spiritual through sensible things it is fitting that God chose modest material things, such as bread, water and wine, as the instruments of our sanctification.[45] Their corporeal nature is like a veil through which we can discern a spiritual reality – not unlike the scriptures in which a profound spiritual meaning can reside within the literal meaning of the text, as Aquinas reminds us.[46]

---

43. *ST* III, q. 46, a. 2; see also III, q. 1, a. 2.
44. *ST* III, q. 73, a. 5, ad 2.
45. *ST* III, q. 60, a. 4.
46. Ibid.

Conclusion

Aquinas offers a number of theoretical responses to the mystery of evil. He adopts, for instance, the traditional notion of evil as privation of goodness, and he appeals to the argument that from a more universal perspective particular evils may actually be good. More important is his Christian-theological approach, which invites us to see the adversities we inevitably encounter throughout our lives in the light of the passion of Christ. Aquinas's views compare favourably, in my view, with today's 'protest-(a)theism'. Aquinas's understanding of providence is richer and more comprehensive than that of modern-day protest theists who implicitly deny the all-encompassing nature of divine providence, thereby perhaps lapsing back into an ancient notion of Fate, if not dualist (Manichean) tendencies. In other words, Aquinas's notion of providence can assist us in discerning the mystery of divine mercy behind the veil of the world and its inevitable, meaningless sufferings. In the words of Simone Weil,

> Those who have the privilege of mystical contemplation, having experienced the mercy of God, *suppose* that, God being mercy, the created world is a work of mercy. But as for obtaining evidence of this mercy directly from nature, it would be necessary to become blind, deaf, and without pity in order to believe such a thing possible. ... That is why mysticism is the only source of virtue for humanity. Because when men do not believe that there is infinite mercy behind the curtain of the world, or when they think that this mercy is on front of the curtain, they become cruel.[47]

Such a dialectical approach which does not deny the reality of affliction and yet discerns the mystery of divine mercy within it is predicated on a number of things. First, it presupposes a belief that affliction does not fall outside the remit of divine providence; secondly, this perspective is only viable in light of the cross and the saving meaning it has. I have suggested that the denial of the centrality of the passion of Christ for our salvation sits uneasily with both the Gospel accounts and the ensuing tradition. As I argued, acknowledging the centrality of the cross of Christ does not mean that we therefore are committed to espousing a penal, substitutionary notion of salvation in which Christ's sacrifice meets the demands of a vindictive, angry god. This view is utterly alien to Aquinas: his comments on divine mercy, as well as his stance that both 'making satisfaction' and 'sacrifice' must be seen in the context of penance, through which our friendship with God is restored, exclude this interpretation. Thus, the passion of Christ does not appease or change God. Like penance, it changes us when we become part of his Body. Accepting the saving significance of the cross does not have to imply that we somehow either legitimize senseless suffering or acquiesce in it. It may assist us, however, in realizing that in the midst of our afflictions we can encounter Christ

---

47. Simone Weil, *Gravity and Grace* (London: Routledge, 1992), 100.

and become incorporated into him. This should not be construed in a *prescriptive* manner. We shouldn't say: 'This is how you should relate to your suffering!' (i.e. by interpreting it in the light of Christ's passion). It is, rather, *descriptive* and simply points to how some Christians, as a matter of fact, relate to their (inevitable) suffering. Whether or not we adopt this outlook is a personal decision, and not something we should impose on others. Nonetheless, the stories of witnesses matter. In emptying the passion of Christ of saving significance, some modern theologians prove themselves unfaithful to both the scriptural witness and the tradition; what is worse, in doing so they are in danger of depriving believers of a ray of meaning in their deepest darkness. In my view, Aquinas's soteriology offers a more sophisticated and rich alternative.

Chapter 7

SUFFERING AND THE DESIRE FOR GOD IN JOHN OF THE CROSS

Edward Howells

John of the Cross's teaching is a *locus classicus* for the discussion of suffering in the Christian life. John of the Cross values suffering for spiritual growth. Two pressing questions arise from his treatment. First, how optimistic should one be about suffering? Second, what status does suffering have with God? The theological dangers of giving divine sanction to suffering are clear, in terms of questioning God's goodness and the goodness of human nature. John has good answers and provides a creative and valuable account of suffering, but to understand him correctly requires some careful work of interpretation.

John of the Cross's 'dark nights' give value to inward states of psychological suffering, in which the soul suffers severely. John introduces suffering in *The Ascent of Mount Carmel* and *Dark Night*, his first two major works, in the specific circumstances of those in the process of spiritual direction who, he says, 'feel lost' on the spiritual path, because they no longer receive the 'satisfaction and consolation' that they had previously in their spiritual exercises.[1] This is a suffering particularly for the friars and nuns of the Discalced Carmelites to whom he is writing, who have dedicated themselves to a life of prayer in a contemplative order – though it can also be applied to others.[2] His account appears to be linked to his own experience of prison, when he was incarcerated by members of the unreformed Carmelite order in solitary confinement for nine months.[3] He focuses

---

1. A Prol. 4-5, p. 71. John of the Cross's works are abbreviated as follows:

   A   *Ascent of Mount Carmel*
   N   *Dark Night*
   C   *Spiritual Canticle (B redaction)*
   F   *Living Flame of Love (B redaction)*

The edition used is *The Collected Works of John of the Cross*, trans. and intro. Kieran Kavanaugh and Otilio Rodriguez (Washington DC: Institute of Carmelite Studies, 1979); for the Spanish original see *Obras Completas de San Juan de la Cruz*, ed. Lucinio Ruano, 14th edn (Madrid: Biblioteca de Autores Cristianos, 1994).

2. A Prol. 9.

3. For an account, see, for example, Colin P. Thompson, *St. John of the Cross: Songs in the Night* (London: SPCK, 2002), 45–50.

on the inner sense of abandonment, especially of abandonment by God, recalling the sufferings of Job and Jesus's cry of dereliction, 'My God, my God, why have you forsaken me?'[4] There are two main 'nights' of suffering: the night of the senses, which is the loss of satisfaction in sensory pleasures, and the more painful night of the spirit, when the soul suffers a kind of disintegration, losing its grasp on who it is and what it wants, feeling terror and the fear that it will die, in a profound and prolonged experience of dereliction.[5]

One might ask why John links these extraordinary feelings that he no doubt suffered in prison to the ordinary process of spiritual growth. He offers little justification for this move, simply asserting that something similar can and does happen to those advancing in prayer, when they move beyond the stage of beginners. They can feel that God has abandoned them. It should be added that John does not think that God has in fact abandoned them – the key point that I shall develop. But the feeling is real and painful, demanding a response. John thinks that when this suffering strikes, it cannot be avoided or cajoled out of people, by asking them to pull themselves together or to see things differently, or by any merely human remedy.[6] Only God can remove it, and John's great pastoral concern is that such feelings are not denied but approached as an invitation to growth, because of this new action of God that they signal. Correctly handled, they lead to growth.[7] It is the growth that John values rather than the suffering, but paradoxically, he notes, both are found in the same place, and this makes it vital that the sufferings are not simply dismissed. The natural tendency to turn away in denial must be resisted, or the gift will be missed. John is particularly critical of bad directors who demand redoubled efforts in spiritual exercises in response, effectively denying the divine invitation and only increasing the suffering, because they imply that it is the directee's fault and something simply to be avoided rather than examined.[8]

John has a theological rationale for why suffering and growth are found together, offering three reasons. First, God is a 'ray of darkness' exceeding our understanding (quoting Dionysius).[9] We can grasp the divine presence from the order and beauty of creation, but as beings made in the image of God, following in the tradition from Augustine, we seek to know God directly, in God's essence.[10]

---

4. A Prol. 4; 2A 7.11.
5. This is to summarize the whole of A and N, but see especially: A Prol. 5; 1.2; 2N 1.1; 2N 6; C 10-11; 12.9. Note that John uses 'soul' in this context to refer to the subject of spiritual transformation, that is, the whole person, soul and body, not just the spiritual part, which I follow in my use of 'soul' here and below.
6. A Prol. 3-6.
7. Ibid.
8. A Prol. 4; F 2.30-62.
9. 2A 8.6; 2N 5.3; C 14/15.16; F 3.49.
10. For the soul's creation in the image of God, see esp. C 1.6; 11.12; 12.1; 39.4; also 1A 9.1.

John makes a strong distinction between 'remote' knowledge of God through creatures and this direct knowledge of God.[11] To know God directly is 'dark' because of God's transcendent nature, so that it is approached through a stage of confusion and disorientation, being too great to grasp. This can feel like suffering, though in fact it is not. Or at least, it is a suffering of delightful excess, rather than of lack. John gives the image of being blinded by looking at the sun.[12] Gradually, with discernment and attention, the soul can become attuned to it, moving beyond disorientation to an awareness that this is the knowledge and possession of God that it really seeks. God is known and beyond our grasp at the same time in this apprehension, possessed and not possessed, thus light and dark.[13] It is knowledge that anticipates the permanent, face to face meeting with God of the beatific vision, and it can be possessed in this life in the state of union with God.[14]

But this is to jump ahead in the process of spiritual growth, for at first other kinds of darkness are felt by the soul, which are truly a suffering. These further darknesses are on account, second, of the soul's nature and, third, of its sin. By nature, the soul is more familiar with created things than with God's uncreated being, so it has a reductive expectation of what it is seeking from God; because of sin, it seeks satisfaction in what is other than and less than God.[15] For both of these reasons together, the soul tends to reduce God to ideas and feelings that it can grasp, reducing God to little more than a figment of the imagination.[16] It then balks at or misses entirely the true presence of God approaching in the darkness. In our language today, the soul prefers what is in its 'comfort zone' to God. Not being a created thing but the creator, God is by definition always greater than what the soul can grasp, extending beyond its comfort zone.[17] John is concerned with the deep roots of resistance to growth, combined with the height of the elevation to be attained by grace in bringing human nature to a supernatural union of equality with God in the Trinity. In this context, growth has the character of being a painful wrench. The problem, he emphasizes, belongs not merely to the exterior appetites of the senses but to the interior faculties of intellect, memory and will, where the image of God resides. The whole natural function of the soul must be denied, in a purification and illumination wrought by grace through faith, hope and love. The process culminates in the hollowing out of the three higher faculties so that they become what John calls the 'void of God', empty of all creaturely images and of the soul's entire orientation to creatures.[18]

11. C 12.5.
12. 2N 5.2.
13. See, for example, C 14/15.8, 16, 24.
14. C 39.6.
15. 1A 2; 2N 5.2.
16. 2A 4.3.
17. 2A 8.3-5.
18. A (in total); esp. 1A 6; 2A 6; also C 13.1.

At this point, a masochistic reading of John is certainly a risk. The denial of created existence can seem so complete in the dark nights that one might assume that the more that the creature is suppressed, the more spiritual a person becomes. But careful attention to John's teaching shows that this is not the case. Concerning how we are to seek God in the darkness, he says, for instance, early in *The Ascent of Mount Carmel*:

> Endeavour to be inclined always ... not to wanting something, but to wanting nothing; ... and desire (*desear*) to enter for Christ into complete nudity, emptiness, and poverty in everything in the world. ... To reach satisfaction in all, desire (*quieras*) its possession in nothing / To come to possess all, desire the possession of nothing / To arrive at being all, desire to be nothing / To come to the knowledge of all, desire the knowledge of nothing ... [etc].[19]

The note of paradox in this passage is vital to understanding John's teaching. He says that the soul should *desire* this nudity and *desire* the possession of nothing. It is not the case that humanity is simply to be wiped out in this negation, but rather that a new kind of desire should come to birth. *Two* desires are involved: there is an *ersatz* desire for God, which reduces God to a created object, which must be denied and reduced to nothing; while another, true desire for God is to be discovered and actively cultivated through this denial. A careful discernment is therefore needed. John calls it the 'difference between dryness and lukewarmness'.[20] The soul feels dry, but it is not lukewarm. False desire is drying up, while a greater desire is emerging. The two desires are in conflict, and it is vital to discern one from the other, rather than to consign both to negation. The one is a superficial desire for satisfaction which, John adds, comes from the 'spiritual sweet tooth', while the second is for God as God truly is, as a ray of darkness.[21]

More than denial, the soul is growing in its capacity as image of God. The 'voiding' of the three higher faculties is their growth, through faith, hope and love, into a greater capacity that can know, remember and love God directly.[22] The soul is being positively transformed. God, John says, 'begins to communicate himself through pure spirit by an act of simple contemplation in which there is no succession of thought'.[23] Intellect, memory and will are not losing God, but rather being invited to let go of their reductive grasp on God, so as to receive the true, 'dark inflow' of God as a non-successive, pure act. The reason for the uncertainty is that there is an epistemological gap between what the soul feels is happening and what is really happening. The soul feels this growth as loss. It feels

---

19. 1A 13.6, pp. 102–3; 1A 13.11, pp. 103–4.
20. 1N 9, especially 9.2-3, pp. 313–14.
21. 2A 6.5, p. 122; A Prol. 8; 2A 7.11.
22. 2A 6 (and see further on faith, hope and love in the remainder of A); C 1.7-18; F 2.34; 3.19-22.
23. 1N 9.8, p. 315.

abandoned by God, rather than that God is coming closer. Against this confusion, various signs for discernment can be given, such as the discernment of dryness from lukewarmness, as already indicated.[24] Further, when the faculties are emptied and void, John points out that even though they cannot yet see God, they do not feel dead but an ecstasy of desire as they move out freely into the unknown. At one level, the soul feels as if it is being torn apart and may die, but at another, it is growing in desire and focusing more precisely on God's greater being.[25]

Is John's teaching then simply that we must grit our teeth and hold out through this highly unpleasant process of growth, for the reward which presumably finally arrives? This could be the conclusion if we stopped only with *The Ascent of Mount Carmel* and *Dark Night*, but if we turn to John's two later works, the *Spiritual Canticle* and *Living Flame of Love*, we see a different picture. In these works, desire for God leads the soul positively from the start: the focus is on the growth of the soul as a creature made in the image of God, with purgation in second place. Much more in these works concerns how, in union, the soul's epistemology catches up with the divine presence, arriving at a secure and direct knowledge of God, beyond the uncertainty of unknowing and the feeling of abandonment. Among a number of passages that could be used to illustrate this point, perhaps the best is to be found in the transition of the thirteenth stanza of the *Spiritual Canticle*, which John introduces with the words from his poem:

Return, dove,
The wounded stag
Is in sight on the hill,
Cooled by the breeze of your flight.[26]

The poem, modelled on the Song of Songs, is a love song between the soul as bride and Christ as the divine bridegroom, on which John comments in terms of the spiritual journey ending in union with God.[27] Christ as the bridegroom first appears 'in sight' at this moment of the journey, as the 'wounded stag'. The image recalls Christ's wounds and the psalm text of the stag who longs for water.[28] John ascribes the figure of the 'wound' to the soul's desire for God, from the Song of Songs's image of the 'wound of love', with which the bride longs for

---

24. 2A 13.1-4; 1N 9.2-3; 2N 8.4.
25. C 11.5-12.
26. C 13.1, p. 458.
27. For a literary and historical–theological study, see Colin P. Thompson, *The Poet and the Mystic: A Study of the Cántico Espiritual of San Juan de la Cruz* (Oxford: Oxford University Press, 1977).
28. John's first scriptural source for the stag is in fact Song 2.9, referring to the swift movement of the stag as a figure for the way that Christ as the bridegroom shows and hides himself in the movement of love (C 1.15); but Psalm 41(42).2-3 is not far behind and is introduced near the point at which the wounded stag appears here (C 12.9).

the bridegroom when he is absent.[29] This feeling of unrequited desire for God dominates the earlier part of the journey. But now John also applies the wound to God: divine desire, God's *eros*, comes out to the soul in love, according to the movement to humanity of the incarnation.[30] Seeing that the soul suffers from its desire for God, John portrays God responding with a similar desire in relation to the soul. If the stag, he says, 'hears the cry of his mate and senses that she is wounded, he immediately runs to comfort her'.[31] In coming to comfort her, Christ shares in her wound, experiencing the soul's abandonment for himself.[32] Christ as the stag is thus 'wounded by [the soul's] wound'.[33] But crucially, in this joining in suffering, the focus is on the meeting between the soul and God at the level of desire, not just on the sharing in suffering. The soul desires God, and God desires the soul, and they meet in love. John indicates clearly that it is love that brings God down to the level of human suffering; God does not desire the suffering itself.

The effect is to subordinate suffering to desire and love, in both God's case and the soul's. As John says, 'Among lovers, the wound of one is a wound for both.'[34] The two desires meet one another and unite in love. The wound becomes a shared wound, and in this sharing, two partners become visible. The effect is that the soul's feeling of abandonment by God, which was her greatest suffering, is now banished in favour of love. The soul sees a sharing in love between two where before she saw only abandonment. The quality of love, as equal and shared, is the very opposite of abandonment. John moves from 'desiring' words to 'love' (*amor*) to signal this change.[35] What is more, the other of this love is none other than the God for whom she has longed, and the soul now knows this other without turning God into an external object, finding God at the level of her own desire. The desire with which she has longed for God is also God's desire for her, and God appears in this desire, not as an object outside it. Enlarging on how the soul knows this, John suggests that she has attained a new kind of knowing possessed directly from the soul's participation in the Trinity. Just as the Father

---

29. C 1.14.

30. John appears to follow Dionysius in speaking of this movement of divine love as desire/eros: see Bernard McGinn, *Mysticism in the Golden Age of Spain (1500–1650); The Presence of God: A History of Western Christian Mysticism*, vol. VI, part 2 (New York: Crossroad-Herder, 2017), 249.

31. C 13.9, p. 460.

32. Christ was 'annihilated' in 'extreme abandonment' at the moment of the cry of dereliction (2A 7.11, p. 124).

33. C 13.9, p. 461.

34. C 13.9, p. 460.

35. This shift was brought to my attention by an excellent student dissertation: Mark Aloysius SJ, 'Does Desire Divide or Unify the Self in the Journey of Mystical Transformation in the *Spiritual Canticle* of John of the Cross' (MTh diss., Heythrop College, University of London, 2017), 31.

and Son are one in the love that is the Holy Spirit, and their difference appears as a distinction made internally to this love, rather than by reference to an object outside it, so God is known now as the other of the love which they share, from within the love. 'For just as love is the union of the Father and the Son, so it is the union of the soul with God,' he says.[36] God puts the soul within this love. As John says in another passage, 'With God, to love the soul is to put her somehow in himself and make her his equal,' so that the soul knows God from within the union.[37] This is the distinctive manner in which Christ appears 'in sight on the hill'. There is an epistemological transformation in which God appears at the level of the soul's immediate inward participation in God rather than externally. God does not appear as the absent object of desire, but more immanently within the desire, at the level of the interior image. In relation to her suffering, this means that God is not found to be as an external agent in terms of either comfort or judgement, but as her inward equal in love.

This possession of God at the deep level of the soul's love, which fulfils the soul's creation in the image of God, opposes suffering in a particular way. John claims that it moves the self beyond the boundaries of the isolated individual to a form of being shared with God, which provides a new 'centre' for the soul.[38] In this 'married' or 'trinitarian' mode, shared in the manner of the Father with the Son, the self shifts from the position of the victim, isolated in abandonment, to a place of permanent inward company with God. Suffering may still be felt in an external way, but inwardly its character is deeply altered. The defining quality of suffering, which for John is abandonment, is undermined by this new selfhood. It is subverted from within the relationality which gives it being by the abundance of love. From this transformation, John asserts that a new agency is given to the soul, in place of her previous passivity. The love of God at the centre 'overflows' into exterior action, directly from God's will.[39] Thus, he says, the soul's 'power to look at God is, for the soul, the power to do works in the grace of God'.[40] Seeing her selfhood differentiated between herself and God and bound together at her centre in love, she moves out towards the world and others, no longer bound by fear. The soul is energized and dignified by this overflow. It is a change of selfhood, in which suffering is truly 'unseated' by the new centre of agency.

---

36. C 13.11, p. 461; C 37.3. On this trinitarian knowing, see Edward Howells, *John of the Cross and Teresa of Avila: Mystical Knowing and Selfhood* (New York: Crossroad-Herder, 2002), 51–5.

37. C 32.6, p. 536.

38. This 'centre of the soul', which is also a 'centre of love', is a new term that John introduces in the *Living Flame of Love* (F 1.9, 12-13; 2.8, 10; 3.10; 4.3). I am grateful to Mark Aloysius SJ for pointing out this distinct shift in John from epistemology to anthropology (Aloysius, 'Does Desire Divide', 16–39).

39. C 18.6; 28.3-8; 40.1; F 1.27, 36; 2.3; 2.22; 3.7, 16; 3.74, 77; 4.4.

40. C 32.8, p. 536.

Conclusion

From this short survey of John's teaching, I would like to draw some brief concluding implications on the question of suffering. John begins from a specific kind of suffering, in the trials of those advancing in the process of spiritual direction, who are learning to relate to God fully as God rather than reductively. But his theological rationale broadens the terms of the discussion into the universal realm of God's dealings with suffering in Christ. From Christ's suffering on the cross, we know that abandonment is the defining element in suffering, and we know that it is opposed by the divine company of the Father and the Son, given to us in the gift of the Holy Spirit, from our creation in the image of God and in spiritual growth ending in union with God. The victory over suffering is therefore the promise of our creation in the image of God and our salvation by Christ, and it can be possessed in this life in the state of union.

John's teaching becomes complex, however, when he asserts that these two opposites – the destruction of the soul in abandonment, and the direct presence of God which fulfils the soul – are to be found together in human experience. The task of spiritual growth becomes one of learning how to distinguish them, so that the direct presence of God can be pursued and the destruction of the soul rejected. Why they are found together remains a mystery: it is a fact of life. But he is clear that they do not *belong* together, and his efforts go into providing means to separate them. These means are given from the perspective of the *viator* – the spiritual seeker on the way – at the level of experience, discernment and growth, rather than in the more distant terms of a theological overview. John's desire to accompany the soul on this journey, as a spiritual director, can make it look as though he is positively recommending suffering or wants the soul to suffer. But in fact he is drawing attention to the need for an honest facing up to suffering, rather than denial, in order to wrest the divine gift from it. He seeks to deal with suffering at its roots, in the destructive inward isolation on which it feeds. To do this, it is necessary to tease out what the soul really desires according to its creation, and to penetrate the hidden form of God's answer in the incarnation and the Trinity. An excavation of the springs of human desire and identity is required, to eject the damage done by the soul's deep sense of abandonment. Against the temptations of denial and self-belittlement, this abandonment must be unearthed by the love of the Holy Spirit. God must be discovered as inwardly present in love, not as a merely external agent, either in comfort or in judgement, but in a personal union like that of Father and Son. The soul then finds this defining experience within itself, at its roots, *before* the experience of abandonment. The result is an epistemological and personal transformation of the self into a new 'centre', which knows and possesses itself out of this love and acts out of its overflow, wholly displacing the abandonment.

Chapter 8

STOP KISSING ME: READING MOTHER
TERESA WITH BONAVENTURE'S HELP

Rachel Davies

Writing some 750 years ago, the great Franciscan Bonaventure spoke of a kiss between two mouths – one that festered and stank with wounds, another endued with life-giving grace.

In the story, Francis of Assisi is met by a man 'whose mouth and cheek were being eaten away by a certain horrible disease'.[1] Overcome with devotion, the man tries to kiss Francis's footprints, but Francis, embracing him, kisses the putrid mouth. As Bonaventure recounts, Francis 'touched that horrible sore with his [own] holy mouth, and suddenly every sign of the disease vanished and the sick man recovered the health he longed for'.[2]

A more recent story about kissing parallels and contrasts the Franciscan account in interesting ways. Near the end of her National Prayer Breakfast address to the United States Congress in 1994, Mother Teresa described meeting a woman suffering from cancer. '"And I told her, I say," said Mother Teresa, "You know, this terrible pain is only the kiss of Jesus – a sign that you have come so close to Jesus on the cross that he can kiss you". And [the woman] joined her hands together and said, "Mother Teresa, please tell Jesus to stop kissing me."'

The story was offered genially, to lighten a speech on the costliness of following Jesus, and over the years Mother Teresa repeated her ideas about kissing in letters to people with whom she was close. To her friend Eileen Egan, an American Catholic social activist, she wrote, 'Sorrow, suffering, Eileen, is but a kiss of Jesus. … I think this is the most beautiful definition of suffering – So let us be happy when Jesus stoops down to kiss us – I hope we are close enough that He can do it.'[3] To her religious sisters she wrote in 1979, 'If I am the spouse of Jesus crucified, He has to kiss me. Naturally, the nails will hurt me. If I come close to the crown of thorns it will hurt me.'[4]

---

1. Bonaventure, *Bonaventure*, trans. Ewert Cousins (Mahwah: Paulist Press, 1978), 195.
2. Ibid.
3. Brian Kolodiejchuk, ed., *Come Be My Light, the Private Writings of the "Saint of Calcutta"* (New York: Doubleday, 2007), 281.
4. Ibid., 282.

It is tempting to reduce a thinker's complexity to particular paradigms or modes of expression we like or dislike. Christopher Hitchens loved to hate Mother Teresa's prayer breakfast thoughts on kissing, and in some circles the new narrative is that Mother Teresa clearly relished suffering and loved poverty more than she loved the poor. Aimed at a woman who not only washed worms from other people's wounds but also established innovative self-help centres for Kolkata's leprosy patients, such readings seem, at the very least, exaggerated.[5]

Yet there is an interesting contrast between Bonaventure's version of the kiss as a medieval scholastic, and Mother Teresa's as a modern passion mystic less immediately interested in systematic theological categories. For Bonaventure the theologian, suffering was a privation, and God was sheer, uncreated Being. When Being met privation through the kiss of Francis, healing was the obvious result. Mother Teresa occasionally affirmed the basic logic reflected in Bonaventure's kissing account. 'In all our lives, as in the life of Jesus', she once explained, 'the Resurrection has to come, the joy of Easter has to dawn'.[6] But it was the passion – not the resurrection – that dominated most of her known writings, leaving the link between kissing's function and God-as-Being sometimes difficult to trace. This presents interpreters with a challenge and a gift: on the one hand, Mother Teresa is both vulnerable to the critique that she inappropriately valourized suffering and at risk of being used to advance distorted forms of spiritual masochism. But reading Mother Teresa in dialogue with traditional, theologically rounded Christian thinkers like Bonaventure, I submit, can help contextualize her passion spirituality within Christianity's larger soteriological framework.

Given the vulnerabilities of Mother Teresa's spirituality, one might well ask whether it is worth reading her at all. The surprising gifts of her charism point in the affirmative. Mother Teresa was undoubtedly influenced by some of the theologies of redemptive suffering deplored by her critics, but the careful reader senses something else at work behind her use of its familiar language – something truthful and, existentially speaking, quite satisfying. Mother Teresa was not a trained systematician promoting well-ordered soteriologies, but a complex thinker and feeler searching for God's presence on the landscape of human adversity. And that adversity was profound, involving not only the physical degradation of Kolkata's 'dying destitute' but also what she often called a 'deeper kind of poverty': the lonely desire for love – for presence – that she met first and foremost in the poverty of her own heart. On one level, divine absence was the guiding motif for Mother Teresa. For nearly fifty years she struggled with feeling unwanted and rejected by God – a personal interiorization, she

---

5. This is not the place for extensive analysis of Mother Teresa's work among the poor. I highlight her leprosy centres here because they are examples of her most successful and least controversial self-help projects. On Mother Teresa's early leprosy work, see especially Nawin Chawla, *Mother Teresa* (London: Sinclair-Stevenson, 1992), 135–54; and Eileen Eagan, *Such a Vision of the Street* (New York: Image Books, 1986).

6. Ibid., 300; cf. 326.

came to understand, of the concrete rejection endured by the world's poor. By preserving a life-long inward space for God's absence, one could say that Mother Teresa was in a sense refusing to varnish the genuine horror of suffering, privation and death. But parallel to this deep, interior truth-telling, Mother Teresa trusted another reality as well: she believed that somehow, God was nevertheless present. The forsaken poor woman or man was Christ in his 'distressing disguise', she often said. As for her kissing accounts – it is of course possible to read these as exhortations to embrace suffering as a good, perhaps for its redemptive value.[7] But they also stand as expressions of her persistent openness to divine presence – a subtle resurrection speech on her landscape of perpetual Fridays. Besieged by the abyss of her own inner anguish, she grasped even at the language of redemptive suffering to affirm God's goodness, and there perceived a kiss.

My claim, then, is that Christian faith is at its best when it grasps the full scope of the paschal mystery – both its this-worldly Fridays and its eschatological Sundays – and that different nuances of this mystery are illumined by the diverse stories and prayer experiences of its believers. Mother Teresa was a Friday believer, perceiving the isolation and devastation caused by suffering with an intensity rarely matched by more systematic thinkers. But this gift bore certain risks – risks best abated by reading Mother Teresa alongside theologians with more comprehensive models of the paschal mystery, grounded in traditional accounts of the doctrine of God. Reading Mother Teresa in this way can enable one to receive the intimacy of Christ's kiss or presence in one's sufferings without that kiss becoming violent – without it turning Christ into the source of suffering so the sufferer feels compelled to say, 'Please tell Jesus to stop kissing me.'

What would it look like, then, to read Mother Teresa with Bonaventure's help? Bonaventure's credentials as a scholastic theologian and mystic of the cross make him a good reading companion for Mother Teresa.[8] While he also emphasized the passion, for him cruciform language and imagery always functioned as the face and door of resurrection, as we shall see. My aim as we proceed, then, will be to illumine the essential connection between Mother Teresa and Bonaventure – to show where they meet experientially, how Mother Teresa intensifies a sensibility already present in Bonaventure, and how Bonaventure unfurls Mother Teresa's Friday kiss into a complete paschal event. By doing this, my hope is to cast Mother Teresa as an original and appealing spiritual theologian who sits within the larger Christian witness to a kiss that ultimately heals.

The motif of kissing offers a useful point of entrance into the heart of Bonaventure's theological vision, which reaches its temporal summit in the

---

7. This aspect of her spirituality deserves fuller treatment elsewhere. I am able to bypass it for the sake of my current argument in part because I disagree with recent popular claims that redemptive suffering was for her some kind of totalizing paradigm.

8. On the centrality of the cross in Bonaventure's thought, see Ilia Delio, *Crucified Love: Bonaventure's Mysticism of the Crucified Christ* (Quincy: Franciscan Press, 1998).

stigmata account recorded in his *Legenda maior*. In the biblical book of Isaiah, a six-winged seraph presses a living coal from the altar of the Lord to the lips of the prophet, and through this kiss-like gesture, Isaiah's sin is purged, and he becomes an expressive self. He hears the voice of God calling and responds with 'Here I am; send me!'[9] In Bonaventure's *Legenda*, the touch of a flaming seraph brings Francis to life by pressing into him the wounds of Christ. The stigmata represent the high point of Francis's spiritual pilgrimage – the full actualization of his growth into the holiness of selfhood. Bonaventure tells us that in the stigmata, 'Christian wisdom' – the expressiveness of the Word – was 'ploughed into the dust' of Francis's flesh.[10]

The appearance of divine Wisdom in the stigmata points to the deeper, transcendent reality onto which Francis's journey maps. The image of a circle is commonly used to describe Bonaventure's soteriology and its relationship to the divine persons. For Bonaventure, God is sheer Being, and for Being to be Good, it must be self-diffusive, that is, a Trinity. The trinitarian shape of Being outlined in the arcs of a circle reveal, for Bonaventure, the pattern of creaturely becoming. The First Principle (or God the Father) is the starting and ending point of the circle. From that Principle the Word or Exemplary Principle proceeds, bearing within itself the infinite possibilities for creation which together reflect God's Being. And the divine circle returns to itself through the upward bend of the Holy Spirit, Love or creation's Completing Principle. Creatures are sent forth from the First Principle as ideas in the Word who 'brings them to birth' in time (as Bonaventure says in his *Collationes in Hexaemeron*), and they are fully actualized on the journey of return in the Holy Spirit.[11] Thus the circle of creaturely becoming mirrors the circular motion of Being itself.

This is the journey Bonaventure traces in his *Legenda*. And the stigmata, in which Bonaventure says Francis was finally 'borne aloft into God' in Christ, represents Francis's spiritual return.[12] Some scholars see the *Legenda* as a commentary on Bonaventure's devotional classic, the *Itinerarium mentis in Deum*. In that text, Bonaventure outlines six stages of spiritual progress that lead to the mind's Passover into the Sabbath rest of mystical union. The *Legenda* likewise outlines six visions of the cross that appear to or somewhere near Francis during his lifetime, marking the various stages of his spiritual ascent.[13] The visions cease when Francis achieves inward perfection, which appears bodily as the stigmata

---

9. Isa. 6.8.

10. *Leg. mai.* 13.10. See Ewert Cousins, ed. and trans., *Bonaventure: The Soul's Journey into God, The Tree of Life, The Life of St. Francis, The Classics of Western Spirituality* (New York: Paulist Press, 1978), 314.

11. *Hex.* 1.17. See Jose de Vinck, ed. and trans., *Collations on the Six Days*, The Works of Bonaventure (New York: St. Guild Press, 1970), 10.

12. *Leg. mai.* 13.3 (Cousins, *Bonaventure*, 305).

13. For a summary of these visions, and Bonaventure's interpretation of their relationship to the stigmata, see *Leg. mai.* 13.10 (Cousins, *Bonaventure*, 313–14).

two years before his death. As Bonaventure writes, there 'the true love of Christ ... transformed his lover into his image'.[14]

One of the most striking things about Francis's journey towards stigmata is the violence of its appearance and of the experience itself. If such an anguished image is the appropriate symbol of divine union, is it not possible that Bonaventure as well as Mother Teresa fetishizes suffering? The possibility of an affirmative answer should not distract one from the appealing refusal of both figures to deny what spiritual maturity often looks like in a historical life. It could be argued that the most realistic examples of heroism are not those figures who triumph over every personal failure and adversity, but people who live lives of moral courage in the midst of ongoing vulnerabilities. So likewise in Bonaventure's *Legenda*, physical and mental strain remain a part of life for the spiritually mature Francis, throwing him 'into an agony of doubt' regarding this stigmatized condition.[15] Thomas of Celano, who offers more to this theme than Bonaventure, recounts how the agonized Francis once pushed away a brother who touched his wounds, 'crying out for the Lord to spare him' (or perhaps, we might say, to stop kissing him).[16] There is, it would seem, a resonance between Mother Teresa and Francis's early interpreters, in that both suggest that it may be possible for spiritual actualization to occur alongside ongoing worldly suffering and brokenness.

But if Bonaventure and Thomas demonstrate a certain existential honesty in this respect, Mother Teresa takes it to an even higher level. Some passages detailing her spiritual struggle are excruciating:

> Lord, my God, who am I that You should forsake me? The child of your love – and now become as the most hated one – the one You have thrown away as unwanted – unloved. I call, I cling, I want – and there is no One to answer – no One on Whom I can cling – no, No One. – Alone. The darkness is so dark – and I am alone. Unwanted, forsaken – the loneliness of the heart that wants love is unbearable – where is my faith? – even deep down, right in, there is nothing but emptiness and darkness.[17]

While suffering confronts individuals for a variety of reasons, God's silence was the consuming burden of Mother Teresa's soul – a silence she encountered daily in the abandoned bodies of the poor. Interestingly, she alludes to divine presence in some of the same passages that highlight her sense of loneliness:

---

14. *Leg. mai.* 13.5 (Cousins, *Bonaventure*, 307).
15. *Leg. mai.* 13.4 (Cousins, *Bonaventure*, 306).
16. Thomas of Celano, 'The Life of Blessed Francis', in *The Saint*, ed. Regis Armstrong et al. (Berkley: New City Press, 1999), 265.
17. Kolodiejchuk, *Writings*, 186–7. This letter was sent to her Fr. Lawrence Trevor Picachy in the late 1950s.

That darkness that surrounds me on all sides – I can't lift my soul to God – no light or inspiration enters my soul – I speak of love for souls – of tender love for God – words pass through my words [sic, lips] – and I long with a deep longing to believe in them. I no longer pray – my soul is not one with You – and yet when alone in the streets – I talk to You for hours – of my longing for You – how intimate are those words – and yet so empty, for they leave me far from You.[18]

Where for Mother Teresa the weight of abandonment presses in and risks suffocating her hearers ('please tell Jesus to stop kissing me'), one senses a greater distance between Bonaventure and the stigmatization of Francis, in that Bonaventure is able to talk freely of suffering and wholeness in the same moment – something Mother Teresa can only do obliquely. Unlike Mother Teresa, Bonaventure is not writing as one who suffers, and one could be excused for feeling that his optimism misses the experiential mark. Here Mother Teresa seems to do a good deal better than Bonaventure. But here, also, the question of whether each figure romanticizes suffering returns and begins to bifurcate. Asked of Mother Teresa, the truth is not immediately forthcoming. Asked of Bonaventure, the question begins to resolve through thoughtful analysis of his metaphysics.

The genius of Bonaventure is the way he incorporates cyclical Being and becoming into the stages of his mystical programme. We have seen how for Bonaventure the summit of Francis's journey involves participation in the passion of Jesus, expressed as the stigmata. But for him the stigmata account maps not only onto Good Friday, the sixth day of creation (which he arrives at just before the stigmata account, having traced six prototypical appearances of the cross throughout Francis's life) but also onto the seventh. In Bonaventure's mystical programme, there is a kind of convergence of days six through eight, Friday through Sunday. One could say that Friday's passion stands as its own reality, and Sunday likewise as a place of eschatological renewal. But in the midst of these realities – on the Sabbath between – the self finds itself at rest mentally in its creative Source, having passed (died) with Christ into the truth of its recreation.[19] The difference

---

18. Ibid., 193.

19. Bonaventure does not offer a hard and fast designation for what happens, spiritually, on days six, seven and eight, but this reading represents one way of interpreting his various bits of commentary. In the *Hexaemeron*, the sixth day is the summit of contemplation, the seventh symbolizes the soul in glory (but deprived of its body) and the eighth represents the eschatological reunion of body and soul – that is, the complete restoration of the human person. In the *Legenda*, the stigmata occur after the symbols of six days have already appeared in the text, while the stigmata signal the seventh during which Francis – still living in this world – 'found [his] final rest'. Bodily renewal (the eighth day) is prefigured in the beauty of Francis's body towards the end of the text. In the *Itinerarium*, the soul reaches perfect contemplative awareness on the sixth day, but the seventh maps directly onto the sixth, also representing the mind's rest. See *Leg. mai.* 13.10, 15.1-3 (Cousins, *Bonaventure*, 312–14, 321–3); *Itin.* I.5, VII; *Hex.* III. 30-31 (de Vinck, *Collations on the Six Days*, 56–7).

between Bonaventure the scholastic theologian and Mother Teresa the modern believer, then, is that while both demonstrate a certain existential honesty in their recourse to the passion, Bonaventure's metaphysical system allows a contrasting but corresponding reality to exist behind the darkness. Because stigmata are the face of a richly articulated human flourishing, Sunday can manifest itself alongside the very real violence of Friday, giving Bonaventure's spirituality a Sabbatarian ethos signaled by the mysterious seventh stage of his *Itinerarium*.

In a system that gives such serious attention to worldly suffering and yet makes wholeness the summit of the human journey, suffering is not only properly acknowledged but also allowed to be transfigured. This can be seen in the extraordinary healing power that Bonaventure gives to Francis's wounds. Like the restoration of the rotting mouth, at Francis's touch, people are made whole, heat enters cold bodies and even animals recover from plague. A cacophony of miracles takes up the end of the *Legenda*, after the saint's passing, when the appearance of the stigmata and of Francis's dead body – mysteriously released from the terms of its worldly vulnerability – finally reflect the physical beauty of resurrection. The wound in his side looks like a 'most beautiful rose', and his skin shines 'with a dazzling [brightness], prefiguring the beauty' of the risen body.[20] Bonaventure's *Life of Francis* mirrors the order of a universe in which all things reduce to God, the Good in whom there is no privation, suffering or death. And Francis functions as a conduit linking God with human neediness through his transparency to both realities.

Whereas Bonaventure's kiss (like his stigmata) bears the whole paschal mystery within itself, Mother Teresa's version of the kiss is more raw. For her the passion is energized not so much by a momentum of Being leading to beatitude as by divine love inviting affective reciprocity. Here she belongs to a tradition that developed from the same Franciscan milieu as Bonaventure, though Bonaventure is unique in that he shares the new devotion to Christ's suffering humanity while articulating the metaphysical realism of the pre-modern period. We see splinters of late medieval passion mysticism coming together in Mother Teresa's devotional practices, private writings and public speeches. Where for Bonaventure the relationship between suffering and salvation exists in the context of Neoplatonic return (*reductio*), Mother Teresa emphasizes the highly personal nature of divine love in a way that tends to minimize God's transcendence. She speaks of 'my love for Jesus, and his tender love for me'.[21] At twenty-one she writes to a friend back home: 'If you could know how happy I am, as Jesus' little spouse ... I am enjoying my complete happiness, even when I suffer something for my beloved Spouse.'[22] To a priest she describes herself as a 'spoiled bride, who lives with Jesus in Nazareth – far away from Calvary'.[23]

---

20. *Leg. mai.* 14.2 (Cousins, *Bonaventure*, 316).
21. Kolodiejchuk, *Writings*, 5.
22. Ibid., 18.
23. Ibid., 20.

Bonaventure is also noted for his emphasis on affect, but for him love's ultimate object is not primarily the human Jesus but the Ground of Being Jesus bears by nature of the Incarnation. After interior darkness engulfs her at age thirty-eight, Mother Teresa's emphasis on the personal nature of God revealed in Jesus develops into a richly sacramental Christocentrism in which the thirst of Christ crucified becomes the energizing motif. On a train in the Himalayan foothills two years before the bleakness settled, Mother Teresa had a series of interior visions or revelations in which Jesus spoke the words 'I thirst' from the cross. More than a thirst for water, Jesus was thirsty for the love of the poor, the dying, the street children of Kolkata, and it was in these individuals that his presence could be found and loved, since as he once said, 'Just as you did to one of the least of these … you did it to me.'[24] For Mother Teresa, then, the journey to God was worldly and immediate, prioritizing sacramental intimacy over ontological transformation.

Thirty-seven years into the darkness, four years before her death, Mother Teresa wrote a moving letter to her sisters on the theme of Jesus's thirst:

> The time has come for me to speak openly of the gift God gave Sept. 10 [what the MCs call 'Inspiration Day'] – to explain as fully as I can what means for me the thirst of Jesus. For me Jesus's thirst is something so intimate – so I have felt shy until now to speak to you of Sept. 10 – I wanted to do as Our Lady who 'kept all these things in her heart'. … Why does Jesus say 'I thirst'? What does it mean? … Until you know deep inside that Jesus thirsts for you – you can't begin to know who He wants to be for you. Or who He wants you to be for Him. The heart and soul of MC is only this – the thirst of Jesus's Heart, hidden in the poor.[25]

Examining how Mother Teresa experienced Jesus's thirst can help illumine the relationship between Bonaventure's systematic project and the practical theology of Mother Teresa. In fact, there is a certain dialectic quality to Mother Teresa's discussion of thirst. On the one hand, her talks, interviews and letters constantly emphasize the infinite nature of divine thirst. She suggests a lack or neediness in God beyond what one normally sees in traditional treatments of divine desire, and if she were a dogmatic theologian well versed in metaphysics, one might argue that she (together with other modern passion mystics) introduces a kind of privation into God by not distinguishing between the divine and human natures of Christ. In an undated note affixed to the original MC constitutions she writes,

---

24. Matthew 25.40. Mother Teresa had a particular fondness for this verse and would often count out the five words 'you did it to me' on the five fingers of whoever she was talking to.

25. This comes from a letter circulated within the Missionary of Charity family, dated 25 March, 1993. The letter is now widely available online. See for example https://blog.franciscanmedia.org/franciscan-spirit/in-mother-teresa-own-words-i-thirst-i-quench (accessed 10 January, 2019).

'I thirst', Jesus said on the cross when Jesus was deprived of every consolation, dying in absolute Poverty, left alone, despised and broken in body and soul. He spoke of His thirst – not for water – but for love, for sacrifice. Jesus is God: therefore, His love, His thirst is infinite.[26]

Mother Teresa imagined divine desire not primarily as a dynamic of Being drawing all things to itself but through the lens of Christ's human need, which got amplified to infinity because of his divinity. Yet while for her God's thirst was infinite, so was the human ability to quench it:

> Our aim is to quench this infinite thirst of a God made man. Just like the adoring angels in Heaven ceaselessly sing the praises of God, so the Sisters, using the four vows of Absolute Poverty, Chastity, Obedience and Charity towards the poor ceaselessly quench the thirsting God by their love and of the love of the souls they bring to Him.

It is this aim that drove her desire, as she vowed early in life, to 'love Jesus as he has never been loved'.[27] In order to answer the desire of an infinite God, Mother Teresa felt that her love also needed to be infinite. So rather than introducing divine privation as though she were conscious of a metaphysics, one might say that Mother Teresa expanded the soul's potential through this dialectic of ceaseless thirsting and quenching – a pretty standard move for thinkers in the mystical tradition and evidence of her intuition for some of the basic ontological concerns that preoccupy a theologian like Bonaventure.[28] But for her, expansion occurred through concrete responsiveness to human need:

> 'I Thirst' and 'You did it to me' [i.e. the least of these] – Remember always to connect the two, the means with the Aim. What God has joined together let no one split apart. Do not underestimate our practical means – the work for the poor; no matter how small or humble – that make our life something beautiful for God. They are the most precious gifts of God to our Society – Jesus's hidden

---

26. Kolodiejchuk, *Writings*, 41.

27. One sees similar overtures in other modern passion mystics. See especially Faustina Kowalska, *Divine Mercy in My Soul: Diary of Saint Maria Faustina Kowalska* (Stockbridge: Marian Press, 2007).

28. It is noteworthy that when she once explained her spiritual longings to Archbishop Ferdinand Périer of Kolkata, and her struggle to achieve them, he responded, 'In what you reveal there is nothing which is not known in the mystical life. It is a grace God grants you, the longing to be His entirely without return on self or creatures, to live by Him and in Him but that longing which comes from God can never be satisfied in this world, simply because He is infinite and we finite' (Kolodiejchuk, *Writings*, 164). Mother Teresa seems to have found a kind of satisfaction by sacramentalizing divine presence within human destitution and then plunging into the darkness herself.

presence so near, so able to touch. Without the work for the poor the Aim dies – Jesus's thirst is only words with no meaning, no answer. Uniting the two, our MC vocation will remain alive and real, what Our Lady asked.

Beneath the pedagogical surface of her 'Inspiration Day' letter, Mother Teresa offers her community a rare glimpse into her own interior life and its relationship to the charism of the Missionaries of Charity. As we have seen through her private writings, Mother Teresa's sacramental sensibility was grounded in the immediacy of her own felt poverty and desire for spiritual intimacy. While Bonaventure was a master in Paris writing with at least some level of academic distance, Mother Teresa's counsels on kissing were a direct outgrowth of her personal contemplative encounters. And because of her historical and practical context, kisses for her contained not necessarily healing, but at least presence. In each encounter she tasted the devastating truth of alienation and yet remained open to Bonaventure's Being.

One need not be a Mother Teresa critic to wince at the idea of her (or any person) telling someone in pain to embrace suffering as the kiss of Jesus. But her difficult pastoral instincts need not be evidence of a sinister fondness for pain, as some have suggested. As with Bonaventure's reading of the stigmata, they may signal her faith in the ability of wholeness to exist mysteriously even in places of great brokenness. To read Mother Teresa in this way would be to read her with Bonaventure's help, but also on her own merit. By living firmly in this world, and confronting the depths of suffering in concrete ways, Mother Teresa leads us into the abyss like few other modern spiritual writers. She allows her readers to be honest about the devastating consequences of affliction, while placing herself in a tradition with resources beyond the scope of her immediate experience. By doing so, Mother Teresa awakens us to the kiss of a fully formed paschal spirituality.

Chapter 9

'THERE IS STILL A LOT OF POLLUTION IN THERE': UNDOING VIOLENT IDEOLOGIES, UNDOING THE SELF

Heather M. DuBois

In 2017, *American Sociological Review* published an article entitled 'Addicted to Hate: Identity Residual among Former White Supremacists'. The opening line of the article's abstract is as follows: 'The process of leaving deeply meaningful and embodied identities can be experienced as a struggle against addiction, with continuing cognitive, emotional, and physiological responses that are involuntary, unwanted, and triggered by environmental factors.'[1] 'Addicted to Hate' presents the findings of a study of eighty-nine former white supremacists in the United States. While the authors are not developing a new clinical diagnosis of addiction, they document what they call the 'substantial lingering effects' after people have disengaged from groups such as the Ku Klux Klan, Christian Identity, neo-Nazis and racist skinheads.[2]

The conversion of destructive politics requires the formation of new identities and the loss of old identities. The intimate, intractable legacies of racism and anti-Semitism – like those of xenophobia, Islamophobia, classism, sexism and homophobia – do not yield to superficial prescriptions. They demand ongoing, painful processes of in-depth inquiry and transformation. In this brief chapter, I offer the metaphor of 'undoing the self' as a stimulus to thinking about what such transformation requires. Specifically, I draw upon the monastic guidance of the sixteenth-century Carmelite mystic John of the Cross to explore the undoing of purgation and the contemporary, psychoanalytically informed sociopolitical theory of Judith Butler to explore the undoing of critique.[3] With this unlikely pair, I examine the undoing of the self in the undoing of violent ideologies.

---

1. Pete Simi, Kathleen Blee, Matthew DeMichele and Steven Windisch, 'Addicted to Hate: Identity Residual among Former White Supremacists', *American Sociological Review* 82, no. 6 (2017): 1.

2. Ibid., 1–2.

3. For more, see Heather M. DuBois, 'To Be More Fully Alive: John of the Cross and Judith Butler on Transformation of the Self' (PhD diss., University of Notre Dame, South Bend, 2018).

First, I will continue to introduce the challenges of identity transformation through the case of former white supremacists. Then, I will sketch the link between their experiences and purgative undoing. Third, I will describe a form of sociopolitical critique that is simultaneously socially and personally transformative. While this chapter focuses on personal transformation, it presumes the importance of ongoing, painful processes of in-depth inquiry and transformation that focus on cultures and structures. Fourth, I will explain that in John's understanding of purgation and Butler's understanding of critique, the undoing of the self is embraced cautiously for the sake of virtue and life-giving relationship. As such, it is notably distinct from overzealous asceticism. Finally, I will return to the language of addiction to offer constructive insights about the process of leaving a violent social movement. This preliminary exploration of undoing in terms of purgation and critique aims to contribute to political theologies that address intractable identity-based violence. Methodologically, it models a way to address violent ideologies with non-violent means.

Groups like the Ku Klux Klan, Christian Identity, neo-Nazis and racist skinheads solidify collective identity through in-group behaviour that ranges from adopting lifestyle preferences to violent acts. Researchers have noted how such behaviour satisfies human needs for belonging and, more besides, provides what sociologist Emile Durkheim called the experience of 'collective effervescence'.[4] Disengagement from such groups is not only a cognitive and social process, as if having the right ideas and hanging out with the right crowd were enough, but also a neurophysiological, psychological and spiritual process. To cease to participate in an 'all-encompassing movement lifestyle' means changing everything from clothing to entertainment to parenting.[5] It means changing deep-seated relationships to self, others and ideals. In the case of movements built through extreme experiences of hate and violence, it means escaping relations that do not want to let you go.

The research findings in 'Addicted to Hate' are based on in-depth life history interviews in which people used the term 'addiction' to describe their struggles to leave 'alt-right' activism and white supremacy. A former member of the American Nazi Party named Melanie, for example, said: 'Somebody needs to do a study ... subject us to the music, to the literature, to the racial slurs and watch what fires in our brains. I guarantee you it's an addiction. I can listen to white power music and within a week be back to that mindset. I know it.'[6] Another former white supremacist named Carter explained that he not only had to avoid certain things or remove them from his life but also had to approach differently things that he desired in his life. 'Since we were religious [Christian] based', he said, 'I had to learn to look at those scriptures differently. That was hard. For years, I didn't even pick up a Bible anymore. I couldn't read it without only reading it from the bad

---

4. Simi et al., 'Addicted to Hate', 8.
5. Ibid., 1.
6. Ibid., 10.

point of view. I just couldn't see another interpretation of that. I didn't want to read it.' Carter continued, 'It took me less than two years to learn to hate and it took me nine years to unlearn it. You don't just stop hating just like that. There is still a lot of pollution in there.'[7]

To call one's self polluted connotes the presence, if not the imposition, of a foreign substance. Getting rid of pollution is not a straightforward process because toxins intermingle with the body (whether a body of water, a human body or the body of Christ). To be rid of toxins is different from emptying a vessel; it requires transformation. If the toxins in question are ideological, they are integrated in human identity. In such cases, one must purge the body and psyche of unwanted ideologies. The challenge is to do so without triggering existential defence mechanisms and without committing violence, understood as cruelty or intense harm, towards one's self.

Purgation denotes cleansing, and it connotes dramatic visceral change, such as vomiting and evacuation of the bowels. For the purposes of this chapter, 'purgation' is preferable to the word 'purification' because it expresses the pain often involved in identity transformation. It also suggests that the process of transformation may not be consciously intentional. Even if the process is embraced, the person purging may find that they have little control over and little foreknowledge of what is to come. On its own, the pursuit of purgation is a daunting, potentially dangerous prospect. Carrying forward spiritual practices related to it is only palatable and responsible if purgation is bound to its classic companions, illumination and union. As part of this threefold process, purgation can play an integral role in non-violent identity transformation.

John of the Cross is the poet of purgation, most famous for 'The Dark Night'. His exposition of purgative contemplation in the commentary on this poem was, in his own estimation, his most significant contribution to spiritual guidance. While many in his time had written about the role of sensory purification in Christian life, few had grasped the need and possibility of spiritual purgation.[8] The difference, he wrote, is that of 'rubbing out a fresh stain or an old, deeply embedded one'. John sought the full cleanse of purgation because he was attuned to the myriad, enduring, surreptitious deformations that result from prolonged or acute vice. 'The stains of the old self still linger in the spirit although they may not be apparent or perceptible.'[9] Releasing the self from these stains enables growth in virtue and positive relationships; thus, it enables new identities.

---

7. Ibid., 9.

8. In John's words, 'Hardly anything has been said of it in sermons or in writing; and even the experience of it is rare.' *The Dark Night*, book one, chapter eight, number two. Hereafter, references to this commentary will be abbreviated to this format: N. 1. 8. 2. All references to John's texts come from John of the Cross, *The Collected Works of St. John of the Cross*, trans. Kieran Kavanaugh and Otilio Rodriguez (Washington DC: ICS Publications, Institute of Carmelite Studies, 1991).

9. N. 2. 2. 1.

Judith Butler is (in)famously associated with a deconstructive approach to social norms and institutions. One might use her work to speak analogously about purgation of oppressive power dynamics in social bodies and collective psyches. However, this chapter highlights the under-appreciated constructive impulse that is at the core of her critical theory. As in the tradition that conjoins purgation with illumination and union, her understanding of critique conjoins deconstruction with the pursuit of truth and the cultivation of alternative relationships. Pivotally, this kind of critique transforms one's own identity; it is not directed only at other people. Like sophisticated portrayals of sin, Butler's portrayal of sociopolitical power demonstrates that we all participate to varying degrees in unjust, violent, social patterns that are manifest structurally, culturally, interpersonally and intrapersonally. Therefore, there cannot be a strong distinction between social critique and personal critique: 'recrafting ourselves' and 'the remaking of social conditions' are inextricable responsibilities.[10]

Looking at John's texts in conjunction with Butler's, it is striking that both authors frequently use the words 'undoing' and 'undone' to describe personal transformation. For example, consider this passage expounding one of John's favourite images for contemplation:

> As fire consumes the tarnish and rust of metal, this contemplation annihilates, empties, and consumes all the [appetitive] affections and imperfect habits the soul contracted throughout its life. Since these imperfections are deeply rooted in the substance of the soul … it usually suffers an oppressive *undoing* and an inner torment.[11]

Elsewhere referencing the biblical Jonah, John wrote that purgation is like being 'swallowed by a beast and being digested in the dark belly'. It 'so disentangles and dissolves [that the soul] feels that it is melting away and being *undone* by a cruel spiritual death.'[12] John described the purgation of vice and imperfection as an undoing of the self, which is a painful yet ultimately life-giving process necessary for union with God.

For her part, Butler focuses on the undoing of the self that is necessary for justice and solidarity across human differences. Critique of social norms and institutions leads to undoing because the self depends upon these for its sociomaterial existence. Even when a set of norms has been identified as destructive and a person is determined to be a part of their alteration, there may be a remnant of desire to maintain them. In her book *The Psychic Life of Power*, Butler wrote about this remnant in terms of norms manifest in law and its impact on conscience:

---

10. Judith Butler, *Giving an Account of Oneself* (New York: Fordham University Press, 2005), 134–5.
11. N. 2. 6. 5. Emphasis added.
12. N. 2. 6. 1. Emphasis added.

For the 'I' to launch its critique, it must first understand that the 'I' itself is dependent upon its complicitous desire for the law to make possible its own existence. A critical review of the law will not, therefore, undo the force of conscience unless the one who offers that critique is willing, as it were, to be *undone* by the critique that he or she performs.[13]

In challenging the law, the 'I' challenges the psychic conditions that have formed and maintained its current life. Even if that law is unjust and the conditions of life deficient, it is not easy to reject law, custom and the relative existential security that they may provide.

Purgation and critique are modes of undoing that engage that which formed and continues to form the self. As such, they are fundamentally destabilizing and uncomfortable, if not painful. Incorporating them into political theologies must be done with caution, not least because the history of Christian mysticism is riddled with cults of suffering that misconstrue ascetic practice. Some critical theories also are complicit in distorted understandings of self-surveillance and fruitless flagellation. Overzealous asceticism of all kinds can amount to violence: self-hatred, confused sacrifice, deadening nihilism or despair. It is noteworthy that John argued vigorously against what he called a 'penance of beasts', reminding readers that penance should be tempered by the use of reason and obedience to one's spiritual guide and religious community. Butler also has warned her readers about severe self-scrutiny and self-beratement. John issued scathing criticism of certain kinds of spiritual guides, and Butler has written about the damage done by certain models of psychological therapy.[14]

Overzealous asceticism is futile in positively transforming the self for three reasons. First, it misunderstands failure to change as primarily a failure of the will. As in recovering from addiction to substances, ceasing to participate in vice and violent ideologies is not simply a matter of deciding to abstain. One can make an informed and passionate commitment to change and still experience 'cognitive, emotional, and physiological responses that are involuntary, unwanted, and triggered by environmental factors'. Indeed, recovery models of addiction treatment emphasize that substance abuse has no cure; rather, recovery is a varying, life-long struggle. Second, violent ascetic practices exacerbate the existential insecurity that accompanies identity transformation. It may be inevitable that people feel insecure while undergoing significant change, but it is not inevitable that people feel desperately insecure or lead into cycles of violence. The third reason that overzealous asceticism is an insufficient, problematic approach to identity transformation is that it is a merely negative intervention. As such, it neglects the

---

13. Judith Butler, *The Psychic Life of Power: Theories in Subjection* (Stanford University Press, 1997), 108. Emphasis added.

14. See especially John of the Cross, *The Living Flame of Love*, stanza 3, numbers 27–67, and Butler, *Giving an Account of Oneself*, 80.

processes of growth that must accompany loss, if transformation is to be positive and sustainable.

For existential insecurity to be experienced non-violently and for the negative intervention of asceticism to be experienced as ultimately positive, the undoing of the self must occur in tandem with being done again anew. As portrayed here, undoing is not to be sought for its own sake, even as the process may bring some relief in itself. Undoing is permitted and perhaps pursued for the sake of a desired new identity, achieved through new knowledge and new relationships. John would have us enter the dark night to grow in virtue. For him, undoing was part of the greater movement towards knowledge of self and union with God.[15] Butler would have us undergo re-crafting of the self to grow in virtue. For her, undoing is part of the greater movement towards knowledge of self and solidarity with sociopolitical others. These greater movements towards God and the other offer life-giving relational support even as the self is destabilized and transformed. Such support is crucial to sustaining the long journey of escape from vice and violent ideologies.

Relational support is necessary to positive, viable identity transformation because relationality is an essential aspect of being human. Although separated by centuries, John and Butler share the observation that the self is thoroughly, constitutively relational. The sixteenth-century friar wrote about a soul formed and transformed through positive relationships with God, other humans, the natural world and bodily affections as well as negative relationships with the devil, representatives of 'the world' of status and wealth, and the unmitigated appetites of the flesh. The twenty-first-century academic and activist writes about the positive and negative effects of sociopolitical power manifest in and through every aspect of life: manifest, for example, structurally and culturally through media communications, economies and symbolic hierarchies; interpersonally through attachments to primary caretakers, teachers and romantic partners and intrapersonally through psychic processes such as conscience formation. Although their cosmologies are vastly different, John and Butler would agree that human perception, affect, cognition, desire, imagination and memory are formed and transformed through interactions with socio-material environments, and this makes us radically vulnerable for better and for worse.

Vice and violent ideologies are not free-floating abstractions presented to the mind in the terms of rational choice theory. They are affect-laden, patterned into daily life, and often embodied in colleagues, friends and family members. To transform identities that have been shaped by vice and ideology, it is not enough to change one's mind. Constitutively relational selves must change the ways that they relate to people and things loved. Understandably, this makes identity transformation exceedingly difficult. Yet, there is a positive corollary to this difficulty: life-giving relationships make it substantially easier to undergo the loss of old identities and to cultivate new ones. The reliable support and accountability

---

15. John wrote that 'the practice of self-knowledge [is] the first requirement of advancing to the knowledge of God'. Ibid., 4. 1.

of a new community can enable departure from a social movement. Identities are not easily exchangeable choices, but neither are they irremediably determined, much less eternally given. The language of addiction used by the former white supremacists underscores that the commitment to ideological change – to ideological sobriety, one might say – has to be renewed again and again. The effort must be ongoing, because relationships occur in and through time; but significant, tangible change is clearly possible.

Continuing with the analogy between addiction to substances and addiction to ideologies, a new, life-giving community is essential, but insufficient. People need the means to do the 'internal work' of transforming spirit and psyche. Otherwise, the void that appears in the absence of former 'fixes' and former relationships will become a vacuum drawing in other potentially destructive ways of life. Even seemingly constructive choices can be distorted to serve destructive patterns, if the root causes that enabled addiction are not addressed. Here, John's classic understanding of the appetites is instructive. An appetite is an inordinate affection that instrumentalizes its object. One can have an appetite towards univocally harmful or univocally beneficial things; the point is not the object of affection. What is at issue is the form of one's desire or the state of the will in the affective attachment.

Like the acknowledgement of addiction, the realization that one has embodied a violent ideology is a first step towards recovery that cannot be taken for granted. Over time, a person becomes increasingly insensitive to alternative ways of thinking and feeling. John was deeply concerned about such insensitivity. In his terms, he was concerned by the damage that habitual, voluntary appetites do to the soul in estranging it from positive relationships.[16] Using biblical metaphor, he wrote, without a 'palate purged and healthy and ready',[17] people are 'unable to taste the delights of the spirit of freedom'.[18] In this state, they will choose 'the food and fleshmeat' of the oppressor because they cannot 'get any taste from the delicate bread of angels', even though it contains 'all savors'.[19]

Furthermore, the difficult realization that one must leave an all-encompassing movement quickly puts a person in a position of heightened vulnerability. Often a 'former' is without strong skills through which to discern who and what can support the new desired identity – if that identity even can be imagined. This vulnerability is intensified by the fact that identity transformation, like all else, has to occur in and through ambivalent socio-material environments. In other words, if humans are constitutively relational, living necessarily through negative as well as positive relationships, there are no pure resources within or without the self. Realistic personal and social change processes cannot depend on futile aspirations

---

16. See especially John of the Cross, *The Ascent of Mount Carmel*, book one, chapters 6–12.
17. N. 2. 9. 3.
18. N. 2. 9. 2.
19. N. 2. 9. 2. Quoting Exod. 16.3 and Wis. 16.20-21, respectively.

of purification; these will only mirror the futile desires of an extremist ideology. As Butler wrote, our only hope is to work together in the 'difficult labor of forging a future from resources inevitably impure'.[20]

In sum, processes of undoing are a vital resource for political theology, and we must be careful in recommending them. Destructive identity politics are gaining traction globally. Given this context, it is imperative to qualify what is meant by purgation and critique. As depicted by John and Butler, these modes of undoing occur in tandem with improved understanding and life-giving relationship. In contrast the phrase 'political purge', for example, conjures images of repression, massacre and genocide. The practices of purgation that John described employ pain in a process of healing, which opens onto an unknown, relationally shaped future. A political purge uses violent means to achieve predetermined, exclusionary goals. Both forms of purgation are transformational; only one interrupts cycles of violence. Re-framing this caution into a productive agenda, the conjunction of Christian spirituality and critical theory offers resources to enable non-violent identity transformation. These resources can be used to intervene in intractable identity-based violence through the cultivation of viable alternatives.

---

20. Judith Butler, *Bodies That Matter* (New York: Routledge, 1993), 184.

Chapter 10

READING SIMONE WEIL IN EAST LONDON: DESTITUTION, DECREATION AND THE HISTORY OF FORCE

Anna Rowlands

The essential contradiction of the human condition is that man is subject to force, and craves for justice. He is subject to necessity, and craves for the good. It is not his body alone that is thus subject, but all his thoughts as well; and yet man's very being consists in straining towards the good.[1]

(Simone Weil)

Simone Weil wrote these words in perhaps her single most luminous piece of writing: her chapter on Homer's *Iliad*. Weil holds up the *Iliad* as a model of intellectual response to suffering. What the poem succeeds in doing, Weil argues, is embodying and revealing a truly tragic sensibility. Yet we can mean quite different things when we invoke the language of tragedy. Weil intends that, via the power of the *Iliad*, we should connect tragedy to the history of force. Force, she argues, holds all in its power – master and slave. Force can be possessed by none, much as we are given to the illusion that it can. Force, Weil believes, is at the centre of human history, a given reality that must be thought and negotiated. Yet she believes that the poem offers a testimony to the history of love that irrupts in intervals (rather than in linear continuous form) and thus forms part of the witness that threads its way through history embodied in acts of hospitality. For Weil such acts of hospitality are a form of, and proxy for, justice. Thus love and force are not two opposing, disconnected movements for Weil, but rather the path to love takes in the history of force. Arguing that confronting the history of force and its invasive misery is a precondition of justice and love, Weil makes the following startling claim: 'Only he who has measured the dominion of force, and knows how not to respect it, is capable of love and justice.'[2] Without contradiction, Weil

---

1. Simone Weil, 'Fragments, London 1943', in *Oppression and Liberty* (London: Routledge, 1965), 150. I am grateful to Professor Lyndsey Stonebridge for originally bringing this passage to my attention.
2. Simone Weil, 'The Iliad or The Poem of Force', in *Simone Weil: An Anthology* edited by Sian Miles (London: Penguin, 2005), 212.

makes her appeal for a counter history of love in the philosophically severe style. She does not plead compassion, empathy or fellow feeling, but rather appeals for a critical attention – attention that is capable of holding experience in thought – to the conditions of suffering and the mutual obligations she believes human beings owe to each other in this light. Alongside Hannah Arendt, as Deborah Nelson suggests, she belongs to the unsentimental school of women thinking suffering in the twentieth century.[3]

This chapter employs Simone Weil's reflections on suffering, force and love to explore the experiences of contemporary destitute and formerly detained migrants and asylum seekers in the UK. It seeks to put Weil's philosophical severity to work in service of articulating the experiences and self-understanding of a small group of people living without citizen status and in destitution in London. According to Weil, human life is conditioned by the tension between the necessity of force and suffering on the one hand, and human orientation towards the good, love and justice on the other. This suffering is manifest in its most extreme form as affliction, which constitutes an attack on the intrinsic nature of the subject's identity that leaves them wordless and loathsome. One result of this affliction is destruction, or the shift from a state of being to non-being.

The chapter builds on interviews with destitute and formerly detained migrants supported by the Jesuit Refugee Service in the East End of London.[4] Focusing particularly on destitution and detention practices, it describes how indefinite detention exerts force to destructive effect on the identity of those within its processes. It describes how it does so through the construction of a discourse of discipline, time-distortion and time-wasting. It also describes how this is enacted through the spectacle of hiddenness. Finally, it notes that, just as Weil describes force as something to which we are universally subject, both detainees and wider society become subject to this discourse.

However, Weil claims that affliction also offers the opportunity for *decreation*, or the recognition of one's being subject to necessity (what *is*). This further enables the subsequent recognition of the nature of God, as understood in distinction to necessity and the creatures subject to it. Similarly, within the total sphere of force, there is the possibility of a moment of reflection in which the history of force is interrogated and the use of force can be suspended by those who wield it, enabling an irruption of love and/or justice. These points of interruption of force and necessity provide the basis for the pursuit of the good.

---

3. To this list we might add Gillian Rose, and as Deborah Nelson – who I draw from here – does, Mary McCarthy, Joan Didion and Susan Sontag. See Deborah Nelson, *Tough Enough: Arbus, Arendt, Didion, McCarthy, Sontag, Weil* (Chicago: University of Chicago Press, 2017).

4. www.jrsuk.net. This period of fieldwork conducted in 2017 has acted as the basis for a series of overlapping short articles, see especially 'Temporality, Dispossession and the Search for the Good: Interpreting the Book of Jeremiah with the Jesuit Refugee Service', *Political Theology* 19, no. 6 (2018): 517–36.

In this vein, the chapter concludes by describing how interviewees utilize Old Testament narratives to construct an identity rooted in the experience of divine love, and a perception of time as a journey which, while indefinite in length, is nevertheless relativized to that love. In doing so, those interviewed are able to find places of action and speech which constitute forms of public appearance and resistance. In this way their account defies and reconfigures some of Weil's assumptions about the wordless nature of affliction and the self-abnegation of decreation.

Returning to Weil

It was unexpected that I would find myself returning to the work of Simone Weil. While I had worked on Weil's writings some years previously and in a very different context, it was the writings of Hannah Arendt and St Augustine that had been my companion through nearly a decade of working on the ethics, theology and politics of forced migration. When I was invited by the Jesuit Refugee Service to undertake a period of empirical fieldwork in the summer and autumn of 2017, I expected that this would deepen and extend my Arendtian work. While Arendt did not disappear entirely from view, as I listened to the two dozen interviewees, their words and the world of meaning they invoked cast me back into the thought-world of Weil. It was Weil's phrases, images and systems of meaning that rose to the surface, strangely and newly resonant. The brief for my research was to seek to understand the experience of destitution and immigration detention and the role played by faith-based organizations as local humanitarian actors. From early in my interview cycle I was struck by the notable parallels between my interviewees' accounts of the asylum system in the UK and Weil's descriptions of what she terms 'affliction', 'decreation' and 'necessity'.

For Simone Weil suffering cannot, in this life, be redeemed. It cannot be made joyful and in its essence it does not produce moral improvement or generate virtue. Suffering cannot, in any direct sense, be 'put to use'. Imagining that each of these things *might* be the case – that suffering might be joyful, redemptive or useful – is a product of a confused Christianity, and evades the properly theological meaning latent in suffering. For Weil there is no incoherence in arguing that suffering lacks any of these qualities or possibilities and yet nonetheless retains theological meaning. She believes that there is meaningful paradox and contradiction at the heart of suffering with which Christian theology must wrestle. Suffering is to be tarried with simply as what *is*. 'I should not love my suffering because it is useful. I should love my suffering because it *is*,' wrote Weil. This intellectual and spiritual struggle with suffering must be had without giving in to the standing temptations to falsely resolve and mediate the tension between the given-ness (and therefore meaningfulness) of suffering and its paradoxical, mysterious inexplicability. While we cannot explain why suffering and affliction exists, its utterly concrete presence challenges us to a politics and theology of recognition.

In practice, such a political theology of recognition centres on an ethics of mutual obligation that sees self and other as bound together as victim, observer and generator of such suffering, connected by the presence of the mediating third partner – the divine creator – who acts redemptively through that which God mysteriously permits. To treat suffering in a political–theological mode is to be determined to look unflinchingly at its horror and its ordinariness, to understand its devastating injustice and its unreasonableness, and to refuse to compensate for this. The proper theological meaning of suffering, Weil proposes, is found in its revealing to us the reality of the fragility and limitation of the world and of human agency. One of the noteworthy but curious features of extreme suffering for Weil is that it seems to gain a near total power – a sovereignty – over the person. It is strange, Weil observes, that a sovereign God should allow such a powerful rival pseudo-sovereign grip for extreme suffering (affliction) over the creature. The genuine sovereignty of God (tenderness and love) refracted in negative form in the puzzling pseudo-sovereign grip of suffering-as-affliction calls the human person – in the positive and negative – away from their own sovereign pretensions towards love and justice. In this sense part of what suffering teaches us is that we need to be de-centred away from fantasies of our own sovereign supreme power, towards more fragile and properly temporal practices of love and attention.

The ethical task is to render suffering meaningful rather than explicable. To render suffering meaningful requires a training of the will (which inclines away from 'thinking' suffering and from attending to its victims) towards attention: attention to the suffering person and attention to the concrete conditions that produce suffering. In this context the deepest theological movement possible for Weil, as sufferer or observer of suffering – and we are all really both across a lifetime – is to dethrone the sovereign self, the self as rival deity, and turn back in love to an absent God. When Weil says God is absent she does not mean to imply a God who does not exist, but rather a God who in love has mysteriously kept open the space or gap between creature and creator, who crucially has also drawn near enough to be born, to die and to rise again from the dead. This gap, between necessity and the good, between creator and creature, is a matter for endless difficult contemplation. Into this space of difficult recognition of limitation, God acts as bearer of a grace that enables what Weil calls the 'decreation' of the person. In her notebooks Weil opposes the theological process of decreation as a conscious act of the human person to the anti-theological movement of destruction of the person as follows: 'Decreation: to make something created pass into the uncreated. Destruction: to make something created pass into nothingness. A blameworthy substitute for decreation.'[5]

In this context, suffering and evil is treated by Weil as simply what *is*. In her writings on suffering Weil distinguishes between what she refers to as the ordinariness of suffering and the horror of affliction. She does not wish to dismiss

---

5. Simone Weil, *Gravity and Grace*, trans. Mario von der Ruhr and Maria Crawford (London: Routledge, 1999 [1947]), 32.

the significance of ordinary suffering, but rather to note a kind of suffering which acts as its limit case: affliction. She argues,

> It is not surprising that the innocent are killed, tortured, driven from their country, made destitute, or reduced to slavery, imprisoned in camps or cells, since there are criminals to perform such actions. But it is surprising that God should have given affliction the power to seize the very souls of the innocent and to take possession of them as their sovereign lord.[6]

Affliction, she argues, 'is not a psychological state; it is a pulverization of the soul by the mechanical brutality of circumstances'.[7] Earlier in the same piece she notes, 'There is no real affliction, unless the event which has gripped and uprooted a life attacks it, directly or indirectly, in all its parts, social, psychological, and physical.'[8]

For Weil, there can be no exemplary state of affliction because people experience the same things in different ways; nonetheless, affliction can be seen and understood by its effects. Weil's characterization of the effects of affliction are particularly pertinent for my purposes: affliction, as Deborah Nelson summarizing Weil notes, 'leaves its victims with a sense of wordlessness, it plunges them into disgust and self-hatred', it makes them feel they are 'incapable of attending to others or feeling union with them, either those afflicted like themselves or those who offer help; it makes them complicit in their suffering by poisoning them with a sense of inertia; it renders them repulsive to themselves and others'.[9]

In this context it is important to note that much of Weil's writing on the conditions of affliction was produced in response to time she spent working in French factories prior to the Second World War. She took leave from her teaching work in order to experience first-hand the conditions of workers. Among the central – and to her initially surprising – insights of this time was the increasing self-perception of a broken relation between thinking and experience. She argued that the kind of suffering experienced by workers produced not immediate lucidity on the subject of their suffering but rather a process through which thought was sent into flight: 'For the first effect of suffering is the attempt of thought to escape. It refuses to confront the adversity that wounds it.'[10] She locates the reason for this fragmentation in the disorientation of factory work, the privation of the good enacted which separates basic human needs from their satisfaction. It is not simply brutality, what Deborah Nelson summarizing Weils calls, 'the impact of the blow',

---

6. George Panichas, ed., *The Simone Weil Reader* (New York: Moyer Bell, 1977), 441.
7. Ibid., 462.
8. Ibid., 440–1.
9. Here I quote from Nelson's sharp summary of Weil on the condition of affliction. See Nelson, *Tough Enough*, 27.
10. Panichas, ed., *The Simone Weil Reader*, 55.

but rather the gradual erosion of 'the ability to make decisions, to possess one's time and one's body, to plan the future' that 'divorce thought from the thinker'.[11]

In *The Need for Roots* she characterizes this process as one of uprootedness, itself a menacing characteristic of modernity. Rootedness, she argues, is the most basic and yet overlooked need of the human soul. Rootedness is defined not in ethno-nationalist terms but rather in terms of participation: 'A human being has roots by virtue of his real, active and natural participation in the life of a community'.[12] Uprootedness is then a social, economic or political process through which the person is displaced from such connections or refused their possibility. In this context one can see enforced stasis and immobility without possibility of participation as a form of uprootedness as much as forced mobility is. By extension, mobility can under some conditions be part of what roots. With interesting echoes of Pope Francis's recent teaching on migration, Weil argues that at the heart of uprootedness in modernity is the 'perverse inversion of means and ends' in which people come to play the role of things and things the role of people.[13]

However, a far greater difficulty in Weil's mind than the challenge of finding language to articulate affliction is our universal tendency to refuse to face affliction, our complex indifference. Indifference for Weil is not lethargy or passivity but rather an endlessly busy, inventive, often monetized and ultimately deadly political process of denial. Great effort is devoted to the manufacture of elaborate mechanisms that enable us to avoid facing the most difficult facts of existence: fragility, helplessness and mortality. In this light, the intellectual task remains to contribute towards the training of the will in attention, making suffering and affliction brutally concrete, to find language to reveal its presence and its conditions.

Negotiating the border: Time, temporality and the asylum system

A proper evaluation of Weil's suggestive and controversial political theology of suffering is beyond the task of this chapter. Instead my more limited task is to draw out the potential resonances between her account and the voices of my London research interviewees.[14] The aim of my interviews was to understand how asylum

---

11. Nelson, *Tough Enough*, 36.
12. Simone Weil, *The Need for Roots*, trans. Arthur Wills (London: Routledge, 1952), 43.
13. Pope Francis has spoken often during the course of his papacy about the disorientation of 'settled' people in failing to respond to the orientation towards survival of the displaced. See his Lampedusa sermon for one notable instance of a repeated theme. This bares comparison with Weil's notion of a cultural uprootedness that uproots and fails to respond to the needs of the territorially uprooted.
14. I do not discuss here Weil's controversial focus on the crucifixion of Christ (rather than the resurrection) as the ethical centre point of her theology of suffering.

seekers in the UK become destitute[15] and how those refused asylum negotiate the process of living in constant interaction with the idea and concrete reality of the border.[16] For some this means lives lived in and out of immigration detention, for others lengthy periods of street homelessness and extreme social and economic instability. Well over half of those who claim asylum in the UK are rejected at the point of making a first claim. Having been issued with a refusal, those claiming asylum then lose access to accommodation and are issued with instructions to leave the UK within twenty-one days, or risk forced removal. There is a prohibition on paid work during any asylum claim in the UK, so dependence on the state, family and networks of personal contacts or civil society is total. The protracted nature of what are perceived managerially as non-profitable immigration claims and the high rate of appeals gives some clue as to the inherent problems with the claims process as it currently stands. As a consequence many asylum seekers remain trapped either between or beyond various stages of the legal process for extended periods of time. For some this is a matter of months, for others a matter of decades.

For those living through stages of refusal – between refusal, appeal, refusal – and without recourse to public funds, survival happens through a variety of means. Most of those I interviewed were reliant on informal arrangements for accommodation with friends or acquaintances. For some this was a huge act of generosity from family, friends or acquaintances. However, some noted that for

15. The Joseph Rowntree Foundation defines destitution as 'lacking the means to meet the basic needs of shelter, warmth, food, water and health'. The literature on destitution makes clear that asylum destitution is a condition that is consciously created by the state as part of its border management and deterrence strategy. Withdrawal of accommodation, privation of welfare support, refusal of work and detention are all used as methods of deterrence and expulsion or of border control. Destitution among asylum seekers is largely driven by the low level of initial successful applications for asylum at first hearing, resulting in protracted appeals processes, the prohibition on paid work during a claim or appeals process, and the lack of access to reliable legal support. Policies of detention and dispersal also feed into dynamics that facilitate social isolation, increase – some would argue manufacture – vulnerability and therefore increase the risk of destitution and magnify its impact. The interviewees in my study also identified poor casework and a disjointed and bureaucratic system that defies comprehension as contributing or aggravating factors.

16. My fieldwork involved several months of visits to the JRS centre in Wapping, East London. I spent a week participating in the work of the centre, including the focal point of the week – a day centre that provides for around 100 men and women living in destitution. I undertook three further visits during which I conducted twenty-five semi-structured interviews and six unstructured staff conversations. The interviews were balanced between male and female participants. In the case of refugee interviewees, the majority identified as Christian, with four identifying as Muslim. No other faith traditions were represented. Refugee interviewees were from West, Central and East Africa, Asia and the Middle East. A further four interviews were conducted with sector policy experts.

destitute people this often involved (out of desperation or a sense of indebtedness) an exchange of accommodation for childcare or sexual or other domestic services. A small number received temporary accommodation for a few weeks or months at a time via civil society hosting schemes. In addition, those I interviewed participated in day centres provided by a range of mainly faith-based civil society organizations (one Jewish, two Christian, one secular). Civil society groups provided a variety of support including night shelters, hosting schemes, legal services, toiletries, second hand clothing, bike schemes, warm meals, small travel allowances, prayer groups and other small-scale essential provisions. Spending the night moving between long distance night buses as places of perceived relative safety, one interviewee described her choices carefully: 'I choose between two or three different night buses that go a long distance so I can sleep for an hour or so at a time, but going to destinations that I think are safer areas for changing buses.' 'You feel worthless and unwanted ... but the bus feels safer to me as a woman than the streets.' Many of those interviewed had been subject to immigration detention at some point during their time in the asylum system. Some interviewees had endured repeated detentions; others had been detained once. One interviewee was detained for several months on the day she took part in the interviews and was later released just as the fieldwork was concluded.[17]

One of the central insights to emerge across all of my interviews concerned the impact of destitution and detention on the way my participants experienced time. I was told repeatedly that the system creates a disciplinary culture that leads to unhealthy and distorted experiences of temporality. In the case of immigration detention this relates to the indefinite nature of detention without time limit and to the enforced idleness that accompanies detention. Time becomes both compressed and yet something you become acutely and agonisingly aware of as it passes. For those experiencing destitution it is the passing of time felt as the wasting of time that caused most mental distress: 'Waiting, reporting, not working, the manner of treatment, sometimes in charities as well as by the Home Office or lawyers, dehumanises. It destroys us. Destitution makes us go mad.' 'Without structure you become susceptible to lots of things: isolation, criminality, addiction,

---

17. In the UK we have held the power to detain immigrants for administrative purposes since 1971. In 1993, there were just 250 bed spaces in UK for immigrants to be detained. At the beginning of 2015 that number had risen dramatically to 3,915 bed spaces for any given night. Thus in the UK we are now routinely detaining 32,000 plus migrants a year in ten detention facilities for periods which range from a few days to several years. Most of those who are detained in the UK have been either asylum applicants being processed through the so-called fast track process (a process recently ruled illegal by the High Court), visa over-stayers, those who are undocumented or stateless or those who have served a prison sentence for arriving with a forged passport or irregular papers. Torture survivors and children are not supposed to be detained, although there is significant evidence that both categories are detained. In the UK there is currently no limit on the amount of time a migrant may be detained. The European limit is generally between 21 and 28 days.

mental and physical illnesses.' Others used the striking and disturbing image of physical decomposition to express their experience of destitution: 'I feel as if I am degrading.' Those giving testimony to a recent cross-party parliamentary inquiry into detention practices in the UK echo these sentiments: one detainee describes the extreme distorting effect detention has on perceptions of time, 'In prison you count your days down, but in detention you count your days up.'[18]

For those who had been detained, the experience was marked by a sense of dispossession and loss, a permanent sense of diminution. As a refugee professional support worker, herself a refugee and previously detained, noted, 'Detention finishes people off. It's a form of mental trauma that takes away skill and capacity. We see this in people who have been highly skilled before – doctors, dentists, nurses, university teachers, but who can't function in these roles even when they later achieve status, because they never fully recover from the trauma of detention.' In all my interviews the trauma of detention was connected quite specifically to the use of force, the absence of a time limit and the mimicking or parodying of a criminal justice process (without process) that conveys the idea of a criminal act or intent that detainees cannot internalize or own as a self-identity. 'Detention is a context that denies love. Staff can be nice but the problem is the use of force, which shapes the whole reality. The system tells you (in all its actions) that you are an identity that you cannot accept.' 'You know you are there because you aren't believed. The culture of disbelief re-traumatizes already traumatised people.' The theme of love denial – denial of the natural human need to be able to give and receive love, dignity and respect – was also central to the experience of detainees. A former detainee (he had been detained twice, the first time for a year aged 19, the second aged 21 for a period of months) described the ways in which the micro-interactions in detention had profoundly altered his character, producing a feeling of self-alienation and self-loathing. He explained that the system only responded to aggression, to get basic supplies of toiletries you had to demand, to become rude and even aggressive. He noted the sense of self-loathing he felt at the realization that, following the second period of detention, he emerged no longer able to feel a naturally empathetic reaction to the suffering of others and was no longer able to trust the motivations of anyone, including previously trusted family. He felt on reflection that this was a result of both internalizing the aggression and suspicion the system enacted and expected of him and a deep inner despair and sense of abandonment he felt in detention. He described the painful process of trying to retrain himself in empathetic instincts a year on from his release.

Given such experiences of privation, it is particularly striking that in two instances former detainees told me about saving the lives of fellow detainees while in detention. In one instance a young detainee, who had just received his own removal papers for a flight to central Africa the following day, witnessed an older

---

18. All Party Parliamentary Inquiry Into the Use of Immigration Detention, see Report https://detentioninquiry.files.wordpress.com/2015/03/immigration-detention-inquiry-report.pdf, 18.

man he knew well tying a noose made from cloth round his neck and jumping from a chair. He dropped his papers and ran to catch the man's body, raising the alarm with staff and saving his life. The man, an Iraqi, told him he was to be returned the following day and wished to die under his own control rather than via torture, and that this way he believed his body would be returned to his family for burial. In the second instance my interviewee had persuaded a fellow detainee not to take a stash of pills. In both cases the suicidal detainees had later been released and achieved refugee status. Both the near suicide and the survival of both men had left profound marks on my interviewees.

A repeated insight was that the experience of destitution and its attendant stresses had led to a permanent loss of skills and capacity and thus a fundamental loss of a sense of selfhood – a permanent form of dispossession. One woman who had been a nurse in her country of origin said, 'Previously I was a nurse. But the asylum process traumatised me. I'm not the same person now. So much time was killed. I can't go back to what I did before. I suffer with heart problems now. I never had those before I came here, even with all the trauma that happened to me back home.' Referring with distress to a friend I was told, 'He was a [health care professional] in his country. But he will never be able to function again like this here I don't think. He has waited too long. He is too unwell now.' Another woman who spent many months sleeping on night buses explained that the chronic sleep deprivation meant that she could feel a sense of her capacity drain away; 'How old will I be when this is sorted? My ability is already not the same. I could have done so much in this country before. But now? I'm trying so hard to be normal.' This woman, a forty-year-old survivor of extreme sexual violence and torture in her country of origin, notes how, in living so many years waiting for an outcome and without access to resources, 'the two halves of life come to feel like they repeat the same thing'. Another woman explained the impact of the lack of nutritious food available to her:

> There are no nutritious things going inside me. The doctor told me he was fed up of seeing me coming in with food poisoning from the effects of eating food that had gone out of date. The system shapes everything. My dream is stability and study to be a midwife but I don't think my brain could take in the study now. Even things I could do before, I am too tired to do.

In one instance I was told that the system had reduced a sense of both capacity and skill but also that my interviewee had given up the dream of becoming an engineer partly as an act of protest: 'I do not wish to give my skills to this country when they have treated me like this (said crossing his arms to his chest). 'I will keep them within myself.'

Repeatedly I was told that the system generates hopelessness. On the one hand this hopelessness relates to the stasis of the system and its non-responsiveness. On the other hand it relates to what a number of interviewees describe as the disciplinary structure of the system. One interviewee described the way that the system feels like it quite deliberately aims to foster a self-identity in the asylum claimant that is the opposite to those that enabled flight: 'Fleeing takes enterprise, courage, determination, judgement. We see ourselves as having these characteristics. But the system creates a sense of ourselves as the opposite of these things.' 'The system makes us in its own image.' This gap between the enterprise of flight and the enforced dependence of the system creates an acute sense of affliction and disconnection from self-identity.

Interviewees describe the ways that the system increases rather than limits the sense of dependence on others or the sense that one is vulnerable and a drain on other people. With some anger one interviewee argued, 'They want to shape the image and shape of asylum seekers. You want to make a particular kind of community, with asylum seekers shaped in that image. The limits you place on us, on pursuing what is important to us, to being human, are about seeking to destroy something.' She continued, 'The system shapes your life, especially as a woman, in such a way that it means you live with no love, no life. Relationships require stability. The system ensures that I have no stability.'

For others it is important that we reflect on the social and economic context of enforced destitution policies. One interviewee expressed his case as follows: 'A capitalist system values the idea of contribution. You need to contribute to get something out – when you are not contributing (in the way society understands contribution) you don't feel like a member of society. This is deliberate. They [the Home Office] know what they are doing.' He continues, 'This isn't just a form of social death but also intellectually you suffer and die because you can't engage, participate or contribute. People don't take this into account when thinking about destitution and what the asylum system sets out to do, but it's crucial to understand.' A sector specialist talked of the ways that asylum policy acts as a complex form of social communication: 'The hostile environment functions not by being enforceable but by sending a message. Whether it's sending a message to the electorate, to the media, or actually to migrants themselves is unclear … but the messaging of it is where the power lies.'

Force as a social relation

This returns us to Simone Weil's treatment of the *Iliad*.[19] Treating the *Iliad* as bearing the hallmarks of generations of refugee writing, Weil presents an extraordinary meditation on the nature of force as a process through which those subjected to it are turned into a 'thing', into something without life. In summary, Weil presents several lines of argument in her chapter on the *Iliad* that resonate with the ways the interviewees in East London sought to find words to capture their experience. First, echoing my interviewees' perceptions of the indignities of detention, the use of sudden immigration raids and hostile environment policies, Weil notes that force seeks its recognition as a form of public spectacle.

---

19. Weil, 'The *Iliad*'.

The exercise of force is used as a means to create (and deny) a sense of public identity both for the agent who enacts force and for the victim of force. In turn the use of force is enacted in the name of a more distant and anonymous group of citizens, whose own identity – and the meaning of this citizen identity – is nonetheless caught up in the drama of force. Weil, as does the testimony of those I interviewed, reminds us that force operates within the space of the social imaginary. For precisely this reason – that the force announces itself as a form of relation – it should not surprise us that the experience of force is taken up as a particularly difficult part of the self-relation of those who are victims of state force. It becomes indigestible partly because the politics it asserts cannot be owned as meaningful by those subjected to it. This is a complex argument to make in the case of immigration detention because we are trying to make a case for force as a form of public spectacle and performance, and yet, detention is, in one sense, defined by its very public invisibility, hiddenness and secrecy. Nonetheless, this turn towards the hidden remains arguably part of a deliberately and irreducibly *public* act, akin in this sense to state policies of disappearance and torture where the act itself is intended both as an action to isolate the victim, to remove the person as a public being, and as a form of visible social action that aims to shape the imagination of the body politic. Similarly, Weil notes that the experience of negotiating necessity as one deals with the consequent disjuncture of being both subject to force and seeking one's good, shapes the experience of both the soul of the person and the politics of the city. It is a move which is felt by the person to be simultaneously intensely personal and inherently social. This act of negotiation of complexity and contradiction indelibly shapes the person. In the case of my interviewees the impact of this reality is clear.

From this point of departure Weil makes two further observations: that force makes victims out of those who possess it as well as those victim to it, and that it takes a miracle to escape what she labels the 'petrifaction of force'. Weil argues that 'force is as pitiless to the man who possesses it, or thinks he does, as it is to its victims; the second it crushes, the first it intoxicates. The truth is nobody really possesses it.'[20] Extending her analysis of force as social relation, Weil drives home her view that political–theological attention to the history of force is vital for the human spirit is endlessly subject to, and modified by, its relations with force in *both* its exercise and reception. The miracle, for Weil, in this context is the possibility of a more truly human(e) moment in the intoxicating exercise of force, the interposing of an interval of reflection, a moment in which the hand that wields the sword is steadied. This was a sentiment echoed in the most ordinary and direct of terms by those I interviewed. A Congolese man, detained and released twice in his early twenties, told me that if he could address the culture of the Home Office he would plead with them to pause, having made a decision, to consider 'whether there was anything they might have missed'. He did not mean

20. Ibid., 191.

an extension in the duration of a claim but rather the insertion of an interval of self-examination.

Weil connects this necessary interval of reflection in the history of force to the possibility of love and justice. Because the exercise of force is a defining and constant social relation, she does not imagine a binary opposition between the pursuit of the good and force, but rather the inevitable negotiation of goods within the endless reinvention of relations of force, where what is possible is the irruption of intervals of love and justice. Therefore confronting the history of force and its misery is a 'precondition of justice and love'. This is the space of decreation – in which the self, recognizing both its agency and its non-sovereignty, is able to open itself to grace and a process of passing into divine co-creativity.

Decreation

It is to this final point that I wish to turn in the last section of this chapter. My interviewees talked readily of a process of both the destruction of self, which they abhorred and lamented, and, more unexpectedly, what I think might be termed the 'decreation' of the self. This latter term has to be used with care. The aim here is not to assimilate the voices of my interviewees into a narrowly Weilian frame but to highlight interesting resonances and to point towards the significance of further exploration of Weil's work.

I will use the word 'decreation' in ways that echo Weil but also move sideways from her. Decreation, as used here, names a way of being in the world that is grounded in a relation of God, self and others beyond narrow claims to self-sovereignty, that is, to self-possession and self-determination. Decreation involves both active agency – often of necessity an act of resistance to dominant cultural frameworks – and attentiveness to the other, always within the concrete conditions of what *is*. What *is* carries within it the various dimensions of what Weil terms – as we will go on to see – the 'impossible': beauty, goodness, loss and terror. To pass into the life of the uncreated, as Weil terms decreation, is not, then, best understood as a passive mystical drift, a kenosis or a self-evacuation. Key, then, is that in the context of this notion of decreation, there can be no discussion of the co-creative relation of God and the human person or the conditions of love and justice which does not foreground the history of force.

To employ Weil's term – especially in the context of the experience of (r)ejection of forced migrants – without some mention of the ethically problematic dimensions of her use of the idea, however, would be irresponsible. Literary philosopher Lyndsey Stonebridge writes of the morally distasteful image of Weil sitting on a stool in Ain-Seba refugee camp in France during her own displacement and writing about giving herself up to her refugee experience as an abandonment that would finally bring her into a decreation, which is 'the cross': she wrote, 'And my greatest desire is to lose not only all will but all personal being.' As Stonebridge writes, commenting on this passage, 'Wishing for your own non-sovereignty came perilously close to saving the Nazis the bother.'[21] There is a kind of self-abnegation in Weil's rendering of the non-sovereignty of decreation that is disturbing to anyone working with displaced persons or on refugee ethics. In this context it is especially striking to me that the narratives offered by those I interviewed provided illustration of the move into forms of 'decreated' non-sovereign ethics without reproducing the self-abnegation that haunts the writing of the disappearing Weil.

To make this case (in two stages) requires that we return for a moment to unpicking the interconnection of Weil's notion of decreation with her writings on affliction. In considering affliction among workers in the Renault factory Weil lays great emphasis on the muteness of suffering workers. She reports that workers tended to talk of their experience either in cliché or in the theory absorbed piecemeal from commentators who, ironically, lacked the workers' direct experience. To break this cycle of banality and to give voice to the afflicted, Weil interposes the necessary mediatory force of the intellectual, one who is capable of paying unsentimental attention to affliction. This dynamic was not paralleled in my own experience of interviewing. While the parallels with the description of affliction are notable, my interviewees were not in the least mute and did not speak of their experience in clichéd or banal terms; they spoke with startling clarity, sharpness and depth about their experiences and usually with the demands of speaking in a second language. It was not clear that 'intellectual' mediation was needed to give 'voice' to these experiences: no intellectual mediator or translator was needed to render what *is*.

Attending to the crystal clarity – rather than the muteness – of what was said repeatedly about the afflicting impact of destitution and detention mirrored Weil's various faces of the 'impossible'. Interviewees moved between speech about the concretely dreadful and the beautiful, the good. A language for both of these was frequently – not always – found in the texts of religious traditions, Christian and Islamic. If we wish to interpret this kind of speech as akin to decreation, but without giving in to the worrying self-abnegating tendencies that lie in Weil's construal of decreation, then we probably need to turn to the very things that Weil herself found difficult: questions about the communal dimensions of identity formation and the role of texts and traditions that enable communal speech about both suffering and the good.[22]

---

21. Lyndsey Stonebridge, 'Simone Weil's Uprooted', in *Placeless People: Writing, Rights and Refugees* (Oxford: Oxford University Press, 2018), 112.

22. Weil is notorious for her difficult relationship to her Judaism and to the Old Testament. Her explicit preference was to locate an ethics of affliction in both Greek thought and in the Gospels, bracketing out the Old Testament completely. She was also an angular, difficult thinker who invoked the significance of communal ties but who also remained uneasy with communal dimensions to thought and action.

Spaces of appearance: Speaking and acting through texts and traditions

Those negotiating lives lived along an ever-present border speak readily of spaces and places that have nurtured survival. While I asked no direct question about faith, belief or religious traditions in my interviews, all but one interviewee introduced discussion of religious texts and ideas, and most talked without formal prompt about the communal contexts that had enabled material and moral survival.[23] For some the notion that a community – either distant or proximate – maintained systems of meaning enacted as prayer, ritual, and/or worship provided a sense of (variously) hope, comfort, mystery and/or sanity. The vicarious performance by a community of others of an identity or belief system under threat for the self from the conditions of affliction was named as a vital source of solace, and a way of maintaining a space of non-sovereign appearance and exchange in a context of disappearance. One interviewee explained, 'If good happens then I just need to be patient. … The testimony of others strengthens. … There were times when my problems seemed overwhelming and then I couldn't pray. The prayer of others enabled my spirit to be lifted up.' Decreation emerges in each of these descriptions as a process facilitated by communal engagement with religious texts and practices, an embodied communal–mystical process.

Interviewees noted the particular importance of the psalms for offering a language through which to make sense of the contradictions of their experience: 'Like the Psalms say, I have walked through the valley of death and I know what it is like, but I also know that God was with me. This was my experience … death and life, evil and protection … like the psalms say … both things are true.' A number of interviewees expressed the view that the psalms were helpful partly because they provided a public (communal) and private (devotional) language for naming the relationship between the realities of good and evil ('the impossible' in Weil's account) that had felt very real during the migration journey.

Others sought to consciously integrate Old and New Testament traditions as narratives that frame and interpret refugee journeys. One interviewee explained to me that while detained he had clung to the writings of St Paul and the Book of Jeremiah, that they had helped him 'keep his mind' in detention. Through participating in chapel groups he felt that he had received in detention a revelation of who he was in Christ. Talking of the prevalence of depression and self-harm in detention my interviewee said that he felt 'we are doomed without this vision'. He explained that this teaching is rooted in the book of Jeremiah: 'God says there are plans I have for you. He says the plan I have for you is for unexpected ends.' My interviewee proposed an interconnected reading of Jeremiah and Paul, arguing that together these writings work to keep one

---

23. Weil outlines the conditions of justice and obligation as they relate to two kinds of human needs: material and moral needs. She views both material needs (hunger, housing, freedom from violence etc.) and moral needs (order, truth, liberty, equality etc.) as the basis of human dignity (which she refers to as 'respect'). See *The Need for Roots*, 4–39.

focused on the possibility of the good in a context where you do not know the ending to your story. Explaining that lots of people think that the problem with detention is that it wastes time he noted that what he had learned was that 'not time, but promise matters'. 'It's about [opening yourself to] unmerited grace.' This was not an attempt to suggest that the experience of detention had not been very difficult, and when asked what changes he would like to see, he was very clear that he would close detention centres. Unlike Weil he did not embrace the conditions of his decreation: rather, his point was to offer a more consciously theological interpretation of his experience. 'Look at the promise to Abraham. It's seemingly impossible. Sarah is looking in the time realm, and time is running out for her [to have a child]. God goes the extra mile and fulfils his promise to her when time seems to have run out.' 'Grace transforms how we experience time.' He concluded his explanation by offering the example of how his own reading of the scriptures had led him to take on a role as a preacher in the chapel in his detention centre and through this public role he had been able to talk with a suicidal man and had persuaded him not to commit suicide. His public speech in an improvised (if still controlled) public space had created a moment of relationship that had, by his account, saved a life.

Explaining that he had seen both 'a beautiful and a terrible side to life in the UK', another interviewee told me of the contrast between his life before he was detained – despite precariousness, he said he felt his life had been focused on the pursuit of money, status and sex. He told me that he realized during the course of the time he was detained, when no one from his former life visited or kept in touch, that these earlier values had left him desolate and without real purpose. In the 'hell' of detention and through attending chapel groups he discovered 'we all deserve to live a good life. I realised I had a love in me.' 'I asked for God's mercy. I realized I was motivated by love and that I could use it to reach out to other people. If you are open to love it brings peace.' 'I read that Abraham was a migrant and he was used by God. This gives encouragement.' Reading Rom. 8:28 that 'all things work together for those who love God ... this helped me to focus on God'. He saw this as Paul's reading of Jeremiah: 'The idea that there is a good plan for each of us ... that we are all here to be players in our divine assignment. ... My main hope became to have a legacy of love. ... Love through works.' He contrasted this with the structures of detention itself: 'Detention is not a context of love. Staff can be nice but the problem is the way of arrest ... the use of force and chaining. ... The system tells you you are an identity you can't accept.'

My interviewees spoke directly of the impossible, using this very language, and they spoke of finding new spaces of appearance, speech and action facilitated in part by communal spaces, texts and traditions. None of these spaces was separate from the history of force; none redeemed the force that caused affliction. All of these spaces involved the agency of fellow refugees. Most notably, none of their narratives suggested a self-abnegation, a desire to disappear. On the contrary they were suggestive of what Weil describes as that which is sacred in each human being: 'At the bottom of the heart of every human being ... there is something that goes on indomitably expecting. It is this above all that is sacred in every human being.'[24] The expecting and the decreating are interwoven in the interview narratives, and in turn the expecting and the decreating involve the creation of spaces of appearance. This appearance takes the form of preaching to fellow detainees, worshipping and praying together, the speech and action that seeks to form new bonds of mutuality and shared life. One interviewee told me that following release from detention a small group of friends who met in detention now meet at the weekend and, smartly dressed, preach the gospel on their neighbouring high street. He described this as a form of citizenship, enacted for the good of the social order.

And so, the long return to Hannah Arendt. Arendt speaks of natality and of the space of the *res publica* as the space of appearance. For her the speech and action that enable us to appear and be seen and heard by non-kin others are conceived as political acts, and they constitute, instantiate or generate the 'public'. Arendt writes in *The Human Condition*: 'For us appearance – something that is being seen and heard by others as well as by ourselves – constitutes reality. ... The presence of others who see what we see and hear what we hear assures us of the reality of the world and ourselves.' It seems helpful to me to explore an account of decreation – of the non-sovereign ethical that takes into account the public history of force – that is sensitive to the multiple ways refugees appear, act and are acted upon, and in so doing constitute what (and who) is 'public'. In this regard Arendt offers to Weil a necessary non-abnegating account of appearance in its public and political forms. Nonetheless Arendt is hostile to the notion that religion (Christianity in particular) is capable of imagining a truly 'public' act or realm. She believes that its vision is, at best, of private experience and common goods. The life of the common good is not, according to Arendt, a truly public life for it does not imagine the hybrid realm 'where private interests assume public significance'. One response to such a critique (other than refuting her reading of the common good tradition) is to engage refugee narratives and writing to widen Arendt's concept of what constitutes the hybrid public. Another is to suggest that we need something more, something of what Weil offers that Arendt does not: an account of something that exceeds the political and cannot be reduced to it, and yet which prefigures and reconfigures it.

Conclusion: Epiphanies of the human, epiphanies of the divine

Simone Weil's work on suffering is not without its problems. I have not, for the purposes of this chapter, addressed legitimate criticism of her doctrinal claims, nor her extreme bodily asceticism, and I have explored only briefly the worrying disappearing self latent in her notion of decreation. But I have in a more limited way suggested the live connections that seem to me to exist between current migration experience and Weil's central claims about the deadening nature of

---

24. Simone Weil, 'Human Personality', in *Simone Weil: An Anthology*, 71.

affliction as a limit case of suffering, about the centrality of handling the reality of force within any Christian theological attempting to grapple with the wider questions of *either* suffering *or* appeals to love and justice, and about the question of the non-sovereign movement of the self who decreates in love. The second and third are perhaps the more counterintuitive and contestable explorations.

However, I also wish to suggest that the value of her work ought not to lie simply in the production of further cartographies of refugee suffering. In this context, recovery of Weil's work offers us an important alternative ethical possibility. The tendency of much public ethical discourse on migration has been to reduce the person of the forced migrant to a figure of either sympathetic or competing suffering victimhood – one who draws out emotions of sympathy in their revelation to us either of a profound otherness or of a self-referring logic (Nussbaum's 'it could be me'), or of a logic of endlessly agonistic competing citizen versus migrant vulnerabilities. A view of refugees as an epiphany (for the viewer) of the simple vulnerability of the other (alone), or a mere projection of our own selves returned to us (it could have been me), is a narrative many refugees rightly resist. Equally, we might wish to resist the disenchanted notion that what is revealed to us in the current politics of forced migration is an epiphany of a necessarily politically austere world in which clashing human vulnerabilities endlessly, hellishly compete. The best of Weil's work is suggestive of a different kind of theo-political epiphany, framed in the negative nonetheless. This is a revelation in several parts. In the first instance the task Weil proposes is less an immediate setting about imagining possible political alternatives and more a formation of the will towards a searing, confronting attention to the concrete conditions of what currently *is*. Our flight from what is and its impossible implications must be acknowledged intellectually, spiritually and politically. Engaging the concrete conditions of the real brings us face to face with the impossible. This includes suffering-as-affliction but also beauty and the good, equally manifestations of the impossible. Each can (differently) render us terrified and tender. Weil believes that such a process of confrontation through attention, if taken seriously, cannot but dethrone the pretensions of the sovereign self – the suffering and non-suffering selves – in favour of a non-sovereign ethics of mutual obligation. Action in the space of limitation is formed on the basis of recognition of relationship, which in turn impels encounter and active response; this is a perpetual temporal movement between gravity and grace. Allowing ourselves to be caught within this movement we are impelled to go 'as far as possible' (which is beyond what we initially imagine to be possible) in response to the uprootedness that uproots. This is the space before, within and beyond the democratic-political. In *Gravity and Grace* Weil writes of this in fragmentary form:

> Necessity. We have to see things in the right relationship and ourselves, including the purposes we bear within us, as one of the terms of that relationship. Action follows naturally from this.

Obedience. There are two kinds. We can obey the force of gravity or we can obey the relationship of things. In the first case we do what we are driven to do by the imagination which fills up empty spaces. We can affix a variety of labels to it, often with a show of truth, including righteousness and God. If we suspend the filling up activity of the imagination and fix our attention on the relationship of things, a necessity becomes apparent which we cannot help obeying. Until then we have not any notion of necessity and we have no sense of obedience.[25]

This is the 'theological turn', which poses as many challenges to a political theology that has analogized divine and political form too neatly as it does to the secular political-theologies which endlessly construct debates about placelessness and migration as an external legitimation debate about sovereign borders.

Weil's work jarred in her own time, as well as in the longer view read against the work of her contemporaries who survived the war and continued to write and think. Nothing in her work (despite her theological fixation with the crucifixion) points us in the direction of a consolatory ethics of a passible God who suffers, nor does she pave the way for a postmodern ethics of identification and empathy. Her severity leaves her a somewhat irascible, jarring, angular thinker of suffering, love and justice. This is her difficult, incomplete gift to us: an account of love and justice that insists we conjure with the history of force, and her insistence on the (im)possibility of an ethics of limit and decreation that speaks to a side of refugee and 'citizen' experience often overlooked, but one that theologians (in particular, but not alone) might do well to be more attentive to. Nonetheless, the kind of critical attention Weil demands to what *is* in the case of forced migrant experiences of destitution and detention illustrated in the small case study in the East End of London implies a response to Weil: that her account of decreation requires a more Arendtian turn, towards the ways in which refugees appear and instantiate themselves within the very spaces and places that would (r)eject them.

25. Weil, *Gravity and Grace*, 48.

Chapter 11

REFLECTIONS ON SUFFERING AND BIPOLAR DISORDER: THREE FORMS OF SUFFERING

John Swinton

The issue of suffering is complex, diverse and contextual. As one, for example, reflects on the literature emerging from disability theology, it quickly becomes clear that people are reluctant to use the language of suffering, and often for good reasons.[1] There is no inherent reason why people should assume that those living with Down's syndrome suffer because of their Down's syndrome. They may suffer because of people's *responses* to their lives, but there is nothing inherent within their disability that necessitates suffering. Likewise, people living with dementia do not necessarily suffer. There is research that indicates that people with dementia even in its latter stages can live lives that are valuable and enjoyable.[2] The problem with the rhetoric of suffering in relation to human disability is that it tends to focus the conversation on that which is negative and in so doing occludes aspects of human diversity that are clearly positive. It is wise to monitor the language of suffering in relation to disability issues. Words matter because they change things. Words create worlds. The words our worlds create shape and form the ways in which we practice within these worlds.

When we come to reflect on issues around mental health and mental health challenges, the language of suffering, at least at times, can seem appropriate. The experience of being in the deep, dark pit of depression is much more than a social construct. Living with voices that constantly taunt and offend you, telling you that you are useless, worthless and have no right to live, is clearly a mode of suffering, although even here we need to be clear and reflexive, realizing that for some people voice hearing, properly framed and managed, can be perceived in a positive

---

1. N. Eiesland, *The Disabled God: Toward a Liberatory Theology of Disability* (Nashville: Abingdon, 1994). A. Yong, *Theology and Down Syndrome: Reimagining Disability in Late Modernity* (Waco: Baylor University Press, 2007).

2. John Swinton, *Living in the Memories of God* (Grand Rapids: Eerdmans, 2012).T. Kitwood, *Dementia Reconsidered: The Person Comes First* (Buckingham: Open University Press, 1997).

manner.³ The language of suffering can be helpful when used with discernment and sensitivity. There remains, however, an ambiguity in relation to suffering and mental health that needs to be recognized and thought through, all the more so as we come to recognize that some of the suffering people experience is in fact socially and as we shall see, theologically constructed. Trying to tease out some of that ambiguity and the reasons for it is the main task of this chapter.

In this chapter we will explore the ambiguity of suffering by reflecting on the experiences of Catherine, a woman who lives with bipolar disorder. Her story will raise some key theological issues around suffering and offers some pointers as to how Christians might respond faithfully to psychological and spiritual suffering. Catherine's narrative is part of a broader practical theological project currently being carried out by the author exploring the spiritual lives of Christians living with three forms of severe mental health challenges: schizophrenia, bipolar disorder and major depression. The project is a phenomenological study in that it seeks to put to one side standard assumptions about any given phenomenon and to get back to the thing in itself, as Husserl has put it.⁴ In this chapter we will put to one side our standard assumptions about what bipolar disorder is and how spirituality 'should' be understood within the context of this diagnosis and try to reflect on the experience as it is lived. Of course, there is inevitably a hermeneutical dimension to the process of reflecting on someone's narrative. As H. G. Gadamer has noted, human beings are basically interpretive creatures; we require our biases and prejudices in order to make sense of the world.⁵ Bracketing helps us to see beyond standard 'natural' assumptions; hermeneutics helps us to come to an understanding of the phenomenon. By utilizing this hermeneutic phenomenological structure within a practical theological framework, it will be possible to illuminate important issues and to develop fresh insights into the nature of suffering.

Catherine's story: What kind of suffering accompanies mental health challenges?

Catherine is a forty-five-year-old medical doctor and a mother of three. She is an excellent pianist, 'a keep fit addict' (to use her own words) and an excellent cook. Catherine also lives under the description of bipolar disorder. Bipolar disorder is a psychiatric diagnosis that is used to explain certain experiences that she goes through, primarily periods of deep depression alternating with periods of great

---

3. M. Romme and S. Escher, eds, *Accepting Voices* (London: Mind Publications, 1993). M. Romme and S. Escher, eds, *Understanding Voices: Coping with Auditory Hallucinations and Confusing Realities* (London: Handsell Publications, 1996).

4. Edmund Husserl, *Logical Investigations*, vol. 2, 2nd edn, ed. Dermot Moran, trans. J. N. Findlay (London: Routledge, 2001), 168.

5. H. G. Gadamer, *Truth and Method* (London: Sheed and Ward, 1989).

elation during which she behaves in ways that are not always helpful for her well-being and the well-being of those around her. Although Catherine does not describe herself formally as a Christian, all of the unconventional mental health experiences she has gone through relate to Christianity. Christianity is therefore important to her, but in a rather unusual way.

Living under a description

The idea of 'living under a description' is important for current purposes. In her work on bipolar disorder, the anthropologist Emily Martin introduces her readers to the term 'living under a description':

> I deliberately use the phrase 'living under the description of manic depression (or bipolar disorder)' to refer to people who have received this medical diagnosis. The phrase is meant to reflect the social fact that they have been given a diagnosis. At the same time, it calls attention to another social fact: the diagnosis is only one description of a person among many.[6]

There are many ways in which we might describe Catherine, only one of which is that she lives with bipolar disorder. This observation is relevant because, as mentioned previously, the way in which we describe things has practical, as well as conceptual, consequences. The philosopher Elizabeth Anscombe points out that all intentional action is *about* something. Unintentional actions such as reflexes simply occur; they are not really about anything. Such actions do not contain *intentionality*. For an action to be intentional it requires to be described. As we describe something so that 'thing' comes into existence in a particular epistemological form. All intentional human actions are thus seen to be 'actions under a description'.[7] Description and practice are closely interconnected. The philosopher Ian Hacking presents the issue in this way:

> Descriptions are embedded in our practices and lives. But if a description is not there, then intentional actions under that description cannot be there either. … What is curious about human action is that by and large what I am deliberately doing depends on the possibilities of description … . Hence if new modes of description come into being, new possibilities for action come into being as a consequence.[8]

---

6. Emily Martin, *Bipolar Expeditions: Mania and Depression in American Culture* (Princeton: Princeton University Press, 2009), 10.

7. G. E. M. Anscombe, *Intention* (Oxford: Blackwell, 1959), 86–7.

8. Ian Hacking, 'Making Up People', *London Review of Books* 28, no. 16 (1996): 23–6, https://www.lrb.co.uk/v28/n16/ian-hacking/making-up-people (Accessed on 18 January 2014).

By indicating that Catherine lives under the description of bipolar disorder, we do at least two things. Firstly, we draw attention to the fact that this is only one of many ways in which we can describe her. Secondly, we become alert to the dangers of subsuming someone to any single description. Catherine lives under the description of bipolar disorder, a description that she is quite comfortable with. However, that description does not define her or overpower every other description we might have of her ... or at least it should not. The other descriptions of her life are impacted by this description, but not inevitably determined by it. This will become particularly important when we begin to reflect on Catherine's spiritual life. Here, we will begin simply by laying out some aspects of Catherine's psychological and spiritual experiences of suffering and of joy, before beginning to think how theology might contribute to both understanding and response.

Bipolar disorder as suffering: A place where God is not

The experience of depression was quite devastating for Catherine:

> Being depressed? Yeah it is kind of like ... I mean you can't breathe underwater, but, it's sort of like breathing underwater or just being lowered into a pit, like just going lower and lower and lower. Being around people is very difficult ... I interact a lot with people, I'm an extrovert, but it's just like when I'm depressed ... everything is on mute or something. And then, it just takes such a tremendous amount of energy to do things, it's hard to describe, but just like putting the laundry in the washing machine is like a monumental task. And as somebody who's quite high functioning generally, it's just so strange.[9]

Living life 'on mute' is hard work. Simple things become major tasks. Finding God becomes difficult and sometimes impossible. Still, she finds some solace and a sense of solidarity in the psalms:

> I mean I have read some things in the Bible that are helpful. I mean like the Psalms. Because some of the Psalms, the ones that are really like 'God, why have You, where are You?' I feel horrible, I'm in this pit, whatever that one is 88? That's so helpful, because it's like it's ok to feel abandoned.

The psalms have given Catherine a language to express her pain and sense of abandonment, but in an odd way; they have provided her a sense of solidarity within the experience of feeling lost and abandoned. Thus, the psalms have helped her to hold on to a hopeful spirituality. However, the hopefulness of her spirituality is always accompanied by a shadow side that can be quite destructive:

---

9. All quotations come from the research projects previously mentioned and are fully anonymized and used with permission.

> When I'm depressed I can get very like confused. I start thinking about the devil. I think, sort of like, why I'm feeling bad, and why I want to kill myself, that might be the devil? When I think like that I generally feel worse. I start asking people, but that can be bad as well.

It is precisely here when her thinking begins to drift into negative spirituality, that she needs a certain kind of spiritual assistance. As her mood shifts her into dark places, so her interpretation of these dark places and the reasons for her being there begins to adopt a negative spiritual shape and form. There is a complex interaction between spirituality and pathology. Understanding this interaction requires sensitivity in relation to the complex interplay between psychiatric and theological descriptions. She needs hopeful affirmation, a way of describing her situation that recognizes the significance of her mental health description but also offers positive possibilities. Unfortunately, what she sometimes encounters is *negative spiritual descriptions* that, while not offered with any real malice, fail in important ways to understand the hermeneutics of her psychiatric description. These descriptions come to her from sources that look upon her with genuine concern, but who do not quite hit the mark in their attempts to understand and explain her situation:

> I have a religious friend and she is kind of, yeah she tries to be nice about it. She's a very religious Christian but she's been like well 'Satan does exist', and I'm like 'what do you mean!' What does that mean? And she's like, 'well I'm just saying.' So that's pretty horrible to think that you're possessed by the devil … . When she said that I just felt terrible. When you're depressed you already feel so terrible. I mean I know this from my work, that people experience it differently, but I always feel very guilty and like I've done something really horrible and I'm terrible, beyond terrible, I don't even know what I've done but it's something that's really terrible. So then if somebody says that this is the devil's work, then it just adds to that.

Catherine's friend may well be just doing the best she can to understand and to help Catherine. However, whatever the motivation, there are side effects to this kind of spiritual diagnosis. By placing Catherine's experiences within a deeply negative spiritual frame, she moves her condition out of the realm of psychiatry (the description that Catherine herself had decided upon as the most appropriate primary description) into the realm of the demonic. Now Catherine does not have a mental health challenge, she is possessed by a demon; something from the outside has invaded her body and is now controlling her experiences. She is not ill; she just needs the liberating power of Jesus! Her medical diagnoses gave her hope and positive opportunities for intervention and hope. This new spiritual diagnosis simply made her feel worse and, in principle, tempted her to leave behind her medical description and to stop using her medication, thus forcing her to face all of the consequences that would emerge from such a re-description. What must it feel like to be told by those who claim to care for you that your experiences are not in fact your experiences, but those of a malevolent force? It is interesting to reflect on the fact that if Catherine had described her situation in this way – my body has been infiltrated by an alien being – she would have been assumed to be psychotic. For an 'outsider' to do the same thing is apparently acceptable, at least within certain communities. 'Whose psychosis counts?' might be a pertinent question.

The dangers of ambiguity

Catherine's friend was not unique in her negative spiritual description and interpretation of her behaviour. Within the realm of professional spiritual carers she had encountered similar difficulties:

> I've had some [other] really bad experiences. Once when I was in the emergency room I felt so depressed I was seriously thinking about killing myself. I asked for a chaplain, and I said to him, 'could I be … is it possible that I'm possessed by the devil?' And he was like, 'I really don't know', which was like, kind of a horrible thing for him to say, I just thought maybe he should have been like no! But I don't know, I guess the answer *was* 'maybe?', but that was pretty negative. Not the kind of truth I wanted to hear. (emphasis in original)

It is not so much that the chaplain was necessarily wrong in terms of the content of his response. The problem was his concept of truth-telling; his desire and perhaps felt obligation to tell a certain kind of truth. The fact that he did not know the answer to Catherine's question could have been discerned as a call to silence rather than a certain kind of honesty that created pathological ambiguity. It is true that Christians are called to 'speak the truth in love' Eph. 4.15. However, perhaps we need to pay more attention to precisely what truth and love are and what they are intended to do? We will return to this issue of the spirituality of truth-telling as we move on. For now, the important thing to note is that responses such as those offered by Catherine's friend and the chaplain led to her becoming alienated from herself and also from Christians:

> I've decided that if this happens again and I'm sure it will, especially if I get psychotic, religious and depressed – that I won't talk to anyone religious … Because I guess you guys (I'm including you [John Swinton] as a religious person) feel the need to honestly answer questions. I don't know how people are trained to be chaplains with people in mental distress, but that experience of that person was just terrible. Even if he thought that, that was not the right thing to say. You just have to be really careful not to invalidate people's experiences. I mean if someone was suicidal and they think they're possessed by the devil it might be best not to not reinforce that even if you believe it! You could just say 'don't worry about that, you're going to be fine.'

Truth-telling for Catherine was complicated.

Bipolar disorder as spiritual joy

The darkness and spiritual confusion of Catherine's lows contrasts quite strikingly with the brightness and spiritual clarity of her highs. Sitting at the heart of many of her experiences of elation was the experience of having beliefs and ideas that others find strange, technically described in terms of *delusions*. Many of these experiences relate to intense encounters with the presence of God:

> Yeah, like I have pretty classic delusions. I become so euphoric that it's hard to describe. Basically, the whole world is connected to me; God is right there and I'm next to Him and we're looking down on the whole world … . I just get like the intense feeling that everything is sort of relating to me, and that's hard to describe, but that's not how you sort of normally feel. I just feel like all of a sudden, I'm a different person than I was before, and like God has chosen me to be His second person. And so, I need to help Him to help others. It's generally very like positive, like I feel I'm able to do amazing things for humanity … . Yeah. God and everything I see has some sort of meaning.

At this level, Catherine's beliefs are pleasurable and encouraging insofar as they give her a sense of being special and having a particular purpose in life. It is true that most people do not experience such a sense of specialness, which does mark her experience out as unconventional. However, from her perspective, and to a certain extent, this is seen as a positive – something worth taking seriously as potentially more than mere pathology. What is particularly interesting about Catherine is the fact mentioned previously that she is not a Christian, at least in the way that the term is normally used. And yet, all of her unconventional mental health experiences relate to Christianity. This is a cause of confusion for her and also for her family:

> It's strange. I have no background in religion. The delusions didn't come from anywhere. And then afterwards I was, and sometimes I still am, just so mixed up about it. I talked to my psychiatrist a lot about it … he is a Christian … and other people, especially religious people, well those that I can trust! I would ask them: 'What does this mean?' Most of them (not my psychiatrist), were like, 'Well if you don't believe in God and Jesus, if something is just there when you're ill then it's not real.' I found that to be really upsetting, because my experiences were so intense and meaningful to me, so I was like, well that's just your opinion. But how do you know? Maybe God was talking to me then when I needed him, who are you to say?

Catherine's point is a fair one. Who are *we* to say that God can only be present if someone has a previous spiritual history within which God is present in an institutional form? The reality or otherwise of religious delusions and experiences in the midst of pathology is a source of great debate and has been discussed at length within the psychiatric literature.[10] We do not have space nor time here to do justice to the complex arguments. It may be enough to suggest that any attempt automatically to subsume a person's description of their religious experience into their diagnostic description risks taking away their voice and holding them back from a potentially valuable source of coping and realignment:

> When people go through hard times they look for stuff, I mean that's obvious right? I mean, people need their faith sometimes when they are going through something difficult. But with me it's more like, I mean, certainly when I'm manic, but also when I'm depressed, I need something to hold on to. I do really believe in God then, and I pray and do things that I wouldn't normally do. And … so I don't know.

Catherine's experience is both challenging and mysterious. Scripture tells us that God listens to the prayers of the righteous. In Jn 9.31 the apostle informs us that 'we know that God does not listen to sinners, but if anyone is a worshiper of God and does his will, God listens to him'. This passage reveals a paradox. Catherine does not describe herself as a Christian, and yet, at her most intensely spiritual times she worships the Christian God with faith and prays to the Christian God in hope. Does the fact that she lives under the description of bipolar disorder annul her description as a praying worshipper of Jesus even if those times of worship are the times when some may consider her to be most unwell? What does it mean that God hears Catherine's prayers? I can only raise the questions here. Deeper reflection on these issues will have to wait until my broader project has been completed.

The shadow side of spiritual joy: Repercussions

Catherine's religious experience does however have a shadow side. Intertwined with her deep sense of connection with God is a tendency towards dangerous behaviours:

> My delusions have repercussions. I mean you just cannot exist like that in the world, in the real world, basically … you end up saying and doing things that are dangerous. I actually have thought I needed to kill myself so that I could be with God. I remember one time I was driving around on the phone to my psychiatrist saying I was going to be going to heaven and stuff, then after that, after I got better

---

10. L. M. Smith, L. C. Johns and R. L. C. Mitchell, 'Characterizing the Experience of Auditory Verbal Hallucinations and Accompanying Delusions in Individuals with a Diagnosis of Bipolar Disorder: A Systematic Review', *Bipolar Disorders: An International Journal of Psychiatry and Neurosciences* 19, no. 6 (2017): 417–33.

just reflecting on it and it was horrible. But even now I sometimes drive my car really fast and close my eyes and do things like that that are very dangerous, so afterwards it's like terrible.

Catherine's spiritual experiences are a strange and difficult combination of religious ecstasy and existential danger, with new spiritual possibilities for both growth and destruction. She is deeply moved by the intensity of her positive experiences with God, but at the same time she remains aware that there can be a heavy price to pay if she does not manage her situation effectively:

> I do miss the high, and I do miss feeling really religious. That's what I miss the most. But I have children so ... and also my husband has made it clear he'll stand by me through anything, but if I stop taking my medicine he won't stand by me for that. And he's like I'll leave you if you do that because it's destructive and we have children and you just can't do it. It would be a huge cost, for an amazing experience. And if I was diagnosed with some other, terminal illness then maybe I would do it. Like if the end of the world was coming. And also I'd lose my job, and that's really important to me.

Catherine works hard to remain within her therapeutic regime not because she wants to get rid of her religious feelings and experiences, but because she realizes that she has to make a choice and she chooses to remain alive and to be with her family. But still she retains a longing for the spiritual.

What kind of suffering accompanies bipolar disorder? Three forms of suffering

This snapshot of Catherine's experience has raised some crucial questions in relation to suffering and bipolar disorder. We might summarize by noting the presence of three forms of suffering:

1. The suffering that emerges from living with bipolar disorder.
2. The suffering that emerges from difficult theological responses to suffering.
3. The suffering that emerges from the threat to Catherine's vocation, identity and desire.

In closing we will reflect theologically on each form of suffering.

The suffering that emerges from living with bipolar disorder

Some of the suffering that Catherine experiences relates to her description as someone living with bipolar disorder. Her experiences of highs and lows fit the established pattern of this description, and she is quite comfortable to accept that the description of fluctuating moods finds its origins in some kind of biochemical issue. As a doctor she is aware of the science of her condition and happy to accept that as an important if not all-encompassing description. However, even here, certainly within the spiritual dimensions of her experience there is a thicker description to be found. Her beliefs can be classified as delusions – false fixed beliefs – but for her they were clearly much more than a 'mere symptom'. It is pretty much impossible to disprove the reality of a religious belief, so there is no firm epistemological basis for attempting to use her mental health description as a way of disproving her religious. Many religious people have beliefs that are fixed, unusual and assumed by some to be false. For the most part these people are not considered to be deluded.[11] Whose apparent delusions are acceptable and why is an important question. However, the issue is more than semantics.

Form and content

The way in which some psychiatrists have tried to discern the truth of a spiritual experience in the midst of psychosis is by drawing a distinction between *form* and *content*. The argument is that if a person has a spiritual experience during a psychotic experience, the validity or otherwise of that experience should be gauged by the following:

a) The form that it takes, that is, whether or not it takes a form similar to the types of one or other of the symptoms laid out in the ICD or DSM criterion.[12] If it does then it is assumed more than probably to be a symptom of some kind of underlying pathology.
b) The appropriateness of the content judged in relation to an established religious or spiritual tradition.

There is a logic in this way of thinking about spiritual experience in the context of mental health challenges. As we have seen, there is a complicated interweaving of the psychiatric and the theological in the experiences of people living with bipolar disorder. However, there are also significant problems with this approach, two of which we will reflect on here. Firstly, there is an oddness in assuming that theology and religious traditions should be the arbiter of the authenticity of religious and spiritual experience. The obvious problem here is the question of whose theology counts. There are some spiritual traditions within which hearing voices, feeling a special calling from God, having visions of Jesus Christ and so forth are considered

---

11. Richard Dawkins, *God is a Delusion* (London: Bantam Press, 2006), and a counter position: Andrew Simms, *Is Faith Delusion?: Why Religion is Good for your Health* (London: Continuum, 2009).

12. American Psychiatric Association, *Diagnostic and Statistical Manual of Mental Disorders*, 5th edn (Arlington: American Psychiatric Publishing, 2013).

to be a normal part of that tradition.¹³ Using religious traditions to authenticate spiritual beliefs is far from straightforward.

Secondly, the form-content assessment process seems to assume that if a person was previously a Christian and, for example, formerly adhered to the teaching of the creeds, he or she should manifest that same faith in the midst of illness. Sound, orthodox theology becomes a criterion for assessing a person's *mental* health as well as his or her *spiritual* health. However, it is clear that people's faith changes over time and according to circumstances, not least in this case because the experience of mental health challenges draws attention to certain theological questions that may not generally be addressed within mainstream theological reflection. Acknowledging the pathological dimension of people's experiences may well be *necessary*, but it is not *sufficient* to work out the value and significance of expressed religious beliefs. The key is to develop strategies wherein we can recognize the reality of pathology, the complexities of suffering and the ever-present love of God in the midst of confusion, without allowing any one of these descriptions of a person's situation to take over the conversation. There is a need for a deeper, thicker theological reflection which requires a creative partnership between theology and psychiatry. Psychiatry needs theology and theology needs psychiatry.

The suffering that emerges from particular theological responses to suffering

The second form of suffering that emerges from our reflections on bipolar disorder relates directly to the theological responses that were offered to Catherine's situation. In response to her encounter with the chaplain's ambiguity about the presence of demons, Catherine commented, 'That was not the kind of truth I wanted to hear.' This is an interesting statement. Both the chaplain and Catherine's friend seemed to feel compelled to 'speak the truth in love' as Paul puts it in Eph. 4.15. In itself this is not a problem as long as we are clear on what loving truth actually is. The question of what constitutes truth is not straightforward. Stephen Plant points out that 'telling the truth is not always a simple matter of accurately reporting facts; it demands that we discern the truth that lies beyond literal accuracy'.¹⁴

This is a challenging suggestion. What exactly does it mean to discern truth that lies beyond literal accuracy? In thinking this through it will be helpful to turn to Dietrich Bonhoeffer and the somewhat unusual and counterintuitive reflections on truth that emerged from his prison experience.

---

13. C. Cook, *Hearing Voices, Demonic and Divine: Scientific and Theological Perspectives* (London: Routledge, 2019).

14. Stephen Plant, *Bonhoeffer: Outstanding Christian Thinkers* (London: A&C Black, 2004), 124.

Bonhoeffer and truth-telling

For Bonhoeffer, telling the truth has not only to do with moral character,

> It is also a matter of correct appreciation of real situations and of serious reflection upon them. The more complex the actual situations of a man's life, the more responsible and the more difficult will be his task of 'telling the truth' … the ethical cannot be detached from reality, and consequently continual progress in learning to appreciate reality is a necessary ingredient in ethical action.[15]

Truth-telling is not simply a dislocated moral act. It has a context – God's ongoing work in the world – and that context shapes the nature of the truth that is told. In this view, the moral responsibility of truth-telling transcends straightforward adherence to moral rules. Sitting at the heart of Bonhoeffer's argument is his concern for the implications of Emmanuel Kant's understanding of truth-telling.[16] Kant argued that truth-telling had to do with adhering to moral rules that determine the nature of what is and what is not true. To tell the truth is to correctly answer questions relating to what did or what did not occur in any given situation. To tell a lie is to break with such a principle and, as such, is morally wrong. Kant offers the example of someone opening their door and finding an axe man who is looking for your friend. The morally correct thing would be to tell the truth: 'He is upstairs in the front bedroom!' Bonhoeffer begs to differ:

> From the principle of truthfulness Kant draws the grotesque conclusion that I must even return an honest 'yes' to the enquiry of the murderer who breaks into my house and asks whether my friend whom he is pursuing has taken refuge there; in such a case self-righteousness of conscience has become outrageous presumption and blocks the path of responsible action. Responsibility is the total and realistic response of man to the claim of God and of our neighbour; but this example shows in its true light how the response of a conscience which is bound by principles is only a partial one.[17]

Telling the axe man where your friend is may be appropriate in terms of Kantian principals, but it fails to take into account the fact that in such a situation, telling the truth increases the possibility of evil and reveals the partiality of principles for responsible Christian life. Truth-telling in Bonhoeffer's view overlooks the fact that it has a deeper moral context and is intended to achieve a goal that cannot be articulated within simplistic moral a + b = c equations. Love is not an abstract principle; God is a living being who is deeply involved with the world. Truth

---

15. Dietrich Bonhoeffer, *Ethics*, trans. Neville Horton Smith (New York: Simon & Schuster/Touchstone, 1995), 359–60.
16. Immanuel Kant quoted in Sissela Bok, *Lying: Moral Choice in Public and Private Life* (New York: Vintage Books, 1989), 282–6.
17. Bonhoeffer, *Ethics*, 359–60.

first and foremost reflects and images this living and loving God. Within this perspective, truth is inevitably relational, always guided by the immediate love of neighbour, rather than by unchanging principles. Christians do not simply have an obligation to tell the truth, they are called to embody and live truth.

In Bonhoeffer's perspective, truth is faithfulness to God whose responsibility shapes and forms our responsibility. God's command comes to us in a fresh and new form each day. God's will does not change, but situations, relationships and perceptions do. Bonhoeffer is not talking here about situational ethics. His ethic is not intended to be ad hoc or occasional. He wants us to see that Christians should take responsibility for discerning the right thing to do, and also take responsibility for doing it. God takes ultimate responsibility for the world and manifests that responsibility on the cross. In a penultimate sense Christians take responsibility for who they are and what they do. We tell the truth in order that we can demonstrate our 'total and realistic response ... to the claim of God and of our neighbour'. Truth is for the 'outcast, the suspects, the maltreated, the powerless, the oppressed, the reviled – in short ... those who suffer'.[18] Our moral responsibility is to learn how to see the world from the perspective of those who suffer and to respond accordingly.

Speaking the truth in love?

If Bonhoeffer is correct, Catherine's friends and the chaplain may have been wise to consider not just the act of truth-telling but its impact. Their truth-telling was misplaced and misdirected for three main reasons. Firstly, neither could be certain that their description of her situation was correct. They 'spoke the truth in love' but didn't really have the 'truth' they claimed needed to be told. There is truth to be told about the demonic. However, it requires knowledge, discernment and the correct context, none of which seems to have been the case here. Ambiguity is not a truth statement; it's a sign of uncertainty. Responsible truth-telling does not speculate or speak out in uncertainty or ambiguity.

The issue here seems to be what we might describe as *casual theodicy*: the ascription of an explanation for the presence of perceived evil without taking time to think it through or explore other plausible descriptions. Like theodicy proper, casual theodicy tries to explain an experience or phenomenon in the world in a way that holds on to the goodness of God in the face of evil, only on this occasion it is not an intentional, considered intellectual endeavour but a passing comment that reflects a desire to find an explanation for an experience that is disturbing and difficult to understand. Like casual racism (the unthinking use of negative stereotypes or prejudices made on the basis of race, colour or ethnicity), causal theodicy is not necessarily deliberately malign in intent. It is often hardly noticed by its perpetrators, but it can be deeply debilitating in its consequences. When there

---

18. Dietrich Bonhoeffer, *Letters and Papers from Prison*, ed. John W. de Gruchy, trans. Christian Gremmels (Minneapolis: Fortress Press, 2010), 52.

are so many medical, scientific and indeed positively spiritual ways of describing Catherine's experience, one has to ask why those in this situation who genuinely desired to be helpful, considered these particular descriptions as more important than the others in defining her experience. Truth-telling is intended to increase our love for our neighbour. Perhaps if they had held that in mind Catherine would not have felt quite so alienated from the body of Jesus.

The suffering that emerges from the threat to Catherine's vocation, identity and desire

The final point of suffering relates to suffering as it is worked out within Catherine's *vocation*. We do not have space here to go into this in detail, but it is worth keeping in mind. At one point in the conversation, Catherine notes that she enjoys the highs but recognizes their danger. The thing that holds her back from simply allowing herself to tumble into the high is the love of her family and the love of her job. She is willing, as far as she has control over things, to sacrifice the beauty of her spiritual highs for the stability of her family. To sacrifice is to give up something valuable for the sake of something else that one regards as important or worthy. In order to achieve her vocation (to become a good doctor) and to maintain her heart's desire (to be a good mother and a good wife) Catherine has to sacrifice the spiritual high. That is not to say that she substitutes her family for God. She retained her belief in God (although without overt commitment to the Christian tradition), but decided to sacrifice something of her perceived intimacy with God. While there may be many aspects of spiritual care that apply to Catherine's situation, it strikes me that issues around *sacrifice* and *vocation* are rarely highlighted as central to the spiritual curfew of people living with mental health challenges. Perhaps this is something we need to think more clearly about for the future?

Conclusion

In this chapter I have tried to show the ways in which theological reflection on the life of someone living under the description of bipolar disorder can uncover fresh perspectives for understanding and practice. My sense is that it is only as psychiatry and theology come together in hospitable dialogue that people like Catherine can find release, understanding and spiritual fulfilment even in the midst of the most difficult of times.

Chapter 12

SHOULD I LOVE MY TUMOUR?

Andrew Graystone

The rhetoric of cancer

A few years ago, in a windowless office in a hospital in Manchester, a young doctor in a tweed jacket looked up from an orange file and said to me, 'You have cancer.' One of the unexpected challenges that unfolded from that statement was the need to work out how I as a person should relate to the cancerous cells I now discovered I was hosting. Of course, rather notoriously, we tend to avoid talking about cancer at all if we can. Cancer is the Voldemort of diseases, the Scottish Play of sickness. As I began to contemplate how my cancer and I were going to get along I found that two themes were dominant in the rhetoric I was offered: enmity and objectification.

There was no doubt that I was expected to see cancer as my enemy, that it was to be feared, and that my cancer cells were an invasive presence that needed to be expelled. The proposed response was both masculinist and aggressive. I was enjoined to 'battle' with my cancer, and to deploy courage against it in the hope that I could 'kick' it. As a Christian with pacifist tendencies I found these concepts unhelpful, and I determined to find out where they had come from, and whether there were more helpful alternatives.

We can date the first uses of the imagery of warfare in relation to cancer fairly precisely. Linguistic analysis of phrases like 'battling with cancer' or 'war on cancer' indicates that their use correlates strongly with periods when Europe and America have been engaged in actual warfare. For example, the US National Cancer Committee placed adverts in publications including *Boy's Life* in 1934 saying, 'We are waging intensive war against cancer. To carry on this great fight we depend on contributions from the public.' In 1938, an editorial in *The Bulletin of the American Society for the Control of Cancer* said, 'It seems high time that the public shook off its readiness to run up the white flag of surrender at the first symptoms of the disease. It is unreasonable. Let us replace this defeatism with militancy and with faith in what science and medicine is achieving in their relentless battle.'[1]

---

1. American Society for the Control of Cancer, 'Editorial', *Bulletin of the American Society for the Control of Cancer* 20 (1938): 20.

Nevertheless, such language appears only sporadically until 1971, when President Richard Nixon signed into law the National Cancer Act, which was central to what he called 'The War on Cancer'. Nixon pledged his administration to a 'national commitment to the conquest of cancer'.[2] He compared the lives lost to cancer annually in America to the death toll of the Second World War. 'The time has come in America,' he said, 'when the same kind of concentrated effort that split the atom and took man to the moon should be turned toward conquering this dread disease'.[3] A biological warfare facility in Maryland was converted into a cancer research centre.

From that point on the language of warfare in relation to cancer quickly gained traction. The rhetoric of Republican politics in early 1970s America was bellicose, and yet Nixon saw himself as a peacemaker in search of a cause. Having won the race to land a man on the moon, Nixon had recently announced the end of the Apollo space programme due to lack of funds. The war in Vietnam was stumbling to its disastrous end. As he began his own battle for reselection perhaps he felt he needed a war he could win, or at least use to inspire the American people. So, in a construction that looks over-optimistic in retrospect, Nixon identified cancer as a new enemy for America to defeat and set a target of eight years in which to do so. From Nixon onwards the rhetoric of aggression gained currency in political and cultural discourse within and beyond America to describe the narrative of medical research into the diseases that are cancer. For example, from 1981 the Australian Cancer Society launched regional 'Cancer Crusade Units', and in 1989 the BBC transmitted a six-part TV series entitled *Fight Cancer*. In September 2009 President Barack Obama used a formulation similar to Nixon's when he announced that 'now is the time to commit ourselves to waging a war against cancer as aggressive as the war cancer wages against us'.[4]

Medical professionals might have favoured a more precise terminology, but the language of warfare was very useful, for example, to medical research charities. In their Race for Life Campaign in 2013, Cancer Research UK ran a series of ads with the slogan: 'Cancer – we're coming to get you.' Their aim was to portray cancer as an enemy that could be addressed directly. Researchers at Lancaster University have shown that objectifying cancer, and using violence metaphors, can be effective at unifying and motivating donors when it comes to fundraising.[5]

---

2. Richard Nixon, *Annual Message to the Congress on the State of the Union*. Online by Gerhard Peters and John T. Woolley, The American Presidency Project https://www.presidency.ucsb.edu/node/240562

3. Ibid.

4. Christine Lennon, 'Ovarian Cancer: Fighting for a Cure', *Harper's Bazaar* (July 2009), 391.

5. Elena Semino, Z. Demjén, J. Demmen et al., 'The Online use of Violence and Journey Metaphors by Patients with Cancer, as Compared with Health Professionals: A Mixed Methods Study', *BMJ Supportive & Palliative Care* 7 (2017): 60–6.

Almost exactly forty years after the National Cancer Act, President George W. Bush declared a 'war on terror'. As Nixon had demonstrated, the language of warfare is useful for rallying public support, even when the enemy is intangible. Fear of terror is tautologous, but it can be used to legitimize the radical suspension of civil rights. Fear of cancer, likewise, might be used to drive people's determination to fight for life, but it is equally possible that the fear that attaches to cancer should be seen as part of its pathology – something that in itself needs to be mitigated, treated and if possible cured.

While there may be some benefit in personifying and objectifying cancer at a cultural level, the same language set may be problematic for the individual with cancer and also for the clinician. Introducing a research report called *Missed Opportunities*, Adrienne Betteley, Specialist Advisor for End of Life Care at Macmillan Cancer Support says, 'We know that "battling" against cancer can help some people remain upbeat about their disease, but for others the effort of keeping up a brave face is exhausting and unhelpful in the long-term. We need to let people define their own experiences without using language that might create a barrier to vital conversations about dying.'[6] Neither Betteley nor I wish to take a fatalist stance towards cancer, nor would I for a moment advocate the majority of patients withdrawing from conventional treatments such as surgery, radiotherapy or chemotherapy. And yet, just as peace is not merely the absence of war, so health is not merely the absence of cancer. The radical 'othering' of cancer enjoins the patient to a civil war on their own body, and it's not clear that this is a just war, since it allows a suspension of many of the norms of medical conduct, tolerates an abnormally high degree of 'collateral damage' and instrumentalizes the patient in a wider narrative of medical victory. As Arthur Frank points out, we don't tend to objectify other diseases like this. We don't treat a stroke as an alien invasion, or go to war on our own heart disease.[7]

The notion of 'physical illness' as supernatural punishment or demonic possession persists in mythology from Homer and the book of Job to the present. Conversely, physical fitness, health and wealth are often associated with divine favour or blessing. Cancer patients may still feel that their illness is a punishment for the secular sins of an unhealthy lifestyle: smoking, poor diet, too much sun or, ironically, not paying sufficient attention to themselves in 'checking' intimate areas. The attachment of the language of warfare to residual notions of divine wrath gives the 'battle with cancer' a cosmic dimension that may account for its almost mythical hold on the public imagination.

---

6. Adrienne Betteley, *'Fighting Talk' Can Leave Cancer Patients Unable to Talk about Death and Dying*, Press release, Macmillan Cancer Support, 15 May 2018. Accessed online at https://medium.com/macmillan-press-releases-and-statements/fighting-talk-cancer-patients-43376148563c

7. Arthur W. Frank, *At the Will of the Body* (New York: Mariner Books, 1991), 91.

The dis-integration of the body

Since the Enlightenment, Western humans have tended to conceive of themselves as rational, and of their bodies as objects of that rationality: for Descartes, body and soul were separate substances; for Kant the body was akin to an animal to be tamed. From this perspective, failure to overcome disease is constructed as a sort of moral weakness on the part of the person. Elisabeth Wendel-Moltmann rejects this dualism, saying that while our predominant experience is of being a person who 'has' a body, in boundary situations such as illness or malfunction, we discover that in fact we 'are' a body.[8] The 'gift of illness' presents the individual with an opportunity for redemptive integration. This is exemplified in Jesus's encounter with a man who was blind from birth recorded in chapter nine of the Gospel according to John, where he indicates that illness is to be seen as a vehicle for God's glory rather than a sign of God's wrath.

When a part of the body such as a cancerous tumour is objectified, a person is forced into the incoherence of disowning or even repenting of a part of themselves. The objectification of cancer as enemy reflects and reinforces a curious Cartesian bifurcation of good-body and bad-body. A linguistic and emotional wedge is driven between the individual and their body, and between their body and itself. The soul is conscripted to subdue the cancer through a mixture of determination and broccoli. This is unhelpful, since, as Elizabeth Wendell-Moltmann points out, 'it is not only my body that is sick. I am sick. I am in my body. I have no other identity.'[9] The body is construed as a battleground, when it might be better construed as a peace conference.

The tendency of New Testament writers to objectify parts of the body only adds to the confusion. In Matthew's Gospel, Jesus says, 'If your eye causes you to stumble, tear it out and throw it away; it is better for you to enter life with one eye than to have two eyes and to be thrown into the hell of fire' (Mt. 18.9). I can almost hear in this the voice of my oncologist outlining his recommendation for a prostatectomy. On the other hand, Paul affirms the unity of the body: 'The eye cannot say to the hand, "I have no need of you," nor again the head to the feet, "I have no need of you"' (1 Cor. 12.21). 'If one member suffers, all suffer together with it; if one member is honoured, all rejoice together with it' (1 Cor. 12.26). So which is it to be? Must I hate my cancerous cells enough to gouge them out? Or should I try to love them even if, for my survival, I need to kiss them goodbye?

If we construct the treatment of cancer as a war, we are consciously raising the stakes. In warfare we accept that the outcome may include a significant number of deaths on both sides, and probably considerable 'collateral damage' (loss and destruction to parties otherwise uninvolved), for the sake of a greater good. In no other area of medicine are the principles of *jus in bello* – just conduct in battle –

---

8. Elizabeth Wendell-Moltmann, *I Am My Body* (London: Bloomsbury Academic, 1995), 1.
9. Ibid., 22.

so markedly tested as they are in oncology. In an age of chemical and biological weaponry it's a rich irony that cancer treatment increasingly depends on the use of toxic chemicals and nuclear material, which, in spite of the promise of more and more accurate targeting, cannot reliably discriminate between healthy and wayward cells. Nevertheless the declaration of war implies that the enemy is sufficiently evil (and the protagonist sufficiently good) that the use of overwhelming force is justified. The proportionality of such force seems to be assessed more broadly in the case of cancer than with other illnesses. In the case of cancerous cells it is not at all clear that a designation as evil is accurate or helpful. Cancerous cells multiply and colonize otherwise healthy organs, but they don't have any moral agency. Cancerous cells are no more intrinsically evil than those we call healthy, nor are they signifiers of the moral state of the person. When Jesus says that the man he meets in John 9 is blind 'so that the works of God can be displayed in him' (Jn. 9.3), he is saying that the disordered body may be and become a place of grace. While healing can be a foretaste of the Kingdom of God, the corollary is that sickness too may be a reminder of the presence of God in a fallen world. The primary dichotomy the cancer patient faces is not between cancerous cells and non-cancerous ones, still less between sin and blessing, but between wellness and illness – between the past, the present and the hoped-for future.

The dis-integration of the body that comes from the objectification of cancer can be seen as an aspect of the power dynamic of medicine within modern culture. In *The Birth of the Clinic* Foucault spoke of 'the medical gaze' by which the clinical establishment simultaneously construes and subdues the physiology of the human body. In *Naming the Silences* Stanley Hauerwas describes medicine as one of the high points in the rationalist project, the theodical project of modernity, part of the task of which is to save liberalism, for which the enduring power of cancer represents a stubborn and irrational problem. Hauerwas and Charles Pinches have written that 'culture forces on medicine the impossible job of bandaging the wounds of societies built on the premise that God doesn't matter'.[10] The language of warfare enlists a second 'supervising regime', placing clinicians in the role of both confessor and military strategist. Surgeons are constructed as heroic warriors, the special forces of the medical world – sometimes fighting hand to hand with scalpels, sometimes using lasers and nuclear ray guns. When this is combined with a sense of the supernatural power of cancer, they can take on an almost godlike status, such that some patients will speak about 'having faith' in their oncologist.

When the treatment of cancer is construed as a battle, the body, or perhaps the whole person, becomes medical territory over which the patient is expected to cede many of their customary rights, so that it is not only the cancer but also the medical establishment that colonizes it. The presence of an enemy permits the doctor to focus solely on the invasive cancer at the expense of the rest of the body,

---

10. Stanley Hauerwas with Charles Pinches, 'Practicing Patience: How Christians Should Be Sick', in *The Hauerwas Reader*, ed. John Berkman and Michael Cartwright (Durham and London: Duke University Press, 1997), 348–69.

and of the person as a whole. Like a general in warfare, their primary relationship is with the invading force, not with the unwilling host. Arthur Frank laments the passivity this imposes on the patient, pointing out how in his own experience the cancerous part of him was depersonalized by clinicians with phrases like 'This will have to be investigated'.[11] The very words 'surgical' and 'clinical' suggest a conscious detachment from the emotional and cultural life of the person. The particularization of cancer is in itself problematic. To the surgeon a tumour is an impersonal, un-gendered 'it', while to the patient, it is inextricably a part of themselves. The excision of the cancerous cells will constitute no loss to the surgeon – in fact if successful it will be counted a triumph. But for the patient, it is the loss of an irreplaceable part of one's self.

Cancer as it is constructed also separates the individual from their community like no other disease. Perhaps the preponderance of marathons, fun runs and mountain climbing to raise money for cancer research and treatment is itself partly motivated by the fear that is engendered by this construction. Is it perhaps a way for the non-sufferer to demonstrate the integrity of their own body in contradistinction to the fallibility of bodies that are diseased?

Towards an alternative rhetoric

In my sojourn with cancer I have been intrigued to discover a number of people exploring alternative rhetoric to describe their engagement with their disease. Some people use dynamic imagery such as walking or journeying with cancer. The late priest and poet Jim Cotter, for example, described his experience of living with inoperable cancer to me as being like a solo pilot flying through the clouds in a rather rickety plane, knowing that he had a limited amount of fuel left, but not knowing how much. Another person with cancer spoke of their tumour as akin to a hitchhiker they had picked up along the road and given a ride to for a time. The experience had not been altogether pleasant or convenient, but they felt they were a better person for it. There's something of the language of pilgrimage here that has a resonance for Christians, and at least it captures some of the narrative force of the illness.

Some have spoken to me of giving hospitality to cancer as an unwelcome lodger. You may not know much about where they've come from, or how long they're going to stay, but you give them a safe space until the time comes for them to move on. St Francis of Assisi, who himself lived with a long-term illness, is said to have embraced his illness like a family member. Perhaps the weakness of these images of hospitality and pilgrimage is that they still envisage cancer as an objective entity rather than as part of the whole body.

Some people with cancer have offered me images of creativity and collaboration. Professor Michael Overduin of the School of Cancer Sciences at the University of

---

11. Frank, *At the Will of the Body*, 51.

Birmingham spoke of cells 'misbehaving' in the playground of the body. He also described the body as akin to a symphony orchestra. At its best it works together to create something beautiful. If one of the instruments is dissonant, you go in and tune it, or retrain the musician, or if necessary ask them to leave. The clear advantage of these organic and creative images is that they construe treatment as a process of working along with the body, not against it.

How might a Christian, and particularly a pacifist, approach cancer? Hauerwas proposes a virtue-based framework focusing on patience and courage as a response to illness: 'We are our bodies and, as such, we are creatures destined to die. The trick is to learn to love the great good things our bodies make possible without hating our bodies, if for no other reason than that the death of our bodies is our own death.'[12] Hauerwas doesn't intend this as a counsel of despair but as an affirmation of eschatological hope. Perhaps the recovery of an integrated, organic and eschatologically focused concept of the body-in-community could offer a more constructive rhetoric for patients and clinicians alike.

Incarnational theology regards the body as a sacrament, a particular place of revelation at a moment in time. That revelation happens in the context of, and as a witness to, the wider community. By contrast, the nature of idolatry is to objectify and particularize matter, to remove it from community and turn it into a focus of worship, fear or self-hatred. It is the body with all its characteristics, including its specific needs, that makes us present to the world and the human community, and reminds us of our dependence on others and on God. For example, the impetus to provide aid to a starving child in a remote part of the world is at least partly driven by the sense that their body should not be a locus of suffering. In that sense, compassion has an eschatological dynamic and represents a real belief in the resurrection of the body. It also has a community dynamic. If one person suffers, we all suffer. What if the body in question is not that of a starving child, but my own body, or at least a part of it, that is located in community and bears witness to suffering? To objectify, fetishize or denounce it would be idolatry; to celebrate its dysfunctionality would be perverse. But to love the parts of me that are dead or dying is to recognize the grace of God and the real possibility of resurrection. Consequently, my cancerous cells remain a very real part of me, not objectified or spiritualized but a tangible reminder of transience and hope. My disease has a prophetic role in the community too, pointing from the present to the future that God has in store. Even my excised tumour has a role to play, leading the way before me to resurrection life. Wherever it is, and in whatever decomposed state, it is part of the earth in which God lives, and in which the remainder of my body will eventually join it. It is the first fruits of my resurrection. My cancerous tumour is not my enemy, but a reminder that none of us are yet what we can be and will be. It is God's thumbprint on the Plasticine of my existence, and it deserves my love.

---

12. Hauerwas with Pinches, 'Practicing Patience', 364.

Chapter 13

DEPRESSIVE SUFFERING AS TRAGIC SUFFERING: THEOLOGICAL INSIGHTS AND TRAJECTORIES

Jessica Coblentz

In the 2006 film, *Stranger than Fiction*, comedian Will Farrell plays the part of Harold Crick, a simple and serious American man who, while brushing his teeth one day, begins to hear the voice of a British woman narrating his life.[1] The sudden presence of her commentary is alarming, and it compels him to seek counsel. Eventually, Harold consults a professor of literature – an expert in narratives such as the one unfolding in his head – and the professor advises him to determine whether the narrator of his life is telling a tale of comedy or of tragedy. As the film progresses, the audience witnesses the high stakes of this literary investigation. The meaning of the events in Harold's life, the possibilities he imagines for his future and the actions he takes, small and large, are bound up with his speculation about whether the narrator has destined him for the happy resolution of a comedy or the ill-fated future of a tragedy. Harold's experience of himself and the world shifts in view of the metanarrative through which he perceives his life.

It is this hermeneutical insight – that the story we inhabit shapes our experiences, our relation to and actions towards others, our capacity for meaning-making and our apprehension of God's work within our lives – that has led theologians to inquire in recent decades about the metanarrative of Christianity. Is history, according to the Christian tradition, a comedy or a tragedy? As a theologian and researcher of depression, the contours and affordances of the Christian narrative are of special interest to me. For years I have immersed myself in first-person stories and phenomenological analyses of an all-encompassing condition that resists meaningfulness and confines its sufferers to a seemingly changeless present. Such suffering does not easily map onto standard Christian portrayals of God's healing grace and the promise of Christian hope. At the same time, many depression sufferers are desperate for meaning-making resources to support their existential survival and disclose possibilities for finding purpose amid this

---

1. *Stranger than Fiction*, directed by Mark Forster (2006; Culver City: Sony Pictures Home Entertainment, 2007), DVD.

chronic, recurring and incurable condition. Many ache for a story that helps them make sense of their lives.

While I concur with Karen Kilby that outsiders are in no position to prescribe meaning to the suffering of others, theologians are uniquely positioned to showcase Christian resources – especially those lesser known – for sufferers to draw on as they interpret their own suffering.[2] This theological task is especially important in circumstances where prevailing Christian theologies fail those who suffer gravely. To this end, this chapter explores the shortcomings of Christianity's dominant comedic world view and shows how tragic articulations of suffering and salvation history can afford valuable resources for those who strive to interpret depressive suffering within a Christian world view. I conclude by suggesting how first-person narratives of depression can likewise enrich these tragic theologies.

Suffering and salvation in comedy and tragedy

Before turning to the specifics of depressive suffering, I will briefly introduce comedic and tragic perspectives on suffering and salvation in recent Christian theology. The narrative world view of Christian theology is most often comic. Comedic plotlines reflect a 'U' structure: they begin in a state of peace and harmony, which is disrupted by a central conflict that spurs a series of unfortunate consequences. Eventually, however, the conflict and its effects are resolved for a happy ending. Flora Keshgegian calls the classic Christian story 'relentlessly comedic: all's well that ends well for the redeemed. And all will end well because God is in charge.'[3]

Like all comedies, this classic Christian story presents an orderly world of cause and effect. As such, only certain forms of suffering appear – suffering that follows from an identifiable source, a negative cause, that is, sin. Comedy's etiological presentation of suffering leads Wendy Farley to associate it with theodicy, which assumes a comedic world view insofar as it is predicated on the possibility of a logical justification for suffering.[4] Theodical thinking, like comedic thinking, assumes that the world is 'rational, orderly, and essentially comprehensible', echoes John Swinton. Suffering, even in its most harrowing forms, is perceived accordingly.[5]

---

2. See Karen Kilby, 'Eschatology, Suffering and the Limits of Theology', in *Game Over? Reconsidering Eschatology*, ed. Christophe Chalamet, Andreas Dettwiler, Mariel Mazzocco and Ghislain Waterlot (Berlin: De Gruyter), 297–2.

3. Flora A. Keshgegian, *Time for Hope: Practice for Living in Today's World* (New York: Continuum, 2006), 158.

4. Wendy Farley, *Tragic Vision and Divine Compassion: A Contemporary Theodicy* (Louisville: Westminster John Knox, 1990), 51–2.

5. John Swinton, *Raging with Compassion: Pastoral Responses to the Problem of Evil* (Grand Rapids: Eerdmans, 2007), 33.

Just as comedy's orderly world view provides a particular lens for suffering, so too with salvation. Within the comedic Christian narrative, the work of salvation is a matter of problem solving: God fixes the problem of sin upon which the plotline of history pivots. Because salvation is ultimately a matter of fixing the problem of sin, the whole of God's salvific relationship to creation is identified with redemption. Furthermore, because suffering is the direct result of sin, God's redemptive overcoming of sin ensures an end to suffering as the fruition of salvation.

Keshgegian observes that the comedic plot 'effectively and rather emphatically excludes ... anything other than a story line that moves inevitably toward a resolution in which what is deemed good, right and true prevails'.[6] Concerned with all that the comedic plotline excludes, theologians in recent decades have questioned its prevalence in Christian theology. Its limited interpretations of suffering and salvation are inadequate because they do not account for persistent, inexplicable and illogical suffering and God's transformative relationship to it.

Tragic narratives appeal to some theologians seeking a more capacious Christian story. Tragedies attend to the complex and manifold realities of suffering in our world and, in doing so, show that a great deal of suffering exceeds the logic of cause and effect. Certainly, there are instances when suffering clearly follows from sinful action – when greed prompts injurious theft, or revenge, painful violence – and while tragedies don't overlook the causal relationship of sin to such suffering, they focus on suffering that cannot be explained so easily. Tragedy confronts audiences with competing goods that lead to unavoidable conflict and strife, or with the coincidental convergence of multiple causes that engender senseless suffering. In Rowan Williams's case for a Christian tragic imagination, he examines how the inescapable opacity of the self and its relation to others blinds us from the ill and unintended effects of our actions, which play out even when we act conscientiously.[7] In such instances, suffering results not from our transparent sinful actions but from our own finitude and inherent relationality. Indeed, what makes the Attic tragedies so fascinating and so horrible is their representation of suffering like this – suffering that evades logical explanation. Tragedies represent this 'inexplicable suffering', and in doing so, they afford Christians a world view capacious enough to contain a wider range of the suffering that fills our world.

Another constitutive feature of the tragic narrative is the irresolution of the suffering within it. This is not unrelated to the elusive suffering at the centre of tragedies, for it is difficult to resolve – or even imagine resolving – suffering that has no clear origin or logic to it. Whereas the comedic narrative facilitates a Christian story in which God inevitably eradicates sin and thus suffering, guaranteeing a happy ending, the tragic world view prescribes no such resolution and thus invites an alternative vision of salvation.

---

6. Keshgegian, *Time for Hope*, 158.
7. Rowan Williams, *The Tragic Imagination: The Literary Agenda* (Oxford: Oxford University Press, 2016), 30–55. Farley also points to this reality in *Tragic Vision*, 44–6.

Depressive suffering as tragic suffering

Like other forms of tragic suffering, chronic and recurring depression evades the causal frameworks of the comedic plotline. Although some attempt to situate it within the etiological logic that characterizes comedy with theories of depression's origin in a gene, or a particular constellation of gut bacteria, or unresolved trauma, or capitalism, the absence of sufficient evidence for any one of these theories has led most scholars to conclude that, at best, depression results from an unidentifiable amalgamation of many causes.[8]

What's more, depression is not *experienced* as the effect of a particular cause. Whereas typical emotions are associated with an object – the loss of a loved one triggers a feeling of profound sadness, for example – depression is not tethered to an object – a cause – within the sufferer's experience or lifeworld.[9] Rather, depression sufferers experience a radical shift in the totality of their way of being-in-the-world. In phenomenological terms, it is an experience that lacks 'intentionality' and thus defies, on an experiential level, the causal explanation for suffering that constitutes the comedic world view. It follows that even if, from an outsider's perspective, we could agree upon a clear-cut etiological account of depression, sufferers would continue to *experience* their suffering as an unquantifiable condition that resists such orderly explanations.

And yet the comedic view of suffering and salvation underlies many of the well-intentioned interpretations of depression that its sufferers resist. Imperatives from 'cheer up!' and 'look on the bright side!' to 'repent from your sins!' and 'pray for God's forgiveness!' – all of which are common responses to depression in Christian communities – assume a clear cause of depression that lies within the sufferer's control.[10] Underlying these and other 'quick fix' prescriptions for depression is a

---

8. For a variety of contemporary etiological interpretations of depression, see *Handbook of Depression*, 3rd edn, ed. Ian H. Gotlib and Constance L. Hammen (New York: Guilford, 2014).

9. See Jennifer Radden, ed., *The Nature of Melancholy: Essays on Melancholy and Depression* (Oxford: Oxford University Press, 2002), 10–12; Jennifer Radden, *Moody Minds Distempered: From Aristotle to Kristeva* (Oxford: Oxford University Press, 2009), 180–7.

10. One need only read a couple of the many Christian memoirs of depression to attain anecdotal evidence of these responses. A number of social scientists have also quantified the frequency of these perspectives in Christian communities. See Marcia Webb, Kathy Stetz and Kristine Hedden, 'Representation of Mental Illness in Christian Self-Help Bestsellers', *Mental Health, Religion & Culture* 11 no. 7 (November 2008): 696–717; Norman Dain, 'Madness and the stigma of sin in American Christianity', in *Stigma and Mental Illness*, ed. Paul Fink and Allan Tasman (Washington DC: American Psychiatric Press, 1992), 73–84; Kristine Hartog and Kathryn Gow, 'Religious Attributions Pertaining to the Causes and Cures of Mental Illness', *Mental Health, Religion and Culture* 8 (2005): 263–76; Lois McLatchie and Juris Draguns, 'Mental Health Concepts of Evangelical Protestants', *The Journal of Psychology* 118 (1984): 147–59.

linear vision of salvation history that pivots on simplistic problem solving rather than the complex realities of suffering and divine transformation in history. Even more 'progressive-minded' Christians who identify depression as a biological illness most often assume a comedic view of suffering and salvation. Though biological interpretations of depression absolve sufferers of moral responsibility for their condition, they still assume a clear cause and straightforward cure for depression that erases the phenomenological complexities of this condition and preclude potential non-linear, life-giving transformations that unfold amid this persistent and incurable suffering. As such, the comedic world view pre-emptively limits the theological resources available to Christians who strive to interpret depression and God's relationship to it.

Alternatively, chronic and recurring depression resonates with the inexplicable and unresolved suffering at the centre of the tragic world view. The persistence and incurability of depression also align it with tragic suffering. These resonances are evident from an objective and a subjective view of depression. Depression is an irresolvable condition by nearly every observable measure. It is constituted by lengthy episodes that can stretch on for months and even years, and these episodes have a strikingly high rate of recurrence.[11] Between severe episodes, sufferers often report continued, milder experiences of depression as well. And, though there are a host of mitigating treatments for depression, there is ultimately no cure for this long and recurrent suffering.[12] The phenomenological reality of depression magnifies its persistence still further. Depression sufferers regularly attest to a shift in temporality that results in an experience of timelessness and thus changelessness. They experience depression as endless, which is more reason to view depression with the irresolvable suffering at the centre of the tragic world view.[13]

Seeing depressive suffering as tragic suffering opens the possibility of situating depression in the Christian narrative while obviating some of the shortfalls of the comedic framework that often dominates and constrains our theologies. It also invites us to bring the insights of tragic theologies to theological reflection on depression. For instance, tragedy's special attention to inexplicable and unresolved suffering informs a different view of God's salvific relation to suffering than that which we perceive in the comedic account of history. First, tragedy challenges the common Christian identification of salvation with redemption alone. According

---

11. See Daniel N. Klein and Anna E. S. Allmann, 'Course of Depression: Persistence and Recurrence', in *Handbook of Depression*, 64–83.

12. For an overview of some typical methods for treating depression, as well as accounts of their respective effectiveness, see *Handbook of Depression*, 492–590. The effectiveness of treatments for depression varies widely, and when they do ameliorate the severity of depression, the reasons for their effectiveness often evade healthcare providers and researchers. This is further evidence of depression's stubborn inexplicability and, therefore, its resonance with the tragic milieu.

13. Matthew Ratcliffe, *Experiences of Depression: A Study in Phenomenology* (Oxford: Oxford, 2015), 33–74, 99–127, 174–200.

to Wendy Farley, the Christian belief that God redeems humanity's sinfulness offers us an account of God's relationship to the sin-based suffering of the comedic milieu, but it does not account for how God relates to the other forms of suffering at the centre of the tragic world view.[14] Even when God fixes the problem of sin, tragic suffering will remain.[15] As such, the tragic world view invites an account of salvation that is broader than redemption. This is not because sin is irrelevant to suffering; indeed, redemption is still a dimension of God's salvific work. Tragedy demands a vision of salvation that is more than redemption, however, because it recognizes manifestations of suffering that exceed the causal origin of sin and thus the efficacy of redemption.[16]

Second, the reduction of salvation to redemption perpetuates the view that God's primary salvific work is problem solving that facilitates the absolute resolution of sin and its effects.[17] This does not resonate with tragic narratives that focus on unresolved suffering like depression. The tragic world view invites an articulation of God's salvific work amid and in response to persistent suffering. I should note that the refusal of tragic theologians to reduce salvation to the resolution of sin and suffering has led some theologians to reject the tragic frame outright.[18] Insofar as Christians believe in the eschatological victory of God over sin, they suggest, Christians must assert some ultimate resolution to suffering in history. In response, Rowan Williams clarifies the difference between tragedy and pessimism.[19] Pessimism responds to tragic suffering with despair; the tragic Christian narrative, in contrast, recognizes tragic suffering and conveys it to a community with the assumption that transformation is possible *amid* persistent and unresolved suffering. In fact, representing suffering in all its complexity is requisite for the actions that can actually affect the suffering of such complicated circumstances.

14. Farley, *Tragic Vision*, 40–4.

15. In dialogue with Farley's argument about tragic suffering, John Swinton resists the theodical (and comedic) assumption that all suffering arises from sin and evil. 'Evil is always accompanied by suffering, but not all suffering is evil,' he asserts. Accompanying this claim is a compelling account of how theologians can delineate among forms of suffering along these lines. While Swinton doesn't adopt the language of 'tragic suffering' due to some disagreements with Farley's project, I believe his attempt to unyoke some suffering from sin and evil may be helpful for theologies of depression and other forms of tragic suffering. See *Raging with Compassion*, 57.

16. Reformed theologian Edwin Chr. van Driel's work on supralapsarian christologies and their soteriological implications appeals to me as a resource that might aid theologians in exploring the distinction between redemption and salvation further. See *Incarnation Anyway: Arguments for Supralapsarian Christology* (Oxford: Oxford University Press, 2008), especially 162–70.

17. Shelly Rambo substantiates this critique in *Spirit and Trauma: A Theology of Remaining* (Louisville: Westminster John Knox, 2010).

18. Williams, *Tragic Imagination*, 108–15.

19. Ibid., 108–36.

Furthering tragic vision with depression narratives

Throughout this chapter, I have tried to demonstrate what the tragic world view can offer Christians who strive to interpret depressive suffering. The tragic world view affords a framework that recognizes the complexities of depressive suffering and discloses possibilities for life-giving transformations amid this unresolved condition. Yet, we know from the study of hermeneutics that interpretation is never a one-way operation; the concrete events we interpret speak back to our hermeneutical lenses, affirming and sharpening them or interrupting them with discontinuities. I have shown how depressive suffering disrupts Christianity's prevailing comedic narrative of suffering and salvation, for example, and I conclude by exploring how depression can, alternatively, affirm and clarify the contours of the tragic narrative lens.

Namely, in response to critics of tragic theologies who exhort a clearer account of Christian hope and the life-giving transformation of salvation, the narratives of depression sufferers provide us with concrete examples. If, as Williams suggests, the resurrection grounds Christians' hope for salvation in a tragic world, then we might look to first-person narratives of depression for glimpses of 'everyday resurrection', that is, for concrete examples to inform the account of our eschatological hope.[20] Based on my study of more than forty first-person narratives of depression, the development of transformative practices that curb the isolation and meaninglessness that sufferers experience amid their persistent suffering often becomes more significant to their flourishing than hope for the eradication of depression itself.[21] These life-giving practices frequently include talking and writing about depression for the sake of supporting fellow sufferers. The vitality that can accompany such practices often surprises sufferers who have previously identified the possibility of flourishing with only the eradication of depression. Eventually, however, many realize that their inescapable condition can nevertheless afford alternative possibilities for situational flourishing.[22] Examples of transformative connection and meaning-making amid depression offer theologians important insight into human flourishing in a tragic world:

---

20. This phrase, 'everyday resurrection', is from Ivone Gebarra, and she uses it to denote the often small, life-giving experiences of poor women in Latin America amid the suffering they experience in everyday life. Gebarra engages these experiences as a resource for theologizing resurrection in history, a methodological move akin to what I exhort here. See *Out of the Depths: Women's Experience of Evil and Salvation* (Minneapolis: Fortress, 2002), 122–7.

21. For a fuller account of the life-giving transformations that regularly appear across first-person narratives of depression, see Jessica Coblentz, 'Depression's Challenge to Theologies of Suffering and Salvation' (PhD diss., Boston College, March 2017), 234–66.

22. This observation is corroborated in sociologist David Karp's *Speaking of Sadness: Depression, Disconnection, and the Meanings of Illness*, Revised edn (Oxford: Oxford University Press, 1997).

salvation, in this context, is not the absolute elimination of suffering, but rather the partial restoration of meaningfulness and connection as suffering persists. This soteriological insight has broader eschatological implications concerning what we deem most fundamental to the human person and its flourishing, I suspect, though the limitations of this chapter leave me to explore this further elsewhere.

I should also note that, certainly, many depression sufferers find no meaning in their suffering. To them, religious narratives are of no aid or are merely detrimental. Some survive in spite of this; many do not. My aim in this chapter is not to impose a theological interpretation upon their pain. Rather, for Christians still grasping for resources to position depression within their religious milieu, I've attempted to relativize the prevailing Christian narrative that so many sufferers find unhelpful and then mine the tradition for another that might be of some aid. My additional hope is that theologians will receive the insights of these sufferers who interpret depression first-hand and allow them to further our theological understandings of suffering and God's transformative relationship to it.

Chapter 14

THE SEDUCTIONS OF KENOSIS

Karen Kilby

Suffering and loss are not good. This is my hypothesis. To say the same thing from a different perspective, suffering and loss are not part of God, or grounded in God's Being, or desired by God. And to say nearly the same thing, in a different way again, suffering and loss are not essentially bound up with love.

At least in its first version – that suffering and loss are not good – this hypothesis is an obvious deliverance of common sense. My proposal, then, in adopting this hypothesis is that theologians should not seek to transcend this common sense: we should not seek to be taken beyond it by a more sophisticated level of thinking, or by a deeper wisdom, or by the scandal of a countercultural Christian faith.[1]

I will not attempt any defence of my starting hypothesis. Indeed it is not clear that an assertion like this – that suffering and loss are not good – *can* be directly defended. The closest one might come would be to show that holding firm to such a hypothesis is compatible with a fully formed Christian vision of things, a vision which can do justice to the centrality of the cross, to the significance of martyrs, to Gospel verses about taking up one's cross and losing one's life to find it, to various themes from Paul, and even perhaps to something in the mystical dereliction tradition discussed at other points in this volume. All this, however, would be too much to attempt in a single chapter. The slightly different and much more limited purpose of this chapter will be to explore a cluster of themes which appear with some regularity in contemporary theological discussion, and which often stand in tension with my starting platitude – themes of kenosis, vulnerability and fragility. I hope to give an account of what is currently making these themes *attractive*, what is giving them their appeal, even if, according to my hypothesis, there is often something misguided in their deployment.

If one aim of the paper is to explore and diagnose a particular contemporary theological fashion, a second is to experiment with an expansion of the method of systematic theology. Over the past several years I have held a series of

---

1. There is of course something properly countercultural in Christian faith, including in its approach to suffering, but I am proposing that we get this countercultural moment troublingly wrong – that we identify the scandal of Christianity falsely – if we understand faith as leading us to see suffering and loss as goods rather than evils.

conversations with a group of religious sisters who belong to the Congregation of La Retraite in England and Ireland. The conversations have been on the theme 'Love and Suffering', and I will draw on aspects of these conversations to develop an analysis of the contemporary lure of kenosis and associated concepts.[2]

In speaking with the sisters, I have not thought of myself as moving into another discipline – some sort of qualitative social science, for instance – in order to study the sisters and then, in a second step, 'do' something theologically with the findings. The conversations with the sisters have instead served to expand, a little bit, two ordinary features of the working pattern of a (systematic) theologian. Theologians almost always, first of all, attend to and wrestle with the thoughts of others as they reflect on any given issue – typically they do so by reading and interacting with historical or contemporary theological texts. In this case, as well as this usual engagement with texts, I sought to enrich and test my thought by listening to and interacting with the La Retraite sisters, women who typically do their theological reflection in a slightly different mode than the one into which I have been trained.[3] So the conversations, first of all, have simply widened the range of those with whom I interacted as I wrestled with ideas. Secondly, since the decisions and directions a theologian takes are always shaped by their experience, one aim of these conversations was to allow my own experience to be a little expanded by attention not only to specific instances of other people's suffering but also to the way in which a group of committed practitioners of the Christian life wrestle with, reflect on and talk about this suffering.[4]

---

2. I spoke with seventeen sisters, both individually and in groups. Financial support for the project, enabling me the time and resources to hold these conversations, and more generally to work on the theme in a sustained way, was generously provided by the Congregation of La Retraite, England and Ireland.

3. The sisters and I understood our project as an experiment in theological collaboration, between an academically trained, academically inclined thinker on the one hand, and a group of people more disposed to reflect in connection with experience and with prayer on the other. It is important to be clear that the contrast is not a sharp one: on the one hand the sisters are well-educated, including theologically well-educated, and on the other hand, I too sometimes think in a way that has links to my experience and even my prayer. The strengths on each side, however, and the emphases, differ.

4. Karl Barth provides a particularly illuminating illustration of this point about experience. Biographers consistently point to two key moments in Barth's life which shaped his theology: the disillusionment with his theological teachers brought about by their support of the German war effort, and his experience of preaching in Safenwil. One cannot it seems tell the story of fundamental decisions and directions he took theologically without pointing to elements of his experience. This does not mean, of course, that he turned this experience into some kind of theological *evidence*, that he made it a source or norm of his theology.

Kenosis, vulnerability and fragility: The issue

There seems to be something peculiarly attractive at the moment, for theologians, in the concept of *kenosis*. The word itself comes from a reference to self-emptying in a verse in Philippians; in adjectival form, it became a technical theological term relatively recently. Kenotic Christology, offering a non-traditional interpretation of the Incarnation, had roots in seventeenth-century Lutheran debates and flourished in the nineteenth century.[5] In twenty-first-century theological discussions, however, kenosis makes an appearance in a range of contexts, playing a role that takes it well beyond either straightforward commentary on the second chapter of Philippians or direct wrestling with contested issues in the theology of the Incarnation. It shows up as a concept in ethics, in spirituality and in ecclesiology, and as a key for thinking through the nature of love, both human and divine. It appears as part of the vocabulary of thinkers of otherwise very different ecclesial styles and orientations, so that – to give examples just from the Catholic world – one can find it not only in the writings of a *Communio* theologian like Hans Urs von Balthasar, who, following the lead of Sergei Bulgakov, presents kenosis as at the heart of the eternal life of the Trinity, but also in the work of more *Concilium*-leaning theologians, such as the Heythrop College scholars who not too long ago edited a book entitled *Towards a Kenotic Vision of Authority in the Catholic Church*.[6]

If kenosis is in the air at the moment, then hovering not too far away are two other terms, 'vulnerability' and 'fragility', together with the sense that these are things which, however difficult this may be, must be embraced, owned and valued. The fascination with kenosis can perhaps be seen as a kind of churchgoing cousin of a more widespread appeal of notions of 'vulnerability' and 'fragility'.

The problem in connection with these theological fashions is not hard to state. Vulnerability means the capacity to be wounded. Fragility means the capacity to be broken. Kenosis means a deliberate self-emptying, a becoming less. It would seem, on the face of it, that to be wounded, or to be broken, or to be less, are not good things. To the degree that we speak about kenosis, vulnerability and fragility in a positive light, then, as things which are good in themselves, we appear to be saying something fairly troubling – something at odds with the opening platitudes of this chapter.

Elsewhere I have developed more detailed examination of these issues in the thought of Hans Urs von Balthasar, and Linn Tonstad has drawn attention

---

5. For a historical treatment of kenotic Christology, see David Law, 'Luther's Legacy and the Origins of Kenotic Christology', *Bulletin of the John Rylands Library* 93 (2017): 41–68.

6. Anthony J. Carroll, Marthe Kerkwijk, Michael Kirwan and James Sweeney, eds, *Towards a Kenotic Vision of Authority in the Catholic Church* (Council for Research in Values and Philosophy, 2015).

to the problematic way kenosis and vulnerability work in the thought of Sarah Coakley and Graham Ward.[7] There would be scope to extend the work of critical analysis to cover further individual cases of the promotion of kenosis and its kin, but criticism alone is not enough: it is difficult to escape from a theological fashion if we cannot identify its attraction, its appeal, *why* it is that so many Christian theologians are currently tempted in this direction. What is at the root of the current fascination with these motifs? What is it that makes them seductive?

There may, of course, be more than one root. The main concern of this chapter will be to follow one possibility – to trace how an attraction to kenosis, vulnerability and fragility can arise from a certain distortion of authentic Christian patterns of responding to suffering and loss – but it is worth touching briefly first on one other possible source of the appeal. One context in which theologians deploy the language of kenosis is when they want to propose that those with power, privilege or authority divest themselves of it, or willingly accept its diminishment.[8] And there are, of course, situations in social, political or church life, where seeking to divest oneself of a degree of privilege and power is the right thing. Typically this is because the accumulation of privilege and power represents an imbalance, probably indeed an injustice. The group of which I am part has, perhaps, historically overstepped, taken too much for itself, and to address this I must find a way to give up what I have become used to thinking of as mine.

What is worth noticing in the invocation of kenosis here is that it suggests an analogy between a group currently in possession of outsized power and privilege, on the one hand, and the divine ('Christ Jesus in the form of God'), on the other, and it suggests a comparison of the powerful group's relinquishing of their power with the pure, unmerited generosity – condescension, even – of the Incarnation of the Son of God. There is a certain irony here: hoping to encourage selflessness and humility, the theologian in fact frames the situation in a way which points in exactly the opposite direction. In a context like this, it may well be more fitting to reach for a term related to repentance than for one which evokes the self-emptying of the Son of God. Of course, it must be admitted, it would not be nearly so attractive: it is surely easier to ask people to forgo power and self-interest – or indeed to persuade myself to do so – if there is a subtle, even subterranean, self-aggrandizement that can be attached to the loss.

---

7. Karen Kilby, *Balthasar: A (Very) Critical Introduction* (Grand Rapids: Eerdmans, 2012), 115–21 and Linn Tonstad, *God and Difference: The Trinity, Sexuality and the Transformation of Finitude* (New York: Routledge, 2016), 58–188.

8. This is at least partly what is at in play in the reference to kenosis in *Towards a Kenotic Vision of Authority in the Catholic Church*, for instance.

Conversations on love and suffering: Some observations

I did not, in my 'Love and Suffering' conversations with the La Retraite sisters, introduce the terms kenosis, vulnerability or fragility as central themes.[9] The conversations, however, circled around broad questions of what can be said positively in relation to suffering and diminishment – how the sisters think about suffering, their own and that which they encounter in others, in relation to love, to God, to grace, to growth and to questions of meaning. Quite a range of types of suffering came up in these conversations: suffering associated with the process of dying, and with the accompaniment of the dying; suffering that comes from living with chronic pain and disability; suffering of frustrated vocation; suffering from tense and fractured family relations; suffering observed in pupils one has taught, or in spiritual directees one has accompanied, or in the lives of migrants or families living with disability; suffering from failure, or guilt, or abuse; suffering associated with the sisters' collective experience of diminishment; the suffering of individuals and communities across the world which we helplessly witness on the ten o'clock news.

There are three strands of reflection that it will be helpful to draw out from these conversations. A first relates to the *manner* in which the sisters were inclined to talk about the positive in the negative – about that which was of meaning and value in or around the experience of suffering, loss, diminishment. The second is about the role that *anger* in the vicinity of suffering played, and some reflections following from that. The third, and most complex, is in relation to a *tension* I stumbled across repeatedly.

When asked about love, God and grace in relation to suffering, the sisters did quite often find positive things to say. Sometimes they would tell of seeming to see in a person dying a purification or distillation, and in the relationship between the dying and those who were with them a kind of growth or deepening or intensification. Sometimes they could tell of moments of surprising, even transforming, grace in the midst of difficult times, where they might have been profoundly touched by the love of another, or by the prayer of a stranger, or indeed by the prayer of one of the other sisters. Sometimes they could speak of the unexpected possibilities that had emerged in the wake of what initially seemed pure pain and loss.

I listened to all this with some anxiety, wondering whether taking seriously the sisters' reflection on their own experience would require me to relinquish my simple, platitudinous hypothesis that suffering and loss are not good. In fact,

---

9. There are two reasons for this. First, while these themes are the central focus of this paper, they are not the centre of the project as a whole – this chapter represents only one strand of the wider project. Secondly, for the sake of a kind of balance in my conversations with the sisters, and in order to get the most, myself, from these conversations, I did not want to root them too heavily in the vagaries of contemporary academic discourse.

however, it didn't seem to. *Why* it didn't might become clear if I say a bit more about the pattern of these conversations.

One thing the sisters' accounts illustrated very clearly is that while there are in the Christian life many testimonies given to the working of grace and the strength of love in the midst of suffering and loss, these are not generalizable. There were stories told to me, for instance, stories which I absolutely believed, of what one might call beautiful deaths, where in the midst of terrible suffering and loss there was growth and depth and reconciliation and peace; but there were also stories told to me of deaths where there was not much other than depression, the sense of meaningless loss and the deepening of family division. There is, it seems to me at least, no formula, no algorithm, by which one can take suffering, and add in a dose of prayer or piety or attentiveness or love, and know that something transformatively meaningful and valuable will appear – this side of the eschaton, anyways.

A second thing I noticed, and which again, once I had identified it, I realize should have been obvious all along, was this: that when the sisters did speak of an encounter with grace in times of suffering, or of having grown through suffering, or growing closer to others in the midst of suffering, they were not generally meaning to suggest that the suffering itself was therefore worthwhile, that its occurrence was *justified* by being an occasion for this grace or growth. People often draw attention to what can be said positively in relation to a negative experience, to whatever element of light in the darkness they can discern, without any hint that what is at stake is the *balancing* of an equation, without any implication that 'therefore it was all worth it', that the suffering itself was therefore after all a good thing. One can speak of love, grace and growth in the midst of suffering, in other words, without being anywhere in the vicinity of a theodicy. As I have come to see it, it is better to understand this sort of attention to grace, growth and love in the midst of suffering as a practice of bearing witness; people are not trying to help make an equation balance, they are not trying to squint with the eyes of faith hard enough until they can see everything as good after all, but they are more simply trying to give witness, insofar as this is possible, and to whatever degree this is possible, to the goodness of God, even in the midst of that which is patently *not* good.

It is worth saying, in connection with this, that at times I found it quite hard to elicit from the sisters with whom I spoke any sort of detailed, concrete account of the 'not good': some would for instance skim in a very minimal way over days, weeks or months of great difficulty in order to tell of the one moment of being uplifted by an unexpected source of support. One might of course interpret this as a form of repression, a British stiff upper lip or its Irish equivalent, but in fact it didn't quite seem that to me, in most cases: it was rather an instinct that suffering itself is not to be denied but it is also not to be dwelt on – what is worth attending to, worth thinking about and coming back to again and again, are those points where something of the work of God is visible, and so those points where there is precisely an opportunity for Christian witness.

One thing I noticed in the sisters, to sum up what I have said so far, then, was an attentiveness to the work of the Spirit in the midst of loss and suffering which was nevertheless *not* any kind of valuing or embrace of suffering itself.

A second interesting thing that came out of these conversations has to do with anger. If one reads around in the literature of pastoral or practical theology about suffering, one frequently comes across the theme of lament, and the need for a reclaiming of the tradition of the psalms, and Jeremiah and Job, a recovery of the tradition of complaining before and to God, and indeed of allowing oneself to be angry with God. So, primed by this literature, in conversation with the sisters, I listened to see if I could hear any hint of this sort of complaint or anger. I could not. I never did hear, either on the surface of what they said or even, as far as I could tell, below the surface, anger directed towards God. Now this does not prove anything at all about the validity or otherwise of that particular theme in pastoral theology – I was talking to a group which was not only relatively small, but which was also made up of people who share a particular spiritual formation. What did seem to me significant, though, was that while I simply couldn't catch any anger, expressed or suppressed, towards God, I did on more than one occasion hear quite clear anger articulated in relation to other *people*, and specifically anger towards others who responded in the wrong way to a situation of suffering – people who, for instance, wanted to fix something which couldn't be fixed, or who ignored a situation of suffering which shouldn't be ignored, or who wanted to force some kind of understanding, some kind of meaning, onto it.

These themes, together with a casual comment from one of the sisters early on that what seems appropriate to say depends on who is speaking, have led me to reflect increasingly on the position of the *onlooker* to suffering, the one who has to respond to a suffering which is not their own, especially the onlooker who is not in a position to 'fix' something. It is clear that it makes a vital difference, in any talk about suffering, whether I am talking about my suffering, or yours, or theirs – whether I am in a first- or second- or third-person relation to suffering. It is not easy to find the right stance towards someone else's suffering – as some of the anger I heard made clear, there are a range of ways in which this can and does go painfully wrong. This is at least partly because there are certain types of things that can be said in relation to *my* suffering – perhaps finding some meaning and value, something positive in it, bearing witness, in the way I have been discussing – that usually can*not* be said in relation to yours or to theirs. So we find ourselves uncomfortable, in relation to other people's suffering, not really knowing how to proceed, not really knowing what to say. Indeed this is a thing which perhaps makes theologians – to anticipate what I will return to in the next section – whose job seems to have to do with explaining and making sense of things and having something to say, particularly uncomfortable.

The last thing I want to explore, in relation to my collaboration with the La Retraite sisters – before returning once again to kenosis – is a particular *tension* that emerged in various ways in our conversations. I first noticed it in the report of a past disagreement, or at least a past discussion, between two sisters, about attitudes to death. Both had nursed their mothers through final illnesses, extraordinarily difficult in one case and even more terrible in the other. One of the sisters had been quite interested by a work of theology she read, which argued that we ought not try to reconcile ourselves to death, but should instead understand it as the enemy, whom Christ came to defeat. The other sister, I was told, had been a little resistant to this, thinking that couldn't be right, because death is organic, part of nature.

A second version of what I consider the same tension came in my own reaction to a range of comments I heard. One sister spoke of imagining love and suffering as like two different colours of yarn, out of which our lives are knit, like a jumper. Joy and sorrow, said another interlocutor, occur in our experience a bit like the movement of a sine wave, always alternating.[10] Diminishment and loss are part of the order of things, they are natural, part of reality, they happen. These sorts of comments were aimed, it seemed to me, towards a kind of wisdom about coming to terms with things, about making our peace with sorrow, suffering, loss and death, seeing and accepting them in the larger context into which they fit.[11] The tension this time arose, as I said, from my reaction to the comments – how is all this consistent with a Christian vision, where Jesus surely *did* come to defeat death; where he healed the lame and the sick, and never once was recorded as counselling them towards acceptance of their loss; where we trust that all shall be well, and that every tear shall be wiped away?

I also saw this same tension – a tension, one might say, between acceptance of and resistance to suffering and loss – in what initially I took to be an inconsistency within the position of a single sister. She was at many points in our conversations an advocate for the kind of acceptance I've just been discussing – indeed she was the sister who referred to death as organic, part of nature. Yet there was one occasion when, in speaking to the group as a whole, and in the context of discussing their increasing frailty, their likely diminishment before next they gathered, she almost casually dropped into the conversation, 'Of course we believe we'll meet again.' It was casually mentioned, not in the sense that the underlying belief came across as in any way casually held, but actually the reverse: the underlying belief was so secure, so much a given and a shared conviction that a passing, light reference was all that was necessary.

---

10. This particular comment came not from one of the sisters, but from a Catholic priest in Port Elizabeth, South Africa, to whom I was introduced by someone the sisters had put me in contact with. This is an example of a certain centrifugal force that seemed to govern the process the sisters initiated with me: during the period of focused, deliberate conversations with the sisters, I also found myself in surprisingly intense conversation with a range of others, including not only friends and connections of the sisters but also neighbours, friends, research students from my department and colleagues I met at conferences.

11. I noticed that none of the sisters to whom I spoke ever spoke in these terms in relation to suffering and loss which are the product of evil or injustice, nor in relation to the serious illness or death of children.

What coherence can there be, I thought, in putting one's spiritual energies into acceptance – acceptance of suffering and loss and death – while also putting one's faith in the resurrection, which, if it is a resurrection in which 'we'll meet again', presumably must involve the overcoming of suffering and loss and death? Should I just suppose that this particular sister, profound though she is, harbours inconsistent attitudes and beliefs? After all, don't we all?

I've come to think, to the contrary, that this tension is best understood if it is contextualized within the broader theme of the relationship of nature to grace. There is in Catholic theology, or at least in the best Catholic theology, always something paradoxical in the relation of nature to grace, the natural to the supernatural. Nature, created by God, is held to be good, to be valued and to be affirmed: it has its own kind of integrity, a certain wholeness. And yet there is also the so-called natural desire for the supernatural: nature is also yearning for something more. It is incomplete, desiring to go beyond itself. It is whole and it is not whole. At the centre of nature is a longing to transcend nature.[12]

The tension that ran through these conversations can, then, be understood as a fairly straightforward outworking or enactment of this Catholic nature/grace dialectic. There is, on the one hand, an entirely appropriate natural wisdom that says all finite beings are limited, frail, part of a cycle that includes diminishment and death, and we ourselves are natural beings, part of all this. If we are grateful for all that is good in life, and appreciate it, then we also have to see and accept its limitations, its cyclical quality, that diminishment and an end are just built into things, that love and suffering do in fact come together, interwoven. Furthermore, though this may be a natural, universally available wisdom, we have to work particularly hard today, as Christians, to re-attune ourselves to it, because we live at a time and in a culture that is often in a kind of rebellion against this wisdom, in denial of diminishment and death, which thinks that with enough Enlightened good will and planning and technology, these things should be avoided – and if, unfortunately, they can't, they are an embarrassment that should at least be brushed to the edges of society and of consciousness.

On the one hand, then, there is a natural wisdom which works to make its peace with finitude, with diminishment and loss and, at least to a degree, sorrow and suffering – a natural wisdom which, under current cultural conditions, we have to work harder to attain. On the other hand, there is also, properly, a hope which transcends this, which longs for the defeat of death and an end to sorrow and suffering, and which becomes, concretely, for Christians, faith in the resurrection and the life of the world to come. Just as the best of Catholic theology, from Aquinas to de Lubac and Rahner, is marked by paradox in the way it holds

---

12. I have explored the paradoxes of Catholic thought around nature and grace in a little more depth in a paper originally given at the Leuven Encounters in Systematic Theology XI Conference, entitled 'Catholicism, Protestantism and the Theological Location of Paradox: Nature, Grace, Sin', which will be published in my *God, Evil and the Limits of Theology* (London: T&T Clark, 2020).

together nature and grace, so we find, when the sisters think about their response to suffering and loss, a certain tension, a paradoxical holding on *both* to a wisdom about the need to grow into reconciliation with some kinds of suffering and loss, *and* to a confident hope which leaps beyond it.

Drawing the strands together: The seductions of kenosis

How does all this help with understanding kenosis? It is possible to draw some of these strands together into a story, a possible account, of how it is that we have got to the point we have, a point where these concepts of kenosis, vulnerability and fragility have become so attractive, so appealing, so widely called upon – how it is that we have come to a point where theologians are tempted to treat loss, diminishment, the capacity to be wounded and the capacity to be broken, as somehow good things.

Let's grant, then, first of all, that the wider Western culture suffers from an excessive fear and denial of suffering, of diminishment and loss, of vulnerability and fragility, an excessive fear of finitude. As a culture, speaking very broadly, we don't know how to conduct ourselves around death. We want techniques to ensure everyone's happiness. We treat suffering as a mark of failure, are most at ease with able-bodied, independent youth, and think of everything which deviates from this as somehow in need of fixing. Christian theologians, among others, quite rightly sense that a corrective, a rebalancing, is necessary. The strand in the La Retraite conversations about seeing and accepting that joy and suffering are interwoven, that our lives are knitted out of both love and suffering, that death and diminishment are natural and something to make one's peace with, are pointers to just this sort of necessary rebalancing – they are efforts to regain, to become reconnected to, a fundamental human wisdom about the nature of creaturely, limited finitude.

It is possible, however, in attempting to offer a corrective to what is wrong in our culture, to go too far. It is possible to go beyond an *acceptance* of limitation and the inescapability of some suffering in the order of things, to its *embrace*. It is possible, that is to say, to go beyond the recognition that vulnerability and fragility are part of the whole that makes up our lives, and that the experience of diminishment is part of the experience of life, to the *celebration* of vulnerability and fragility – to the celebration, under the title of *kenosis,* of diminishment.

Why might this happen? Here I think it is worth returning to the difficulty of second- and third- person relationships to suffering, the problematic situation of not knowing what to do, or what to say, in the face of the suffering of another, especially when one has no cure, no fix. I think this is something theologians may sometimes feel in a particularly acute way. We are, after all, in the *business* of having something to say, of contributing something by way of understanding and new perspective. In the face of massive suffering in the world, it doesn't feel right to remain dumb, silent. Theologians of our era, I suspect, feel this in a particularly acute way, not because there is more suffering in our time but because certain frameworks for understanding suffering which seemed to bring intellectual satisfaction in the past will not quite do the job for us anymore.[13]

So theologians of our time feel they have to have something to say in relation to suffering, by way of making things meaningful, or offering some consolation. What is arguably the most drastic example, at a theoretical level, of trying to find the meaning, the good news, in other people's suffering, is the attempt to provide a theodicy, a justification all at once of all the suffering there is in the world, an understanding of how all the apparent evil in the world is really in one way or another in service to a greater good. Even theologians who do not go all the way to a theodicy, however, who do not try to tackle the whole thing all at once, can still feel the burden, perhaps the pressure, of having *something* to say, something to contribute, *some* way to bring consolation to the situation and to be seen to be taking it seriously. Perhaps, then, it is this pressure which explains why it is so appealing to find some way to perform a kind of *flip* with at least some kinds of suffering, to find a way of discovering that what we had thought bad is really secretly, subtly good. This is what makes it so appealing to go beyond that common sense platitude with which I began, to discover value in emptying and loss, in vulnerability or fragility.

And of course, in doing this one is doing something which sounds reassuringly quite *similar* to a familiar and authentic Christian practice. As the sisters' testimony exemplified, Christians do at times find that growth and grace are given in the midst of suffering and diminishment, that in our times of weakness the Spirit can work, and Christians do bear witness to this, telling of whatever it is they can spy of the goodness of God and the working of the Spirit, the power of love, in the midst even of the darkest times. It can sound only a very small step to go from this to something which is in reality quite different, to go from 'in our diminishment, we have encountered grace, discerned the workings of the Spirit' to 'diminishment is grace, it *is* the working of the Spirit'; it can sound only a small step from 'even in the darkness, we met something of the light' to 'the darkness is, after all, in its depths, the light'. In a similar way it can sound only a very small step to go from 'much that we value in life is fragile, and there are goods that make us vulnerable' to 'fragility is a value, and vulnerability is good'.

So theology can be seduced into valuing kenosis, and vulnerability and fragility, through a combination of factors: first of all, we know that there is something wrong in our culture somewhere near these issues, some too-great fear of suffering and loss, and we can fall into thinking that it is a unique contribution of the Christian faith to provide a corrective, to go in exactly the opposite direction, reacting against the flight from suffering by instead undertaking an embrace of suffering. Secondly, we can feel that we *have* to have something positive to say

---

13. The primary framing of suffering in much of the pre-modern Western tradition was as consequence of and punishment for *sin*, particularly original sin. Within the space opened up by this primary answer it was then also possible to say various things about God's providential use of suffering, to strengthen, mature, test and so on.

about suffering, we have to find a goodness and meaning and value in it, because that is our role as theologians: to contemplate all that suffering of others without having something positive to do in relation to it, some way to contribute towards making things better, is just very uncomfortable. Finally, we can be seduced into valuing kenosis, vulnerability and fragility because to do so sounds so familiar, sounds so similar to authentic practices of bearing witness to the goodness of God, the working of the Spirit, even in the midst of diminishment, woundedness and brokenness.

What shall we do instead? What shall we do, in relation to suffering, specifically as theologians? If one asked the question in relation to all Christians, there would of course be a huge range of answers: I avoid suffering where I can, I bear it patiently where I can't, or I do not bear it patiently but lament and complain and struggle with God as does Job; I work to eradicate suffering where I can; I repent of my contribution to the ills of the world, the suffering I have caused; I seek to listen, to be present, to accompany those who suffer; I accept suffering if it is necessary for my vocation, for the life of discipleship; I look for ways, even in the midst of this suffering, that I can continue to grow, if there are such ways; I look out for the presence of God, the gifts of the Holy Spirit, even in times that seem most desolate; and so on. But specifically as theologians, what shall we do in the face of suffering, if it is not that we find ways to make it secretly good, to allow ourselves to be seduced into valuing kenosis, vulnerability and fragility? Perhaps, again, there are many things, but I want to suggest two in particular. First, we have to cultivate a certain ascesis, a certain restraint, the capacity not to find meaning where it does not exist, or where we have no right to it. This does not come automatically: such an ascesis is a genuine intellectual work, which requires attention, effort and education. Secondly, we have to cultivate a certain incompleteness; we have to remember to keep a place in our theological systems, or our theological reflections, for hope in that which goes absolutely beyond anything these systems can offer or grasp, hope in the eventual triumph of love over suffering, joy over loss.

Chapter 15

ON VULNERABILITY

Linn Tonstad

The concern driving this chapter is the frequency with which theologians and cultural theorists invite us to affirm vulnerability. The need to affirm vulnerability has become very nearly a theological and theoretical truism, insistently prescribed as a remedy for any number of contemporary ills. The reason we need to affirm vulnerability, we are told, is found in some version of the following story, sometimes told more and sometimes less explicitly: The autonomous, rational, self-determining, self-transparent subject of modernity was built upon the denial and externalization of certain fear-inducing features of human existence onto those made, through that projection, somewhat less than human: women, animals, colonized peoples and so on – all of whom were associated with excessive bodiliness in different ways. That is, unable to deal with his own vulnerability, the modern subject – usually traced to Kant, Descartes, or both – distinguished himself from a variety of others by associating them with the vulnerabilities the modern subject could not admit to himself. That autonomous, rational, self-determining, self-transparent subject of modernity – I will from here on call him Man, with a capital M – is a destructive fiction that continues to determine, or at least affect, differential distributions of political, economic and social power, based on the closeness or distance variously classified persons and creatures have to this fictional ideal. Thus, Man must be overcome in order to open the door to new, or previously denied or denigrated, ways of being human together. Overcoming Man requires, it is assumed, recovering the vulnerability that the production of Man denies. Thus, prevalent responses to the problem of Man – at least the genre of problem that concerns me in this chapter – use one or both of the following strategies to bring vulnerability back.

In the first strategy, one demonstrates just the pattern I've briefly summarized: Man is produced by projecting his own vulnerabilities onto his others, thereby distinguishing himself from them. His autonomy is thus always a false autonomy, predicated on the subjugation of others and the denial of his dependent relationality to and with them. *Man* cannot, then, be a theory of the human as such, nor can he serve any longer as a regulative ideal for how human beings ought to live. Man needs to be destabilized, made visibly dependent, and so overcome. It is sadly easy to find illustrative examples of the pattern this story describes. For instance, one might point to Immanuel Kant's dependence on racialized theories of both literal and symbolic blackness (or maybe his 'literal' blackness was always already symbolic) to distinguish the rational, Enlightenment-made Man from his others. Justifications of colonialism depended on theories of the human that positioned the colonized subject as a less developed, often more child-like, kind of human being who needed to be tutored, classified and ruled so that he might learn to rise even to the (limited) heights that were his full capacity. There are plenty of other examples one might mention. Once the dependence of Man on his others is shown, the hope is that such demonstration will contribute to loosening the hold of Man on the sociopolitical imagination. Man was always already dependent, and in that dependence always already vulnerable – but the production of Man required a denial of just that vulnerability.

Which suggests, immediately, what the second strategy will be (I'm distinguishing them analytically, though they are often found together). The second strategy requires the *affirmation of vulnerability* – and here, vulnerability refers not just to the dependence of the idea of Man on the others made yet more vulnerable by Man's projection of his vulnerabilities onto them but to an affirmation of vulnerability as a feature of human, particularly bodied, existence *as such*. The theological incarnations of this second strategy often insist also on *divine vulnerability*, a point to which we'll return later. At a minimum, the affirmation of vulnerability insists on vulnerability's inescapability for finite, bodied creatures. In this version, affirming vulnerability probably means something more like *recognizing* vulnerability – with a positive affect attached. That is, we need to recognize vulnerability because we are prone to forget it, and in recognizing vulnerability we need to approach it with a *subjective attitude* that it is good, even if we are discussing its possible ambivalences. Since we know that we tend to forget or deny vulnerability, we need to associate it with goodness – to make it desirable – as a corrective to our temptation to forget or deny it. In maximalist incarnations of this strategy, vulnerability is not merely inescapable, requiring recognition but a positive good, requiring active affirmation. Vulnerability, here, *is* good. Typically, it is good in several ways.

The first way is that it provides a counter to sovereignty. That is, the goodness of vulnerability is not just that it *shows* sovereignty to be a fiction, as in the strategy above – the goodness of vulnerability lies also in the effects of recognizing its significance. In valuing vulnerability, we devalue sovereignty, and devaluing sovereignty helps to prevent some of its destructive effects. This is a strategy of reversal. But strategies of reversal may not always be effective, because they are prone to accept the terms on which a problem is posed *within the system of value that the strategy of reversal seeks to correct*. What is changed is primarily which member of a contrastive pair is placed where, or made more valuable, not whether the contrastive distinction is the right place to start when trying to change what needs to be changed.

The second way vulnerability is *good* is that it makes various *goods* possible, or that it is an associated condition of various desirable goods – including the good of bodied being itself. Ed Farley – about whom more later – is a leading proponent of this strategy. He emphasizes that many of the goods of bodied being, of temporal existence, of relationship, even of the particular ways we exist – since we are part of evolutionary processes – require or entail vulnerabilities that are often enacted in ambiguous or highly destructive ways. By implication, if we want to affirm goods like bodied being, which, presumably, we do, we *must* affirm also the vulnerabilities that make them possible, without being too distracted by their tragic ambiguities. So far, we might be dealing only with logical entailment: we'd be reminded not to deny the conditions of possibility of the goods we want to examine or uphold. Since bodied being is the condition of our existence and bodied being entails certain vulnerabilities, we must not pretend that those vulnerabilities don't exist or forget that we couldn't have bodied being as we have it without those vulnerabilities.

But the situation is, I think, a bit more complicated than that, and it is those complications that interest me. We are told that we want to deny vulnerability because we are ruled by a cultural ideal of Man. Therefore, neither recognition nor reversal is sufficient unless accompanied by a subjectively intense appropriation of vulnerability. The subject, it is assumed, does not know its vulnerability, or, if it knows it, seeks to flee its recognition. Therefore, the subject must be reminded, impressed, intensely riven by reminders of vulnerability. The insistence of vulnerability must be impressed upon the subject (hearer or reader), written into the flesh. I want to note three typical, though not universal, aspects of such insistence. First, the sense that vulnerability needs to be impressed upon the hearer means that the one who wants vulnerability to be recognized and valued needs to keep upping the ante, as it were, so that the presumptively resistant hearer will come around to the required subjective appropriation of vulnerability. Second, the hearer, who needs to be convinced of vulnerability and its value, is – precisely because that hearer needs to be convinced of their own vulnerability – placed at a distance from vulnerability, a distance that then needs to be traversed. Third, insisting on vulnerability in distinction from sovereignty or self-possession can reinstantiate the centrality of sovereignty or self-possession as that which always needs to be overcome – and at the same time it can also intensify rather than ameliorate the relationship between vulnerability and self-securitization. Let me develop this last point a little.

The affirmation of vulnerability is intended to have political effects, to provide the basis for a new political solidarity of the vulnerable. To learn the vulnerability that one has denied will dismantle attachment to the hope of sovereignty and so allow for solidarities that will then transform the conditions of political action. If we could acknowledge, rather than deny, our vulnerability, the solidarity that would emerge would avoid the differential positioning of subjects along lines of the more or less human. The hoped-for effect of a solidarity of vulnerability would be the end of the differential enforcement of *specific kinds* of vulnerability on different segments of the population: the degree to which health care access is determined by personal and national wealth; the intensified policing, incarceration, and, at least in the United States, state-sanctioned killing of Black and Brown populations; the common practice of siting pollution-emitting chemical plants near resource-poor communities and on and on.

However, the contemporary socioeconomic and political order doesn't necessarily work by denying vulnerability, but by intensifying it. We're not told that we are safe and secure and have nothing to worry about. Instead, we're told that our way of life is under threat, that we need to protect our borders – because we are vulnerable, that we need to work harder and accomplish more because our futures are unstable and insecure. So making the intensification and appropriation of vulnerability one's project can – it doesn't *have to*, but it can – make the project of self-securitization more rather than less subjectively powerful. What's more, the project of affirming our vulnerability, rather than fleeing it and seeking security, may require us to be what one theorist calls 'ethical intentionalists who can make cognitive decisions to short-circuit foundational affective attachments'.[1] Does, in other words, requiring a transformative relation to vulnerability require or engender something much like the very project of mastery vulnerability intends to undo? I will return to that question at the end of this chapter.

In sum, then, I've suggested that an emphasis on vulnerability, and the need to affirm it, is found in both theological and theoretical conversations; that the emphasis on vulnerability is intended to have salutary political, economic and social effects, though it may not always work as hoped; and that emphasizing vulnerability is taken to be necessary because of its denial in modernity, particularly in the production of the figure of Man. I've also pointed out that this narrative requires vulnerability to be affirmed in both affectively and substantively intense ways as a response to its presumed denial.

In the next section of this discussion, I turn to developing this general picture through a somewhat more detailed examination of vulnerability's workings in contemporary theological discourse, with respect to human beings as well as God.

A classic theology of vulnerability is found in Edward Farley's 1990 book *Good and Evil: Interpreting a Human Condition*. Farley emphasizes the constitutive character of vulnerabilities in human existence, which are neither sinful nor 'bad', even though they are often conflictual and lead to tragic effects or suffering.[2] Yet pain, negativity and suffering are not themselves evil; they are unavoidable aspects of creation that have to be accepted and affirmed if the goodness of creation is to be held at all. In other words, Farley moves many features of human existence that theologians have often ascribed to the effects of sin *away* from sin and into the arena of what has to be affirmed if we are to hold to the goodness of creation.

Farley defines vulnerability as 'an entity's capacity of being damaged, distorted, or even eliminated. [Vulnerability's] realization is always some kind of suffering. The absolute vulnerability of any living thing is the vulnerability to death.'[3] What he means by vulnerability's realization is the difference between vulnerability as

---

1. Lauren Berlant, *Cruel Optimism* (Durham: Duke University Press, 2011), 182.
2. Edward Farley, *Good and Evil: Interpreting a Human Condition* (Minneapolis: Augsburg Fortress, 1990), 29, 62.
3. Farley, *Good and Evil*, 57. See also 43.

potential – the potential to be damaged – and vulnerability as realized – damage made actual.

I want to draw attention to that distinction – vulnerability as potential damage, and vulnerability as the experience of damage – because it concerns the effects affirmation of vulnerability is intended to have, and it often seems to be neglected or underplayed. Vulnerability as a fundamental condition names a state in which all beings live – even the rich die, and not always of old age (sometimes they die in small plane crashes, or of liver cancer). Any bodied being is *potentially* vulnerable to harm, whether from violence, disease or accident, though (and crucially) not all of us are *equally* vulnerable to specific kinds of harm.[4]

Farley's distinction between vulnerability as potential and vulnerability as actual harm is not always held as carefully as one might like, and the distinction opens some other questions as well. The first concerns the relationship between vulnerability and harm. Second, we might ask about the relationship between vulnerability and contingency.

Returning to Farley's definition, to be vulnerable is to have the capacity or potential to be damaged or distorted. This is true of any finite existent. That capacity is a permanent state; because of the multidimensionality of human existence, it is almost certainly being realized in some dimension of our existence at every time. When vulnerability is *realized*, when it moves from the potential to the actual, the event or experience is one of suffering. The realization of vulnerability is always suffering, in Farley's account, because the realization of vulnerability is the actualization of harm. Now, not everyone who wants to affirm vulnerability takes seriously what Farley says here, I think – perhaps because of a possible confusion (or elision) between contingency and vulnerability that I will come back to in a moment.

Farley includes in the harm that defines vulnerability 'both the frustration of the needs and desires of [the] creature and the pain and suffering that accompany that frustration'.[5] As a result, harm – the realization of vulnerability – becomes an extremely broad term, one that slides across a range of meanings from the non-actualization of some desire of mine all the way to physical and emotional violence, including their worst aspects. Vulnerability, when not accepted in all its tragic ambiguity, can lead to sin and evil, but because the tragic ambiguity of vulnerability is neither sin nor evil in itself, Farley argues for less destructive ways of living with vulnerability.

Farley worries about specifically theological denials of vulnerability: one names the tragic structure of human existence as an effect of sin rather than a necessary

---

4. Ruth Wilson Gilmore defines racism as 'state-sanctioned or extra-legal production or exploitation of group-differentiated vulnerability to premature death', so it is just the enactment on some populations of vulnerabilities shared by all that constitutes racism on her account. See *Golden Gulag: Prisons, Surplus, Crisis and Opposition in Globalizing California* (Berkeley: University of California Press, 2007), 28.

5. Farley, *Good and Evil*, 43.

condition of the realization of all the goods of created being, while the other denies the inescapability of these tragic effects by projecting an impossible-to-realize ideal of harmony rather than advocating the fragile work of reconciliation *within* ambiguity. Farley's concern is that such theological denials remove the possibility of grappling with the reality of the human situation in order to transform it. Farley's analytic – which is worthy of far more attention and critical consideration than I give it here – allows us to *consider some differences.*

First, as we have seen, vulnerability is in a certain sense a constitutive, inescapable condition of all bodied being. Yet *vulnerability as such* covers a vast range of affectively, emotionally, physically and socially differentiated (but of course connected, as human beings are not divisible into distinct parts) experiences, threats and types of suffering and harm. When I am asked to affirm vulnerability, what am I being asked to affirm, and what does it mean to affirm it? That is, what kind of relation to vulnerability is its affirmation, and what is the difference between affirmation and recognition? What does it mean to affirm something that is the basic condition within which I live? Do I affirm the air I breathe? Do I affirm my bodily dependence on my environment (material and relational), and so my vulnerability, when I go on existing? Or must I do something more to affirm it – and if so, what understanding of the self's relation to itself is required when that demand is made? That is, is the self-transparent, self-determining subject that the affirmation of vulnerability was intended to overcome being brought back in at another point – the point at which I can knowingly, intentionally make the affirmation of vulnerability a project for myself – to produce a more authentic self?[6]

Vulnerability as a condition is absolute (because we all die), but that condition is also made up of many different vulnerabilities that are not absolute in the way death is. To take a trivial example: not getting into medical school, as one desired to, and becoming a dentist instead. Who or what is it that is harmed in that experience of actualized vulnerability? There's a certain harm, perhaps, in the disappointment of a desire and the loss of the anticipated satisfactions that, in the imagination, accompanied the decision to become a doctor rather than a dentist. But let's say that it turns out that I love being a dentist, and that I meet the person I end up marrying as well as several lifelong friends in dental school. Reading such a situation through lenses of vulnerability and harm, rather than contingency, may also require a vision of the human being as non-conflicted and aware of her desire – rather than inwardly conflicted and composed of all sorts of desires and imaginative visions with different levels of lived seriousness or depth.[7]

Examples like this turn our attention to the relation between vulnerability and contingency. The *actualization* of a particular vulnerability is often a matter of contingency: it might or might not have happened, but it did. It might have

---

6. It's clear that Farley doesn't intend anything like this.

7. It may also entail imposing a temporal frozenness and determination by abstracting from the lived reality of desire's development.

happened another way, but it didn't. The experience of vulnerability's actualization – that is, the experience of actual harm – is therefore closely bound up with contingency. But contingency and vulnerability are not the same, and some difficulties in theological approaches to vulnerability are due to a lack of attention to such differences. Vulnerability is, as Farley made clear, tied to the capacity to be harmed: to be vulnerable is to be harmable. But vulnerability is not necessarily *lived* or encountered as harmability all the time, because vulnerability is often negotiated through the possibilities, the goods, that specific vulnerabilities accompany – the goods, not the vulnerability, are the point, the focus – at least until the point of loss. Vulnerability's actualization involves a change; vulnerability as a condition involves the capacity to change or be changed for the worse – to be harmed. But contingency maps both the possibility of being changed for the worse and the possibility of being changed for the better – of new, unexpected possibilities arising, of a change that might involve a dramatic disidentification with what and who one was *without harm* being an illuminating lens through which to consider that change.

Some changes – changes for the better[8] – involve loss only in the sense that life is lived in time. Thus, I want to suggest, it would be better to see vulnerability and contingency as related, but non-identical, aspects of human existence. Vulnerability, the capacity to be harmed, and contingency, the capacity to change – or the being-only-as-becoming that is an intrinsic feature of human life until death – aren't the same, even if they both derive from the bodied and temporal nature of finite existence.

What, then, is the relationship between demands to affirm vulnerability in the human case and discussions of divine vulnerability? The versions of divine vulnerability developed in the twentieth and twenty-first centuries are almost innumerable. Traceable perhaps to certain lines from the Heidelberg Disputation, at least in one form, the turn to divine vulnerability accompanies the worries about sovereignty, self-possession and self-determination that we discussed earlier in terms of the human, but many of these discussions of divine vulnerability are also often doing something else. I said above that the affirmation of vulnerability for human beings is intended to have salutary social, economic and political effects. What are discussions of divine vulnerability intended to do?

A standard trajectory of argument for the necessity of divine vulnerability departs from Aquinas's denial of a real relation between God and the world, on the God-side, and argues that a God that cannot be related to the world, affected by the world, is also a God that cannot love, that cannot experience compassion and sympathy. Any first-year student of Thomas typically knows the correct answers to that charge, which have very little to do with whether God can love and have compassion on the world, and a great deal to do with what a *relation* is thought to be in a Thomistic sense. But for many, such technical answers are either

---

8. Leaving aside for now the obviously significant question of how one knows that something is a change for the better.

insufficient or irrelevant. For others – I'm thinking here of typical trajectories in process thought – divine vulnerability and relationality are the result of the adoption of certain metaphysical principles that are thought better to exemplify real dynamics in the world and universe than those on offer in 'classical' Christian thought. Divine vulnerability in its contemporary forms emerges primarily as a response to the dilemma so important in modernity: What does it mean to say that a perfectly good God loves a world as marked by vulnerability, harm and suffering as the one we inhabit – and what, in particular, does it mean to say that within a *Christian* narrative in which, in some sense, suffering is not the end – even though for so many untimely struck down, it so evidently appears to be?

In Emmanuel Katongole's *Born from Lament: The Theology and Politics of Hope in Africa*, which focuses on post-conflict Congo, he offers a thoughtful examination of the role of lament as an enactment of hope in relation to God amid horrendous suffering and the wreckage it leaves behind. For now, I want to look only at a small section in the middle of this rich book, where he draws some conclusions that illustrate the concerns driving much talk about divine vulnerability. Lament, Katongole points out, is a complaint to God: 'God has not delivered; [God] has hidden [God's] face from the people.'[9] The one who laments calls God to account in situations where God is not acting as the saving God that God has covenanted to be. But, as Katongole points out, calling God to account (as the lamenter does) risks that God may *still* not answer. And when God does not answer, one's trust in God's faithfulness and justice may be put to so stringent a test that it does not recover.

> The fact that God quite often remains silent and hidden in the midst of the people's anguished cries for deliverance raises serious questions, not so much about God's saving power, but about what kind of God would remain silent and unresponsive to the peoples' pleas. Might God's silence point to a God who may be in some ways 'powerless' in the face of human evil … a God who … suffers and laments with [God's] people? If we grasp this possibility, … what begins to emerge … is the reality of a vulnerable and suffering God.[10]

Katongole sees 'immense personal, social, and political possibilities' emerging as a result. When God is recognized as vulnerable and suffering, then 'the silence of God in the psalms of lament cannot be interpreted as that of an uncaring God'. Instead, God's silence is *because* God 'suffers and laments with [God's people]'.[11] Katongole amasses some biblical evidence for his view of a suffering God: the God who hears the cries of God's suffering people and has compassion on them; Jesus who 'weeps at the death of Lazarus' and cries out from the cross to the God who has

---

9. Emmanuel Katongole, *Born from Lament: The Theology and Politics of Hope in Africa* (Grand Rapids: Eerdmans, 2017), 111.
10. Ibid., 111–12, partly following Ellington; quote on 112.
11. Ibid., 114.

abandoned him.¹² None of that evidence necessitates, or even I think quite justifies, the notion of a 'vulnerable and suffering God' without further qualification, unless one has already defined compassion as a quality that can only be shown by those who are not just vulnerable to suffering but who indeed *suffer*. The exception is the cry of dereliction, but as the history of theological reflection shows, that cry can be interpreted in a variety of ways. But Katongole's vulnerable God is not, I think, really supposed to be justified by the biblical evidence. Instead, it is the only road he sees open to avoid positing an uncaring God, in order to *save faith in a saving God* in a context of vast suffering.

Katongole speculates that resistance to a 'vulnerable/hidden/crucified God' – note that these are not necessarily the same – in African theology is because Africans 'expect their gods to be bigger, stronger, more powerful, and more enduring than humans', as he puts it.¹³ I don't know whether that's a fair assessment, but Katongole misses that his account of God makes the same kind of mistake: measuring divine power by its size, on a human scale of what power must be and how it must act. Katongole misses this point for reasons that are quite understandable and bring us back to what we cannot understand – even as we live in its midst. The missing premise of his argument is that if God could act, God would, in ways that would be recognizable and predictable, and that would prevent the horrendous suffering humans experience. Because God has not, as far as we can tell, acted to prevent or to heal the situations of terror and suffering that Katongole examines, God must be either uncaring or, in some sense, vulnerable and 'powerless'. (It's worth noting the association between vulnerability and powerlessness here, as their converse accompaniment, what they're being distinguished from, is that which is powerful and invulnerable – which is just the problem.)

Katongole's basic dilemma is an existentially powerful incarnation of the well-known theodical dilemma: God is good, God is all-powerful, evil exists – which one are you going to give up? The standard answer, given by almost every systematic theologian of the kind that I am, is that *none* of them should be given up: they should stand there, in their contradiction, with all the concomitant challenges for faith and understanding – because otherwise one is trying to understand something that precisely eludes understanding; one is rationalizing both evil and God, neither of which (for very different reasons) is rightly rationalizable. But God's power, in classical Christian thought, is of a different kind than all other kinds of power and so cannot be measured by its purported presence or absence within creation's gaps.

Katongole opens up the response not of protest atheism but of protest theism: lament, calling God to account, as one of the forms that faith takes in contexts of suffering. But there is more: Katongole helps us see that the effect vulnerability-talk is intended to have is not just solidarity among humans, achieved by learning one's own vulnerability, as we saw earlier. The people Katongole discusses do not

---

12. Ibid., 113.
13. Ibid., 120.

need to learn that they are vulnerable; in many cases, they have been given the opportunity to know little else. Divine vulnerability is intended, by Katongole, to address just that fact: humans are *so* vulnerable that the only alternative to an uncaring God that he can find is a God who cares by co-suffering.

The potential consequences of such a move become even more evident in another theologian, Paul Fiddes, who shares some of these concerns. Fiddes, like Katongole, wants the outcome of divine action to be certain, at least in some sense. Katongole has no doubt about God's transformative work and salvific power, but he wants to say something to contexts within which God's transformative work seems invisible or absent. Fiddes – I focus here on his discussion in *The Promised End*, though he has canvassed these themes several times – wants to avoid the inverse problem that concerns Katongole. If Katongole is worried that God seems uncaring in situations of tremendous suffering, Fiddes is worried about triumphalist reconciliations that posit divine overcoming of all suffering and unreconciliation as well as about the apparent destruction of freedom, contingency and choice in human existence if God's final plan is known from the beginning and carried out as writ. Fiddes's solution is illustrative for the concern that's appeared several times in this chapter, that emphasis on vulnerability can also bring mastery back.

Fiddes argues that,

> a God who depends upon nothing outside God's own self for existence (is self-existent, having *aseity*) may still, *out of pure free will*, become dependent upon others for enrichment of the divine life. The Creator who is perfect in the sense of having no deficiency at any stage of relationship with creation, may still *choose* to be in need and to be completed by those who are created.[14]

Note how *intensified* divine sovereignty becomes in this sequence. God *freely chooses to become dependent*. I don't quite understand what dependence means here, but its meaning may be illuminated by looking at what Fiddes wants divine dependence to accomplish. Fiddes wants God's victory over evil to be certain, but he wants the road to that victory to allow room for plenty of contingency *and* for the possible non-reconciliation of parts of reality.[15] God takes what Fiddes calls a 'limited risk': there is no danger that the end will be total tragedy and futility (although I don't quite see why that would be true on Fiddes's account – he calls it a 'wager' that Christians make on 'love as the strongest power in the universe'[16]), but there is still some risk of a 'possible tragedy … that there will be an absence of some good that might have been produced'. God knows where God intends to go, but 'what is reconciled may be less than it might have been. … God may see,

---

14. Paul S. Fiddes, *The Promised End: Eschatology in Theology and Literature* (Oxford: Blackwell, 2000), 174. This 'suggests a vulnerable God, whose power is when in loving persuasion and not coercion' (174–5). First emphasis added.

15. Fiddes, *The Promised End*, 23.

16. Ibid., 178.

as finite persons will not, that some possibilities have not been actualized, some potentials have not been fulfilled.'[17] There are three problems that concern Fiddes. One, if humans don't contribute significantly to the realization of divine purposes, then human existence is empty and meaningless waiting. Two, the contingency of events along the road to reconciliation – the contributions that humans make – mean, due to the nature of finitude, that some goods won't be realized because others will have been chosen. And three, the non-chosenness or non-actualization of some goods constitutes Fiddes's 'possible tragedy'.

I think Fiddes makes some mistakes here. He makes substantial the 'nothing' out of which creation is made, so that the actualization of one good rather than another becomes an actual *lack* (the absence of a good that could have been). His vision of God is one in which God, tragically, has an 'eternal vision of potentials that have not been actualized.'[18] If this means only something along the lines of the difference between going to medical school and becoming a dentist, as in my earlier example, it's hard to understand what the problem is. That's contingency, not tragedy. Why would God's vision focus on what didn't happen rather than on the goods that *were* realized? In a way, it's as if God's vision of humans were eternally made tragic because humans aren't the dragons, unicorns or elves that God might equally well have created.[19]

If the problem is that some people, some events, might not be reconciled – thus making divinity vulnerable to what Fiddes terms 'the humility of being willing to be rejected'[20] – we run into a problem with two sides. On the one side, it's not clear how Fiddes can posit that God's risk is only limited rather than total. On the other side, if Fiddes can and does hold to that posit, he is operating with a distinction between God's *potentia ordinata* and *potentia absoluta* that makes God's sovereignty potentially so absolute that God becomes a hidden terror who we'd have little reason to trust. Let me explain. If the potentials that haven't been actualized mean not that some goods rather than others were in fact realized along the way – that is, that humans were humans rather than elves, dragons or unicorns, or dentists rather than doctors, then the problem is just that Fiddes is reading the realization of one equally valuable good rather than another as tragedy, which doesn't seem at all right. But if the problem is that some may resist reconciliation, and God can't overcome that because of how God has chosen to make Godself dependent on us, then God's decision to become vulnerable must in reality be a total risk rather than a limited risk: if God is holding something back, some power that God could have deployed but didn't (very loosely said), God's sovereignty is not just total but terrifying. Indeed, some have charged that that distinction, between God's power as such and God's power as deployed, is precisely the origin of the sovereignty that vulnerability is intended to undo.

17. Ibid., 179.
18. Ibid., 195.
19. The point is that you can't lack something not properly yours.
20. Fiddes, *The Promised End*, 195.

I've suggested, then, that divine vulnerability (1) can be a way to hold onto faith in situations where faith is sorely tested – but that positing such vulnerability risks rationalizing what cannot and should not be rationalized – and (2) can conceal a deeper sovereignty.

This brings us, in the final section of the chapter, to the ambiguity we've encountered several times, about the relationship between vulnerability and mastery. Let's return to the difference between *affirming* vulnerability and *recognizing* it, and the variety of self-images that can be negotiated by way of a relation to vulnerability. In her wonderful book *Tough Enough*, Deborah Nelson examines six women – from Diane Arbus to Simone Weil – who were known for their toughness or what Nelson terms 'unsentimentality'. Unsentimentality, Nelson argues, describes a relation to suffering that seeks to get the self out of the way of the recognition of suffering. That is, the authors she discusses are worried about the self's tendency to obtrude, to introduce its self-regard in a way that blocks the recognition of suffering. The obtruding self, as I'll loosely term it, wants its passion in the face of suffering to be recognized – it wants to perform its empathy, its compassion, in relation to the sufferer.[21] Empathy in the face of trauma, in the face of vulnerability, is often taken to be the condition of an ethical response to suffering. Nelson's unsentimentalists were, in contrast,

> drawn to suffering as a problem to be explored and yet remained deeply suspicious of its attractions. ... They sought not relief from pain but heightened sensitivity to what they called "reality". ... They imagined the consolations for pain in intimacy, empathy, and solidarity as *anesthetic*. Their toleration of pain, indeed their insistence on its ordinariness, is a part of their eccentricity.[22]

The intensification of vulnerability and the affective and subjective appropriation of vulnerability – rather than *recognition* of vulnerability – can, Nelson's study suggests, be a way to put the self in the centre, to let the self's sensitivity to suffering become the point of attention to suffering.

A second risk that accompanies the 'maximalist' affirmation of vulnerability is found in Nelson's reading of Joan Didion. For much of her career, Didion's concern is to avoid 'self-pity and self-delusion' by looking unflinchingly at vulnerability. But as Nelson shows, Didion's desire to avoid sentimentality runs aground when she discovers 'the grandiosity of hardness',[23] what I describe as the affirmation of vulnerability as a practice of mastery. To insist not only on one's own vulnerability, but to make a project of the 'affirmation of vulnerability' in both practical and theoretical terms can become a way to steel oneself against the *discovery* of

---

21. See Leslie Jamison, *The Empathy Exams* (Minneapolis: Graywolf Press, 2014) for critiques along these lines.
22. Nelson, *Tough Enough*, 8.
23. Ibid., 10.

unexpected vulnerabilities.[24] Paradoxically, then, the 'maximalist' affirmation of vulnerability can, as a strategy for negotiating life, be transformed into a management strategy of the very vulnerability by which one sought to be undone.

The bestselling memoir in which Didion comes up against the limits of her earlier strategy, *The Year of Magical Thinking*, starts with lines that Nelson quotes several times: 'Life changes fast / Life changes in the instant / You sit down to dinner and life as you know it ends / The question of self-pity.'[25] You sit down to dinner and life as you know it ends: those of us who have, literally or not, experienced such a dinner know the lostness, the dislocation and self-dissolution that result. One should not run from such knowledge. But the experience of its realization – the actualization of the vulnerability built into the form of life in which life as one knew it can end during an ordinary day's dinner – ought rather to be *acknowledged*, recognized, than affirmed. And acknowledging it would require acknowledging just how destructive such an experience can be. The ordinariness of suffering's capacity to destroy the ordinary is not, I think, something to be celebrated.

Those who posit divine vulnerability, especially when that vulnerability is made to contrast with power, may also be at risk of taking away the only part of Christianity that would make it more than an admittedly useful philosophy or aesthetics for negotiating daily life. The reason Christianity exists is that people thought they saw the *resurrected* Christ. They did not see a human being who had survived great trauma, emerging scarred, but with his capacity to love intact. They did not see yet another instance of suffering vulnerability. They saw the one who was dead *alive*. That is *not* a story of invulnerability, by any means. But it is a story of life beyond death – beyond the vulnerability that Farley termed absolute.

Like many who worry about vulnerability, Rowan Williams wants to avoid both Christian triumphalism and final despair. Therefore, he suggests in *The Tragic Imagination*, 'the schism … for a Christian imagination is … between God as the eternal will for healing and God as the compromised and vulnerable agent within history who can change history only by renouncing power or security or success'.[26] What does it mean to consider those distinctions a 'schism'? The sheer 'quantity' (and quantity is not at all the right word) of suffering – actualized vulnerability – in the world is overwhelming. Christian faith in God – not, I think, only as the eternal *will* for healing – may not be existentially satisfying much of the time, or easy to hold in the face of suffering. It may also render

---

24. This is the charge Eve Kosofsky Sedgwick brings against the paranoid reader in her influential chapter, 'Paranoid Reading and Reparative Reading, or, You're So Paranoid, You Probably Think This Essay Is About You', in *Touching Feeling: Affect, Pedagogy, Performativity* (Durham: Duke University Press, 2003), 123–51.
25. Nelson, *Tough Enough*, 169.
26. Williams, *The Tragic Imagination*, 133.

Christianity vulnerable to all the charges that have been brought against it in modernity: escapism, triumphalism, a comedic resolution, the foundation of sovereignty. But where Williams sees a schism, Christian theology typically sees there not a schism but an identity: an identity of the different (divine and human) beyond difference, a paradox that transcends and explodes its own paradoxicality on the day of resurrection.

Chapter 16

LIVING SACRIFICE: IS THERE A NON-PATHOLOGICAL WAY OF LIVING SUFFERING AS SACRIFICE?[1]

Paul D. Murray

> I appeal to you therefore, brothers and sisters, by the mercies of God, to present your bodies as a living sacrifice, holy and acceptable to God, which is your spiritual worship.
>
> (Rom. 12.1)

Introduction

The aim of this speculative chapter is to sketch a theological position rather than develop a full argument: to open up some lines of thought which are incomplete but, I hope, suggestive, perhaps even provocative. In some respects it might be likened to a kind of Pascalian or Teilhardian meditation.[2] It is aimed at encouraging us to think differently about something familiar. More specifically, it is aimed at unsettling what I, along with many others, regard as a damaging constellation of

---

1. Here 'pathological' is meant in its primary medical sense of that which is damaging to the body – in this case, the ecclesial body of Christ – rather than its subsequent extended use as a term of societal and even ethical disapproval. Behind this lies a particular understanding of the systematic theological task, versions of which recur throughout my writings, as consisting in something like the attentive analysis of Christian life and the questions and problems which arise there, with the aim of offering constructive repair and thereby enhancing the quality of Christian life. This is systematic theology understood as an intentional ministry of healing to the stresses and strains in contemporary ecclesial reality and the pathologies, paralyses and wounds which disfigure the living ecclesial body of Christ. It represents a praxis-inflected version of St Anselm's far more elegant *fides quaerens intellectum*.

2. See Blaise Pascal, *Pensées*, trans. A. J. Krailsheimer (Harmondsworth: Penguin, 1966) and Pierre Teilhard de Chardin, 'Pensées', in his *Hymn of the Universe*, trans. Gerarld Vann, O.P. (London and New York: Collins and Harper & Row, 1965), 69–141.

ideas about God's salvific work and the place of suffering in that work. It seeks to do this by showing such ideas to be unnecessary.

Prompting this meditation was a conversation I had with Karen Kilby during the course of the Love and Suffering Project on which she was engaged with the Sisters of La Retraite. Karen mentioned a reflection of one of the sisters, that whereas previous generations had been helped to find and express the meaning of their suffering in the language of 'offering it up with Christ' and of 'looking at Christ on the cross', this does not seem right to us.[3] But nor, the sister had further reflected, have we found any replacement. For her own part, the sister was not passing judgement on previous generations; more simply both noting that while the notion of 'offering it up' had worked for them, helping to carry them through, it does not seem to do so for many of us today, and regretting the apparent lack of an alternative mode of proceeding.

I draw two things from reflecting on this. First, that the theology and spirituality of 'offering it up' no longer works for us. Second, that the lack of an alternative ready means of transmuting the endurance of suffering into a prayerful act of faith and of seeking to live suffering as an act of love is indeed a serious lack in much contemporary Christian theology and spirituality. Indeed, I wish to press this contrast somewhat more sharply than the sister herself was doing. For my own part, I do in fact consider the constellation of ideas which tends to lie behind the spirituality of 'offering our suffering up' to be unhealthy and damaging, distorted and distorting. I also, however, hold – both on account of its inescapable role in human life and on account of its central relationship with the Christian tradition – that we urgently need to find an alternative, non-pathological and convincing way of positively and actively integrating suffering into our spiritual lives, in a manner which flows from the heart of the tradition.

My key assumption is that in Christian spirituality it is uncontentious to think of prayer as a means of sharing in the one act of God's trinitarian love, which act is always creative and transformative in this order. In turn, my core

---

3. Typically feeding into the once-standard Catholic spirituality of 'offering-up' one's sufferings as a participation in the redemptive work of Christ was a specific constellation of ideas and influences, in particular: (i) the assumption, from Anselmian satisfaction theory, that for the infinite offence of sin to God's dignity to be satisfied, there must be either an infinite debt of honour rendered or an infinite debt of punishment endured, (ii) the assumption, from Col. 1.24 ['I am now rejoicing in my sufferings for your sake, and in my flesh I am completing what is lacking in Christ's afflictions for the sake of his body, that is, the church'], that we are called not only to be taken into the movement of Christ's redemptive work but to emulate and extend it in some way in order to help make good on the aforementioned debt and (iii) that this can be done through the intentional endurance – the 'offering up' – of such things as suffering, self-denial and penance as privileged means of sharing in this manner in the redemptive work of Christ.

constructive suggestion is that we can choose to live unavoidable suffering as a space of bodily prayer, akin to fasting, which can similarly be a channel for the movement of this creative-transforming act of love, both in our own lives and in the lives of others.

The meditation is in four movements. First, a number of other principles are identified which are woven into my constructive proposal. At this point, little by way of supporting arguments or evidence is provided for these. In any full treatment of the proposal this lack would clearly need to be rectified. Second, brief indication is made of the family of ideas which, despite their strong pedigree in Christian spirituality and theology – particularly Western Christian spirituality and theology – is here rejected as profoundly problematic. Third, a somewhat different constellation of ideas is traced, with different presuppositions. Finally, it is suggested that this different way of thinking provides a way of re-appropriating the practice of living unavoidable suffering as sacrifice but as a non-pathological loving, *life-giving, self-giving* rather than as a self-emptying, self-renouncing, offering-up as part of the price of redemption.[4] So, in T. S. Eliot-style, we come back to where we started but, hopefully, now seen afresh.[5]

Assumed principles

§1 *About God, the Trinity:* Christian tradition understands God as the fully actualized eternal act of joyous love, in which there is no lack, no un-actualized potential and no possibility of diminishment. As such, Christian tradition maintains that the life of the Trinity is unchanging –

---

4. Although quite independently developed and here distinctly focused on the question of how we might seek to live unavoidable suffering positively as an act of love, in relation to the underlying critique and re-appropriation of the understanding of sacrifice in Christian tradition there are some points of resonance with the recent interesting argument of Asle Eikrem, *God as Sacrificial Love: A Systematic Exploration of a Controversial Notion* (London and New York: Bloomsbury T&T Clark, 2018), particularly Chapter 6, 119–74. One of the distinctive points in the present proposal, however, is the central place given, as will emerge, to this original core concept of 'life-giving, self-giving' love as a felicitous means for thinking of the fundamental divine dynamic at work in the being-in-act of the Trinity and, by analogy, so much else.

5. See 'We shall not cease from exploration
And the end of all our exploring
Will be to arrive where we started
And know the place for the first time.'
T. S. Elliot, 'Little Gidding' (1942), 'Four Quartets', in *The Complete Poems and Plays of T. S. Eliot* (London: Faber and Faber, 1969), 191–8 (197).

because already absolutely fully actualized – and without need, risk or suffering.[6]

§2 *About creation:* Christian tradition understands creation as an utterly gratuitous, contingent act held within the one eternal fully actualized act of the Trinity. In accordance with this, Catholic Christian tradition understands creation, in each and every part and in its totality, as only existing through participation in and orientation towards this one, absolutely fulfilled act of joyous love, in which creation's destiny lies.[7]

§3 *About created action:* As brought into and held in being by nothing other than the one eternal act of the Trinity, all created action is made possible by, dependent upon and situated within this one act. With Julian of Norwich, 'Everything that is done is well done, for it is our Lord God who does it. How God functions in creatures was showed me at this time; not how they function in themselves. God is the focal point of everything and does it all.'[8]

§4 *About relative created freedom:* Moreover, as brought into and held in being by nothing other than the absolutely free being-in-act of the Trinity with a view to sharing variously in this one being-in-act and as, therefore, variously

---

6. In assuming this principle, of understanding the Trinity as the fully actualized act of being, I am aligning myself with the classical Augustinian-Thomistic Catholic tradition. In emphasizing this one eternal act of love as 'joyous' love, I am aligning myself more specifically with this tradition as drawn upon and freshly voiced by Julian of Norwich in the fourteenth century, see Julian of Norwich, *Revelations of Divine Love*, trans. Clifton Wolters (Harmondsworth: Penguin, 1966). As Karen Kilby explores, adherence to this principle distinguishes the line assumed and developed here from the approach adopted by Hans Urs von Balthasar, who views the demands of love to be such as to introduce suffering and risk into the very trinitarian life of God and not simply as a matter of God's identification with us and bearing with us in Christ and the Spirit. See Karen E. Kilby, 'Julian of Norwich, Hans Urs von Balthasar, and the Status of Suffering in Christian Theology', *New Blackfriars* 99 (2018): 298–311.

7. See '(v) God who made everything because of love, by the same love sustains it in being, now and for ever, (vi) God is all that is good, as I see it, and is the goodness of all good things.' Julian of Norwich, *Revelations of Divine Love*, §8, 74, adapted to gender-neutral; also 'God showed me all this to my great happiness, as if God were saying, 'Look, I am God. I am in all. I do everything! I never cease upholding my work, and I never will. I am guiding everything toward the end I ordained for it from the first, by the same might, wisdom, and love with which I made it.' Ibid., §11, 80–1, adapted.

8. Ibid., §11, 80, adapted. In this Augustinian-Thomistic understanding of the concurrence of divine and created action and in contrast to the central premise of free will defence theodicies, the realm of creaturely action does not strictly stand over against and in absolute distinction from the realm of divine action but is always situated within the latter as the ground of its possibility.

reflecting something of God's trinitarian being, creation necessarily has a relative freedom about it and is a sphere in which relative freedom is necessarily possible.[9] If this is variously true of all creation, it is true in a particular way of embodied, self-conscious human creation, which in Judaeo-Christian tradition is understood as being created in the 'image of God' (Gen. 1.26). As situated within and oriented to the absolutely free being-in-act of the Trinity, it follows that the fulfilment of relative creaturely freedom consists in freely willed alignment with this free being-in-act of the Trinity. Divine freedom and creaturely freedom are not locked into a zero-sum relationship.

§5 *About sinful creaturely action:* As both held in being by and granted a relative freedom within the one absolutely free and fulfilled act of the Trinity, it is possible, if incomprehensible, for creaturely action to resist and contradict the joyous loving orientation of the one eternal act on which such creaturely action depends for its very possibility and consummation.[10]

§6 *About God's presence to and in creation:* Given that creation only exists as contingent participation in the one eternal act of the Trinity, in Catholic Christian tradition God in Christ and the Spirit is closer, more intimate, to each created thing than created things are to themselves.[11] As present to and within each experience as the one act of existing, God in Christ and the Spirit knows each experience from within. This is true in a unique way of the Word incarnate in the Spirit in the human nature of Jesus. By analogy, however, it is also more generally true of the most intimate presence of

---

9. This is also to reject another standard premise in free will defence theodicies: that God had a real choice to make between a created order with relative freedom and a deterministic created order without any such freedom. By contrast, the assumed position here – although I am not claiming that this particular assumption is generally made explicit within standard articulations of the Augustinian-Thomistic classical tradition – is that the only real choice open to God was between either creation with relative freedom, and all that could be anticipated in detail as following from that, or no creation at all. Given that creation only exists within and so reflects something of the one being-in-act of the Trinity and given that freedom is an essential attribute of the Trinity, then creation – if it is to exist at all – must, I am suggesting, have something of a relative freedom about it.

10. Again this is in line with the Augustinian-Thomistic understanding of sin and evil as a privation of the good and, as such, a lived lie and self-frustrating self-contradiction. In Julian's terms, 'From this I gathered that sin is not a thing that we do, not a deed, for in all that was *done*, there was no sin shown.' *Revelations of Divine Love*, §11, 80; also 'All this was shown in a flash. ... But I did not see *sin*. I believe it has no substance or real existence. It can only be known by the pain it causes.' Ibid., §27, 104.

11. See 'God is nearer to us than our own soul, for God is the ground in which it stands, and God is the means by which substance and sensuality are so held together that they can never separate. Our soul reposes in God its true rest, and stands in God, its true strength, and is fundamentally rooted in God, its eternal love.' Ibid., §56, 161, adapted.

the Spirit to and within each created thing. As St Paul writes, 'The whole creation has been groaning in labor pains' longing to 'obtain the freedom of the glory of the children of God' (Rom. 8.21-22).

§7 *About the human vocation:* With creation understood as originating from, existing within and being oriented to the Trinity's one fully actualized act of joyous love as source, sustainer and consummation, the classical Christian tradition views embodied, self-conscious, communicating humanity as the place where this comes to conscious recognition, articulation and response. In the *imago Dei* tradition this suggests an understanding of humanity – every human – as priest of creation, called both to voice creation's praise and pain and to enact and embody the creator's loving purpose. As will be developed here, this might also include voicing and embodying the creator's rejection, through embrace and transformation, of the pain and suffering which creation entails. In this understanding, life in the Spirit, the life of grace, consists in becoming sensitive, attuned and fluent in this participation; and contemplative prayer and living similarly consists in learning to be within this one act in the particular circumstances of our lives. Again with St Paul, 'We ourselves, who have the first fruits of the Spirit, groan inwardly while we wait for adoption' (Rom. 8.23).

§8 *About physical pain:* Physical pain is a consequence of finitude, material bodiliness, sentience and creaturely frailty in a relatively free created order capable of producing and sustaining relatively free sentient beings. The potential for physical pain is the inevitable consequence of created material existence.[12] This is not to say that any specific event of pain is inevitable, for each specific event is always contingent on myriad contingent factors. Indeed, even though all such contingent factors and specific events might be 'anticipated' and known from all eternity in God's omniscience, that still does not necessarily make any such specific event inevitable. What is inevitable in a relatively free material creation with sentient beings is both the basic potential for pain and that some such pain will be experienced by all sentient beings, even though its specific realization will be contingent on all sorts of factors.

§9 *About emotional pain:* Emotional pain is the more specific consequence of our being interdependent creatures made for joyous love who have to tread this path in a frail and finite world marked by sinful failures in love. Taken together, pain in all its forms is the consequence of our being created for joyous love in a relatively free sentient material order marked by sin.

---

12. This is a contested presupposition. For its sustained rejection in favour of a theological apophasis which declines any answer to 'Why suffering?' while both maintaining that God does not do death or deathliness in any way and resisting any resort to providential explanation, see John E. Thiel, *God, Evil, and Innocent Suffering: A Theological Reflection* (New York: Crossroad, 2002).

§10 *About God's permitting of the possibilities of pain, suffering, sin and evil:* The account I am tracing here – of the capacity for pain and suffering being consequential upon a sentient material creation and the possibility of sin being incomprehensibly consequential upon the necessary relative freedom of creation – requires us to say that at some level the trinitarian God of inexhaustible love has said yes to a world such as this existing in which pain and suffering is foreseeable; and perhaps even foreseeable in specific detail and not just as a general possibility. That, however, does not ipso facto equate with the dangerous and damaging claim that any specific event of pain or suffering is ever specifically positively given as a deliberate means of achieving some good or other. That particular idea is here rejected. We can say that 'from all eternity God might anticipate how various non-compensatory goods of redemption and consummation might ultimately be drawn from the various specific ills which can be anticipated as being undesirably consequential upon creation' without having to say that 'such ills are to be understood as having been specifically and deliberately given for such purposes'. The first statement neither requires nor should lead us to think the second statement. By contrast, in the line of thought being explored here, such ills are the divinely foreseeable undesired surd of creation which are only permitted in the knowledge that they will be redeemed. Again with Julian of Norwich, 'All shall be well, and all shall be well, and all manner of thing shall be well.'[13]

§11 *About resisting suffering:* Whenever we are able to resist, alleviate or overcome suffering without infringing integrity or causing further harm to others, we have the responsibility so to do.[14] Pain and suffering can never properly be seen as goods in their own right.

---

13. Or in Wolters's rather more prosaic translation, 'It is all going to be all right; it is all going to be all right; everything is going to be all right.' Julian of Norwich, *Revelations of Divine Love*, §27, 103–4.

14. The caveat about not infringing integrity includes the integrity of personal vocation and mission. On the one hand, the Gospels both record a number of occasions on which Jesus either gave his opponents the slip or avoided going up to Jerusalem, thus showing that crisis and suffering do not need deliberately to be sought out when they are otherwise avoidable. On the other hand, all four Gospels bear consistent witness to Jesus's resoluteness once it was clear that the integrity of his vocation could not be satisfied except by embracing and making central act of the passion which was the unavoidable consequence of his life and message. The political and liberationist theologians have done a great service in enabling us to understand more clearly something of the ways in which Jesus' death was consequential upon the life he lived and the options he made. For a thoughtful mediation of such thinking to a broad-base English-language readership, see Thomas Cullinan, *The Passion of Political Love*, 2nd edn (London: Sheed and Ward, 1987). It is notable that Eikrem, again independently, also adopts a consequential approach to the death of Jesus, see *God as Sacrificial Love*, 108–11.

§12 *About resisting the legitimation of suffering*: Any way of thinking, Christian, pagan or secular, which diminishes resistance to suffering is to be rejected: for example, fatalism, the maximization of profit, claims that the suffering of non-human animals is irrelevant, convictions about the necessity of suffering for God's redemptive activity, or claims for its irrelevance when compared with the joy of eternity.

A dangerous family of ideas

At work in many theologies and spiritualities of suffering, sacrifice, self-renunciation, desolation and dereliction is a problematic assumption which is frequently also at work in the notion of 'offering up one's sufferings' as a share in the redemptive activity of Christ. It is the assumption that human suffering – or some of it at least – is a necessary and directly divinely willed means both of our disciplining in the way of holiness and of God's pardoning and freeing us from sin.[15] As such, far from being resisted on the occasions when it is avoidable, suffering is to be embraced, even deliberately sought out, as a core mode of Christian living.

As already noted, the reception of St Anselm's satisfaction theory of the atonement has exerted immense influence here.[16] Of course, in the context of then contemporary feudal dignity codes, Anselm's theory was intended as an account of God's gracious, loving determination to overcome the problem caused by sin. That accepted, Anselm nevertheless straightforwardly shares the standard feudal assumption that offence to a superior's dignity can justly only be satisfied either by the rendering of an otherwise un-owed honour in

---

15. As identified in conversation with Walter Moberly, a full development of this argument would have to show how it configures with the recurrent scriptural tradition of testing through adversity. Distinctions would here need to be drawn between being exposed to diabolic testing (e.g. the temptation narratives, Mk. 1.12-13 and parallels), being subjected to testing by a 'counsel for the prosecution' within the heavenly council (e.g. Job 1.9-11), and being tested directly by God (e.g. Gen. 22.1-18, of Abraham, and Deut. 8.2, of Israel in the wilderness). In keeping with the principles articulated in 1.§10 here, my inclination is to suggest that while life is indeed testing in ways which we can imagine as having been foreseen in specific detail within the omniscience of God, we are not required to think of such occurrences as having been positively willed within God's loving providence. Moreover, even though we can experience ourselves as sustained by God's love in such situations and, possibly, as growing in love through them, we are not required to think of them and are best advised not to think of them, as having been specifically and purposefully given for this.

16. See St Anselm, 'Cur Deus Homo', in *St Anselm Basic Writings*, 2nd edn, trans. S. N. Deane (La Salle: Open Court, 1962), 191–302; also n. 2 in this chapter.

proportion to the offence committed and in excess of what is otherwise already owed to the superior party or by the undergoing of appropriate punishment as payment of penalty.[17] So, for Anselm, if God is to be able, as God wills, to forgive humanity for the infinite offence caused by sin then either an infinite un-owed act of honouring must be performed or an infinite debt of punishment must be undergone which God in Christ does on our behalf. In turn, we can then share in this by identifying our sufferings with the redemptive sufferings of Christ. Something of this is expressed in H. A. Williams's comment on suffering that 'the more of a dead-end it feels the more is it an invitation to join in Christ's sufferings'.[18]

It is this set of assumptions which, in one form or another, subsequently dominated the Western Christian soteriological imaginary for over a thousand years, with Protestant penal substitutionary accounts representing both a development and a narrowing of it. But there have always been counter-narratives, whether Abelard's sketching of an exemplarist approach in the twelfth century[19] or Gustaf Aulén's *Christus Victor* in the twentieth century.[20] Further, although satisfaction and substitutionary accounts can draw support from certain strands in the New Testament, the New Testament witness is far more plural than that, utilizing many different, even conflicting, images for God's salvific work in Christ and the Spirit.

I concur, then, with those who judge the dominant Western approaches to be both unnecessary and damaging beyond redemption, on account both of their valorization of suffering and the permanent tension they can leave us with in the

---

17. See ibid., Bk 1, §24, pp. 247–51.

18. H. A. Williams, *Some Day I'll Find You* (London: Mitchell Beazley, 1982), 177 [cited in Esther de Waal, *Lost in Wonder: Rediscovering the Spiritual Art of Attentiveness* (Collegeville: Liturgical Press, 2003), 109].

19. See Peter Abailard, 'Exposition of the Epistle to the Romans (An Excerpt from the Second Book)', trans. Gerald E. Moffatt, in *The Library of Christian Classics. Vol. X. A Scholastic Miscellany: Anselm to Ockham*, ed. Eugene R. Fairweather (London: SCM, 1956), 276–87, particularly 283:

> Now it seems to us that we have been justified by the blood of Christ and reconciled to God in this way: through this unique act of grace manifested to us – in that his Son has taken upon himself our nature and persevered therein in teaching us by word and example even unto death – he has more fully bound us to himself by love; with the result that our hearts should be enkindled by such a gift of divine grace, and true charity should not now shrink from enduring anything for him.

20. See Gustaf Aulén, *Christus Victor: An Historical Study of the Three Main Types of the Idea of the Atonement*, trans. A. G. Hebert (London: SPCK, 1931).

Trinity, between one who is bound by justice, even wrapped in wrath, and another who, moved by mercy, endures the price of assuaging this.[21]

Let me seek to clarify what I am and am not maintaining here for, as I have indicated, I am minded to accept that all that occurs in time is 'anticipated', permitted and ultimately transformed in the one fulfilled act of trinitarian love from all eternity. With this, I am also minded to trust that from eternity it has been anticipated how some non-compensatory goods might be drawn from some specific ills. As St Paul says, 'We know that all things work together for good for those who love God, who are called according to God's purpose' (Rom. 8.28).

However, while being minded to think in these ways I nevertheless reject the notion that suffering is ever intentionally given to us as a lesson, or as a punishment, or as a test by God. We may indeed learn things through suffering, suffering may indeed be consequential upon our sin and folly and the endurance of suffering may indeed test our resources. But the God of Jesus Christ is not capricious, nor vengeful, nor manipulative but faithful, trustworthy and endlessly abundant in love, regardless of what the experienced frustrations of love might at times appear to be suggesting to the contrary:

> If God is for us, who is against us? ... Who will separate us from the love of Christ? ... For I am convinced that neither death, nor life, nor angels, nor rulers, nor things present, nor things to come, nor powers, nor height, nor depth, nor anything else in all creation, will be able to separate us from the love of God in Christ Jesus our Lord. (Rom. 8.31, 35, 38-9)

---

21. For a recent critical discussion which resonates with the line of argument here, see Elizabeth A. Johnson, 'Book I: Wrestling with Anselm', *Creation and the Cross: The Mercy of God for a Planet in Peril* (Maryknoll: Orbis, 2018), 1–30. By contrast, for a body of writings arguing that when correctly understood satisfaction-based approaches, and penal substitution in particular, do not in fact fall foul of the criticisms which are levied against them and actually perform ethically useful functions, see Stephen R. Holmes, *The Wondrous Cross: Atonement and Penal Substitution in the Bible and History* (Milton Keynes: Paternoster, 2007); also Holmes, 'Of Babies and Bathwater? Recent Evangelical Critiques of Penal Substitution in the Light of Early Modern Debates Concerning Justification', *European Journal of Theology* 16, no. 2 (2007): 93–105; Holmes, 'Can Punishment Bring Peace? A Reconsideration of Penal Substitution', *Scottish Journal of Theology* 58, no. 1 (2005): 104–23; and Holmes, 'The Upholding of Beauty: A Reading of Anselm's Cur Deus Homo', *Scottish Journal of Theology* 54, no. 2 (2001): 189–203. Also of significance specifically in relation to Anselm is Fleming Rutledge, 'Anselm Reconsidered for Our Time', in her *The Crucifixion: Understanding the Death of Jesus Christ* (Grand Rapids and Cambridge: Eerdmans, 2015), 146–66. It is particularly to be noted that Anselm explicitly seeks to guard against the charge of their being any intra-trinitarian tension, see 'Cur Deus Homo', Bk1, §9 and Bk2, §18, pp. 206–11 and 287–93.

Thinking differently about suffering

Turning to my central constructive idea, it might be worth pausing briefly in order to identify some other helpful ways of thinking in situations of suffering which resonate with points made earlier:

- Suffering is not divine punishment or affliction but the consequence of our being finite, sentient, material beings in a relatively free created order marked by sin.
- When we are suffering we know that those who love us seek to do so in specific ways in order to help sustain us – well given we are told that 'the Spirit helps us in our weakness' (Rom. 8.26), we can trust that when we are suffering, the threefold God of love is also loving us and sustaining us in quite specific ways, even when the precise mode and character of this bread daily given as viaticum is not transparently clear to us.
- Suffering is not a state of God-forsakenness but, as revealed in Jesus and known in the Spirit, a place of God's intimate presence who, in Word and Spirit, bears with and knows our suffering and the cost of creation from the inside – as Gerald Vann writes, 'We know that love cannot but be involved in the suffering of what it loves; but God is love; therefore God cannot but be involved in the suffering of what God loves; but God loves all God's creatures; therefore God cannot but be involved in the sufferings of all God's creatures.'[22]
- Being faithful in the context of suffering means not allowing our understanding of God to be distorted by what our suffering might be falsely suggesting to us and maintaining steady gaze on what we truly see of God in Christ and the Spirit, such that the appropriate question is not 'Why is God doing this to me?' but 'How is God specifically loving and sustaining me in this situation?'[23]
- We should not be resigned to avoidable suffering but should protest and resist it – not only in relation to ourselves but also on behalf of others and, indeed, on behalf of the whole of creation – and so, as priests of creation, give voice and witness to the protest and resistance of the Spirit of Christ at work in the world.[24]

---

22. Gerald Vann, O.P., *The Pain of Christ and the Sorrow of God* (London: Blackfriars, 1947), 63, here adapted to gender-neutral. I am grateful to Sr Ann Swailes, O.P., of Fisher House, Cambridge, for drawing my attention to this work.

23. Remembering, again with St Paul, that 'hope does not disappoint us, because God's love has been poured into our hearts through the Holy Spirit that has been given to us' (Rom. 5.5).

24. This is to take Edward Schillebeeckx's recognition of the protest which 'negative contrast experiences' of suffering evoke and to read this in explicitly pneumatological vein as an aspect of the movement and acting of the Holy Spirit in creation. For Schillebeeckx on 'negative contrast experiences', see 'Church, Magisterium and Politics', in Schillebeeckx,

- With this, in relation to unavoidable suffering, on behalf of creation and in the Spirit of Christ we can voice lament for the costly, consequential surd of creation – a lament which might even cry forth as reproach against God but in the course of which we might also come to understand ourselves as actually voicing the Spirit's own lament and assurance (e.g. see Mk. 15.34 cf. Ps. 22).
- An experience of suffering can be of varying intensity, like the British weather, and sometimes we just need to hunker-down and endure with fortitude until a particular pulse of intensity subsides.[25]
- In looking for and waiting upon the possibility of transformation we need to follow scripture's exhortation to 'be patient in suffering' (Rom. 12.12), for it generally appears that the imperceptible normal mode of God's action in our lives is pebble-smoothing slow rather than wave-crash quick.[26]
- In Catholic understanding, part of the explanation for the normality of the pebble-smoothing slow character of grace in our lives is that while this is throughout – from start to finish and all between – properly God's achievement in Christ and the Spirit, and not ours, the story of salvation must nevertheless come to real and not just notional effect in the details of our lives such that it genuinely becomes our story: the intensity of the exceptional – the occasional impact of wave-crash quick effect – is in service of this ordinary integration of our personal narratives of desire, will and act, not in place of it.
- While in situations of enduring suffering we should still seek actively to attend to and to take solace and joy in tokens of love and beauty, even in small things for in such small things something of the infinite goodness and glory of God can assuredly be revealed to us.[27]

God the Future of Man, trans. N. D. Smith and Theodore Westow (New York: Sheed and Ward, 1968), 141–66 (153–6); also Schillebeeckx, *The Understanding of Faith: Interpretation and Criticism*, trans. N. D. Smith (New York: Seabury, 1974), 91–5; Schillebeeckx, *Christ: The Experience of Jesus as Lord*, trans. John Bowden (New York: Seabury, 1980), 817–19; and Schillebeeckx, *Church: The Human Story of God*, trans. John Bowden (New York: Crossroad, 1991), 5–6 and 28–9. For drawing the pneumatological freight of this more clearly into view, I am grateful to Ross Jesmont.

25. As St Paul also tells us, 'Suffering produces endurance, and endurance produces character, and character produces hope' (Rom. 5.3-4).

26. Of course, these apparently different modes of action – pebble-smooth slow and wave-crash quick – are more closely related than might at first appear. It is a matter of perspective: the action of pebble-smoothing slow is in fact the cumulative effect of zillions of wave-crash quick movements over time; and observing the intensity of wave-crash quick is but to feel and to recognize in a moment the drama of the ordinary. Transformation can be happening in the imperceptible.

27. Gerald Vann, O.P., expresses this well: 'What the great lovers of God tell us again and again is this: that we must not despise the *small* things, the small events of everyday. On the contrary it is through them that we can learn to share God's life because it is out of them that goodness is made.' *The Pain of Christ and the Sorrow of God*, 11, also ibid., 11–12.

- Without denying or diminishing the fact of current suffering, we need to keep our hearts and minds focused on being created for a joyous love which ultimately will not be thwarted, even if transformation is not possible in this order: 'Neither death, nor life, nor angels, nor rulers … will be able to separate us from the love of God in Christ Jesus our Lord' (Rom. 8.38-9) and 'the sufferings of this present time are not worth comparing with the glory about to be revealed to us' (Rom. 8.18).
- In the context of unavoidable suffering, it can be helpful also to ask what we can learn there – in medias res – of the way of love and how we might even live such suffering in and as prayer, enfolded in the one act of God's love, and assured that although 'we do not know how to pray as we ought … [the] … Spirit intercedes with sighs too deep for words' (Rom. 8.26).[28]

That last point brings me to the key constructive idea at work in this meditation on living sacrifice. I offer once again a series of thoughts and summary claims without, at this point, attempting anything approaching adequate justification.

Living suffering as loving, life-giving, self-giving – or living sacrifice differently

§1 We can identify a divine dynamic of life-giving, self-giving at the heart alike of the Spirit-impelled life and ministry of Jesus unto death and resurrection and – as revealed and understood in Christ and the Spirit – of the eternal Trinitarian life of God. This is the inexhaustible eternal act of creative-transformative perfect joyous love, the unified unfathomable threefold being-in-act of the Trinity, in which we are situated, exist and participate.

---

28. The 'it can be helpful' references an important distinction which Karen Kilby draws between what is variously appropriate and inappropriate in first-person, second-person and third-person forms of speaking in relation to suffering, see Kilby, 'Eschatology, Suffering and the Limits of Theology', in *Game over? Reconsidering Eschatology*, ed. Christophe Chalamet, Andreas Dettwiler, Mariel Mazzocco and Ghislain Waterlot (Berlin: Walter de Gruyter, 2017), 279–92. Accordingly, I recognize that while the approach I trace here to living suffering as prayerful act can potentially be found helpful and can be witnessed to as such (first-person) and even offered, on occasion, in general second- and third-person fashions as a potentially constructive resource for and within the tradition, it cannot appropriately be presented either as a necessary solution to or as a requirement for second- and third-parties who are enduring – and perhaps being utterly broken by – specific instances of suffering. This pertains particularly but not exclusively to instances of what Marilyn McCord Adams refers to as 'horrendous evils', see McCord Adams, 'Horrendous Evils and the Goodness of God', in *The Problem of Evil*, ed. Marilyn McCord Adams and Robert Merihew Adams (Oxford: Oxford University Press, 1990), 209–21, at 211. I am grateful to Karen Kilby and Timothy J. Murray for discussion of this point.

§2 This notion of there being a divine dynamic of life-giving, self-giving love enables us to speak of a wide number of related things in their interrelationship. For example, it enables us to speak of the movement of the divine relations and life in the Trinity, of the movement of divine act *ad extra* in grace/the Holy Spirit and the incarnation of the Word, of the central movement disclosed in the life unto death and resurrection of Jesus, of the creative, saving and sanctifying act of God in Christ and the Spirit, of the movement of sacrifice and Eucharist, of the life of prayer and of the core Christian ethic of self-giving love.[29] The same movement recurs throughout not because it keeps being duplicated and repeated but because it is quite literally the one movement, the one life-giving, self-giving act, of the trinitarian life of God in which all things live, and move, and have their being (Acts 17.28). In creation the trinitarian God of life-giving, self-giving love opens space within the life of the Trinity for that which is not God to be in God; in redemption this same act of life-giving, self-giving love overcomes and transforms the bonds of sin and death and liberates creation 'from its bondage to decay' and for 'the freedom and glory of the children of God' (Rom. 8.cc21).

§3 Given that the Trinity is the fully actualized act of joyous love, in which there is no lack, no un-actualized potential and no possibility of diminishment, this divine dynamic of life-giving, self-giving should not be understood as a self-emptying but as always being from fullness unto fullness in the one eternal act of God's trinitarian love. It genuinely is 'the gift which keeps on giving' and without any diminishment in the process. On the contrary, as the life-giving, self-giving that is the inexhaustibly abundant joyous love of divine life, it is always generative, whether in the Trinity, in creation, in redemption or in consummation.

§4 However, when transposed into the conditions of finitude, materiality, temporality and a sin-strewn world, this dynamic of life-giving, self-giving love does bring inevitable risk, likely resistance, and the potential for suffering in its wake – as seen in the life of Jesus – whilst also still always being ultimately creative and transformative, as definitively shown in the resurrection. If in the created order as it actually exists, the life of love is a locus for suffering, we see in Jesus that such consequential and unavoidable

---

29. This central integrating notion of there being a fundamental divine dynamic of life-giving, self-giving love is in some ways analogous to Karl Rahner's notion of the unfathomable proximity of the 'self-communication of God' which similarly recurs throughout his theology and across many loci, most notably Trinity, incarnation and grace. While recognizing that Rahner did not intend 'self-communication' in a merely cognitive or data-transmission sense, I find 'life-giving, self-giving' more readily suggestive of action, practice, life, love and relation; and more suggestive too of the inextricable interwovenness of the pneumatic and the Christic.

suffering can also become an intensified place of living this one act of life-giving, self-giving love and so, in turn, can become a locus for love's transforming effects.

§5 My proposal, with some intentional resonance with St Thérèse of Lisieux's 'little way', is that we are called to enter into and to live out of this divine dynamic of life-giving, self-giving – this one eternal act of joyous love – in and through the details and circumstances of our lives and to become there living prayers and effective channels of God's sustaining and transforming being-with creation and the cost it entails.[30] Pierre Teilhard de Chardin expressed something similar in his own 'Pensées':

> It was a joy to me, Lord, in the midst of my struggles, to feel that in growing to my own fulfilment I was increasing your hold on me; it was a joy to me, beneath the inward burgeoning of life and amidst the unfolding of events that favoured me, to surrender myself to your providence.[31]

This learning to become living prayers and effective channels of the Trinity's sustaining, transforming being-with creation is the fundamental schooling for eternity – 'each person's core purpose in life' – which is taking place in every moment of our lives.[32] In its regard we are remarkably recalcitrant slow-learners relative to the infinite patience and mercy of the God of Jesus Christ, who *is* the perfect being-in-act of life-giving, self-giving love.

---

30. See especially her emphatic realization, in the context of meditating on 1 Cor. 12–13, 'I understood that LOVE COMPRISED ALL VOCATIONS, THAT LOVE WAS EVERYTHING, THAT IT EMBRACED ALL TIMES AND PLACES … IN A WORD, THAT IT WAS ETERNAL! Then, in the excess of my delirious joy, I cried out: O Jesus, my Love … my *vocation*, at last I have found it … MY VOCATION IS LOVE!' St. Thérèse of Lisieux, *Story of a Soul: The Autobiography of St. Thérèse of Lisieux*, trans. John Clarke (Washington DC: ICS Publications, 1976), 194. I am grateful to David F. Ford for reminding me of this striking passage in his *The Drama of Living: Becoming Wise in the Spirit* (Norwich: Canterbury Press, 2014), 125.

31. de Chardin, 'Pensées' §30, *Hymn of the Universe*, 94. I am grateful to Elizabeth Johnson for reminding me of this and other passages in Pierre Teilhard de Chardin's 'Pensées' and for drawing my attention to their part resonance with what I am suggesting here. Surprisingly, however, Teilhard makes little or no mention of the role of the Spirit. Indeed, his Christocentric cosmology is so total that Christ is spoken of as both the 'divine energy' and as the form, or expression, of that energy, see 'Pensées' §30, *Hymn of the Universe*, 95. I prefer to think of the inextricable association of energy and form as the inextricable interweaving of Spirit and Christ respectively.

32. As Ford writes, 'I think it is important to see vocation as embracing everyone. It is about each person's core purpose in life, to be carried out by him or her in their own unique way.' *The Drama of Living*.

§6 We can draw from this that one possible sign of the authenticity, or otherwise, of Christian prayer might be as to whether it leads to a greater sensitivity to the suffering of others and an increased ability to stay with such suffering, to attend to it and to bear with it rather than serving as protection and flight from it. As the poet Micheal O'Siadhail reminds us, after Coleridge, 'He prayeth best, who loveth best.'[33]

§7 In turn, the more specific proposal here is that we can sometimes learn even to live unavoidable suffering as just such a conscious act and lived prayer of sharing in and being conformed to this loving, life-giving, self-giving of the Trinity and God's bearing-with the cost of creation in Christ and the Spirit; moreover, that we can do this in the conviction that any such costly sharing in the Trinity's boundlessly generative love will ultimately be transformative for ourselves and others in the, generally, pebble-smoothing action of grace. The conviction is that in Christ and the Spirit the threefold God of love can take us in our suffering into the life-giving, self-giving movement of God's life and so transform our suffering into a place of redemption.[34] Again with Pierre Teilhard de Chardin,

> And now that I have discovered the joy of turning every increase into a way of making – or allowing – your presence to grow within me, I beg of you: bring me to a serene acceptance of that final phase of communion with you in which I shall attain to possession of you by diminishing within you.[35]

§7 Alternatively stated, the conviction here of faith is that when we are able to choose to live unavoidable suffering as an embodied act of love – as we can similarly seek to live prayer and fasting as acts of bodily love – it can become a transformative means of the Trinity's life-giving, self-giving being at work in the world.

§8 Embodied acts of prayer, such as fasting, are useful as they can be operating in background mode while other programmes (e.g. domestic duties, running a meeting, teaching, reading etc.) are running front of screen. Further, background-mode embodied acts of prayer will keep breaking through to front of screen, frontal lobe consciousness – for example, when fasting, we keep becoming aware of our hunger – serving as a recurrent opportunity

---

33. Micheal O'Siadhail, '1. Making, Canto 5: *Abundance*, vii', in *The Five Quintets* (Waco: Baylor University Press, 2018), 51, citing Samuel Taylor Coleridge, *Poems*, ed. John Beer (London: J. M. Dent, 1991 [1963]), 189.'The Rime of the Ancient Mariner'.

34. The simplest expression of the basic idea proposed here might be 'finding ourselves sustained by the creative-transforming love of God in situations of suffering and, in such situations, actively orienting ourselves on our real sharing in that love'.

35. de Chardin, 'Pensées' §30, *Hymn of the Universe*.

to orientate intention and desire explicitly towards living in accordance with the life-giving, self-giving act of divine love. So also, the constructive proposal here is that we can similarly sometimes choose to live the experience of unavoidable suffering as a recurring opportunity to orientate ourselves towards the movement of trinitarian love and to ask that we be taken more deeply into its dynamic in a way that will be sustaining and, ultimately, transformative for ourselves and others.

§9 Indeed, the act of fasting – and, similarly, the decision to seek to live suffering as an act of prayer and love – is not merely instrumental, a useful training ground for conforming and attuning us more closely into the future with the movement of trinitarian love. Such acts, such decisions, are themselves already really held within, drawn and prompted by – indeed only possible on account of – this movement. As such, in some small way they not only provide opportunity to be more deeply conformed to the movement of life-giving, self-giving love. Before this they are to be understood as already actually embodying and enacting this very movement in the specific circumstances of our lives; and in as much as they instantiate it and do not simply articulate towards it, then we can trust that they will indeed be generative and transformative, even if in imperceptible, pebble-smooth slow ways.

§10 The suggestion here, then, is that perhaps our priestly calling is not only to voice creation's praise and pain but also to be places, living sites, living temples, where the transformative life-giving, self-giving bearing-with of Christ and the Spirit is given contemporary form, expression and actuality. It is not that we add anything to the sufferings of Christ. It is not even that we join our sufferings to those of Christ. It is that in our unavoidable suffering, when intentionally lived as act of love and prayer, we can be more deeply taken into and become effective channels of the one movement of God's creative-transformative, life-giving, self-giving love. This is at once the one movement of the Triune life; the one movement of the Trinity's acts *ad extra* in creation, incarnation, grace and redemption; the one movement of Jesus' life; the one movement of his passion; the one movement of the Eucharist and the one movement of Christian life.[36]

§11 None of this, however, means that our consciously seeking to live unavoidable suffering as embodied prayer, as an intentional means of sharing in the one movement of the Trinity's life-giving, self-giving love,

---

36. Again something of this is suggested by Gerald Vann, 'Christ did not die merely for the sins that were then being committed or had been committed in the past, it was the total evil of the world, past, present and future, that was responsible for Calvary. And as with the sin, so with the suffering that is the effect of sin: wherever you find it, there is the Cross, sharing it in order to redeem it, to bring good out of it.' *The Pain of Christ and the Sorrow of God*, 65.

can become a technique which we can manipulate for making things better in our own preferred timescale. It simply means that we can ask that in our bodies and in our bodily circumstances we be taken more deeply into the divine dynamic of self-giving, life-giving love, that we become more closely conformed to living in accordance with it, and that our living and effective channelling of it be generative for ourselves and others.

§12 With this altered and reclaimed perspective on the living of suffering as sacrifice in view, we can give the last word to Karl Barth, who commenting on Rom. 5.3-5 said,

> Thus our tribulation, without ceasing to be tribulation or to be felt to be tribulation, is transformed. We must suffer, as we suffered before. But our suffering is no longer a passive, dangerous, poisonous, destructive tribulation and perplexity ... but is transformed into a tribulation and perplexity which are creative, fruitful, powerful, promising. ... By tribulation we are braced to patience. ... The road, which is impassable, has been made known to us in the crucified and risen Christ.[37]

---

37. Karl Barth, *The Epistle to the Romans*, 6th edn, trans. Edwyn C. Hoskins (London: Oxford University Press, 1933), 156–7.

INDEX

abandonment. *See* dereliction, mystical
Abelard, Peter   197
action
   creaturely   83–4, 192–3
   divine   192 n.8
   intentional   135
Aeschines   28–9
affliction, general   117, 126
affliction, mystical   57. *See also* dereliction, mystical
   in Angela of Foligno   60–1
   in Gregory the Great   58–9
   in John of the Cross   68–9
agape   23
Angela of Foligno   60–1
Anscombe, Elizabeth   135
Anselm   80, 190 n.3, 196–8
appetites   111
Aquinas. *See* Thomas Aquinas
Arendt, Hannah   114, 129
asceticism   109–10
asylum seekers   119–20, 127–8. *See also* immigration detention
atonement   80, 190 n.3, 196–8
Augustine
   on afflictions   79
   on knowing God   88
   on sacrifices   81
Aulén, Gustaf   50, 197

Bake, Alijt   63–4
Balthasar, Hans Urs von   192 n.6
baptism   9–10
Barth, Karl   206
Battista da Varano, Camilla   64–5
beauty   41
Betteley, Adrienne   149
bipolar disorder. *See also* depression
   personal priorities and   146
   spiritual experiences and   141–3
   as spiritual joy   139–41
   as suffering   136–8
   truth-telling and   143, 145

Black, Clifton   8
blessedness   37–8
body (*soma*)   11–14
Bonaventure
   on Francis of Assisi   98, 99
   spirituality of   100–1
   as theologian   97–8
   on Trinity   98
Bonhoeffer, Dietrich   143
   on truth-telling   144, 145
Burnaby, John   32
Butler, Judith   108–9

Camus, Albert   71
cancer
   aggressive responses to   147–52
   evil and   151
   pacific responses to   152–3
chance. *See* contingency
Christ
   death   4–5, 8–9, 31, 205 n.36
   devil and   50
   Holy Spirit and   203 n.31
   kenosis of   48–9
   love of   24–5
   passion   56, 76, 82–4
   resurrection   8–9
   self-gift of   26, 31–2
   suffering and   15–20, 55, 56, 95, 101, 202–3
   thirst of   102–3
   union with   5–7
Cobb, L. Stephanie   33
Colossians, letter to the   190 n.3
comedic world view   157
contingency   179–81, 185
Corinthians, second letter to the   3
Cotter, Ian   152
creation
   definitions of   18
   God and   193–4
   gratuitousness of   192
   groaning of   18–19

darkness. *See* night of the senses; night of the spirit
da Todi, Jacopone   61
death. *See also* dying
   attitudes towards   170
   definitions of   8
   gift-giving and   30–1
   levels of   7–8
   life and   9–11
   self-gift and   30–1
   sin and   9–11
De Boer, M. C.   7
decreation
   definition   114
   destruction and   116
   self-abnegation and   125–6
delusions   139–42
demons   45–6. *See also* powers of opposition
depression. *See also* bipolar disorder; mental health challenges
   effects of   136–7
   flourishing and   161
   meaning and   162
   night of the spirit and   68
   spiritual responses to   158
   as tragic suffering   158–60
   tragic world view and   161
dereliction, mystical. *See also* affliction, mystical
   in Alijt Bake   64
   in Camilla Battista da Varano   65
   in Jan van Leeuwen   63
   in John Tauler   61–2
   in Mechthild of Magdeburg   59–60
   in Mother Teresa of Kolkata   70, 96–7, 99–100
   night of the spirit and   88
   spiritual growth and   88–91
   spiritual growth beyond   91–3
   in Teresa of Avila   65–6
   in Thérèse of Lisieux   69–70
Derrida, Jacques   31
destitution
   asylum seekers and   119 n.15
   definition   119 n.15
   personal skills and   122
   sense of time and   120
   social participation and   123
   suffering and   120–1
detention, immigration. *See* immigration detention
devil. *See also* powers of opposition
   suffering and   48–50
   titles for   45, 46
Didion, Joan   187
disability   133
disease. *See* illness
divine attributes. *See under* God
divinization   47, 49
Dodds, Michael   82
doxa (glory)   16–18
dualism   150
dying. *See also* death
   with Christ   6–10, 16–17
   suffering and   5–6

Eastman, Susan   14
Eckhart   61, 75
emotional suffering   37
empathy   186
eros   23
eternal life   39
Eucharist   84
Evagrius Ponticus   45–6
evil
   definition   74, 193 n.10
   God and   35, 74
   goodness and   73–5
   kinds of   72
   mystery of   75
   natural   74
   pain and   35
   possibilities of   195

faith   199
fall, the   41, 46–7
Farley, Edward   176–7
Farley, Wendy   156, 160, 178–80
fasting   204–5
Fiddes, Paul   184
flesh (*sarx*)   12–14
force
   identity and   124
   love, justice and   113–14, 125
   reflection and   124–5
   victimisation and   123–4
Ford, David   203 n.32

forsakenness. *See* dereliction, mystical
Foucault, Michel   151
fragility   165
Francis de Sales   69
Francis of Assisi   95, 98–9, 152
Frank, Arthur   152
freedom   192–3
friendship   28 n.21
fulfilment   36–7, 203. *See also* vocation

Gadamer, H.-G.   134
Galatians, letter to the   26, 31
Gebarra, Ivone   161 n.20
Genesis, book of   35, 47
Gennadius of Marseilles   80
gift-giving
   death and   30–1
   spirit of   28–9
   structures of   29–31
   value of   27–8
glory (*doxa*)   16–18
Glucklich, Ariel   57
God. *See also* providence
   causality and   83–4
   creation and   193–4
   desire of   103
   evil and   35, 74
   freedom of   193
   justice and mercy of   76–8, 85
   love by   101–2, 198, 201–2
   opposition to   45
   power of   185
   self-communication of   202 n.29
   self-emptying and   202
   suffering and   199
   Trinity   98, 191–2
   unchangeableness of   191–2
   vulnerability of   181–7
goodness
   evil and   73–5
   sense perception and   35
   senses of   34
   sin and   73–4
grace   167–8, 194
Gregory of Nazianzus
   career   43–4
   on Christ and devil   50
   on the fall   46
   on illness   52

   on *kenosis* of Christ   49–50
   on powers of opposition   47–8, 51–2
Gregory of Nyssa
   on martyrdom   39–42
   on pain and pleasure   35–6
   on persecution   36–9
Gregory the Great   58–9

Hacking, Ian   135
hatred. *See* violent ideological groups
Hauerwas, Stanley   151, 153
healing   189 n.1
hedonism   35–6
hermeneutics   134
Homer   113, 123
hope   38

identity transformation. *See* personal
   transformation
ideologies, violent. *See* violent ideological
   groups
illness
   effects of   52
   hope and   153
   integration of   150
immigration detention
   empathy and   121–2
   hope and   122–3, 127–8
   personal transformation and   128–9
   procedures in   124–5
   society and   123, 124
   suffering and   120–1
injustice   108–9
Isaiah, book of   98

Jenson, Robert   43
Jeremiah, book of   127
Jervis, Ann   20
Jesus. *See* Christ
job   58, 73
John, Gospel of   140, 150
John of Damascus   84
John of the Cross
   on appetites   111
   career   66–7
   on personal transformation   108
   union with God in   91–3
   various nights of   67–9, 87–91
John Paul II   55–6

Julian of Norwich 192, 193 nn.10, 11, 195
justice 75

Kant, Immanuel 144
Katangole, Emmanuel 182–4
kenosis
   definition 165
   privilege and 166
   salvation and 48–9
Keshgegian, Flora 156, 157
Kilby, Karen 156

lament 182–4
Leclercq, Jean 58
loss 37, 163
love
   force and 113–14
   by God 101–2, 191 n.4, 198, 201–2
   self-sacrifice and 23–6
   suffering and 190–1, 201–6
Ludlow, Morwenna 45
Luther, Martin 62

Marie de l'Incarnation 69
Martin, Emily 135
martyrdom 38–42
Matthew, Gospel of 150
Matz, Brian 48–9
Mechthild of Magdeburg 59–60
mental health challenges 133–6.
      See also affliction, mystical; bipolar disorder; delusions; depression; derliction, mystical
   spiritual experiences and 57, 141–3
   truth-telling and 137–8
merit 81–2
mourning 37, 163

Nelson, Deborah 186–7
night of the senses 88
night of the spirit 88
Nixon, Richard 148
Nygren, Anders 23–4

O'Collins, Gerald 76
O'Siadhail, Micheal 204
Overduin, Michael 152–3

pain
   definition 56
   emotional 194
   evaluation of 40–2
   evil and 35
   physical 194
   pleasure and 35–6
   possibilities of 195
   salvation and 39
   transformation of 39
Paul. *See specific letters of Paul*
penance 78–80. *See also* asceticism
persecution 36–9
personal transformation
   asceticism and 109–10
   injustice and 108–9
   support for 110, 111
Philippians, letter to the 48–9
Pinches, Charles 151
pleasure
   evaluation of 39–42
   pain and 35–6
   salvation and 39
pneuma (spirit) 13–16
Pomerius, Johannes 63
powers of opposition 44–6
   God and 45
   persistence of 47–8
   victory over 51–2
prayer 190–1, 204–5
providence 73–5
Psalms, book of 76, 81, 127, 136
punishment 196 n.15, 198, 199
purgation, spiritual 107–8
purification, sensory 107–8

racism 179 n.4
Rahner, Karl 75
redemption 159–60, 202
resurrection 171, 187–8
Romans, letter to the
   chapter 5 4–5
   chapters 5 and 6 6–10
   chapter 7 11
   chapter 8 12–20, 194, 198–9, 201–2
   chapter 12 200
   chapter 15 24
rootedness 118

sacraments   84
sacrifices   81
salvation. *See also* Christ, passion
   redemption and   159–60
   sin and   157
   suffering and   162
sarx (flesh)   12–14
satisfaction   80, 190 n.3, 196–8
Schillebeeckx, Edward   72, 76, 83, 199 n.24
Schweitzer, Albert   5–6
self-gift   26, 28–31, 81
self-interest   25 n.9
self-love   25 n.10
self-sacrifice   24, 25, 32
self-subtraction   25, 32
Seneca   26–31
sentimentality   186–7
sin
   atonement for   196–8
   body and   14
   comedic world view and   157
   death and   9–10, 11
   definitions   72, 193 n.10
   effects of   78
   goodness and   73–4
   possibilities of   195
   responsibility for   47
   salvation and   157
   as sickness   78
   suffering and   46, 160, 173 n.13
   tragic world view and   157
Sisyphus   71
slavery   9 n.28
soma (body)   11–14
spirit (*pneuma*)   13–16
Spirit, Holy
   Christ and   203 n.31
   as helper   199
   life in   194
stigmata   98–9
Stonebridge, Lyndsey   125–6
Stranger than Fiction (Forster, dir.)   155
suffering. *See also* affliction, general; affliction, mystical; cancer; Christ; death; dereliction, mystical; destitution; disability; fragility; immigration detention; injustice; *kenosis*; loss; mental health challenges; pain; persecution; punishment; slavery; vulnerability
   acceptance of   170–1
   anger and   169
   avoidance of   172, 195, 200
   definition   56
   desire for God and   90–3
   devil and   48–50
   distribution of   75
   embracing of   172
   endurance of   190, 197 n.19, 200
   ethics and   116
   faith and   199
   fulfilment and   203
   glory and   16–18
   God and   199
   grace and   167–8, 173
   honour and   18
   hope and   174
   indifference to   118
   integration of   190
   lament and   182–4
   love and   190–1, 201–6
   meaning and   55–6, 72, 115, 116, 162, 174
   New Testament pillars of   55
   offering up   190, 196
   ordinariness of   116–17
   perspectives on   156–7, 169, 172
   politico-theological aspects   116
   possibilities of   195
   prayer and   190–1, 204
   as a privation   96
   privilege and   3
   punishment and   198, 199
   resistance to   195, 196, 199
   resurrection and   171
   salvation and   72, 162
   sin and   46, 160, 173 n.13
   solidarity in   82
   spiritual formation and   44 n.5
   as test   198, 199
   thought and   117–18
   tragedy and   184–5
   transformation and   101, 200, 201, 204, 206
   value of   38–9, 53, 163
   virtue and   4

will and 205–6
witness and 168
Suso, Henry 61
Swinton, John 156, 160 n.15

Tannehill, R. C. 6
Tauler, John 61–2
Taylor, Charles 44–5
Teilhard de Chardin, Pierre 203, 204
Teresa of Avila 65–6
Teresa of Kolkata, Mother
  attitudes towards 96
  on Christ's thirst 102–3
  dereliction in 70, 96–7, 99–100
  mission field of 96
  spirituality of 96–7, 101–3
testing 196 n.15, 198, 199. *See also* suffering, offering up
theodicies 156, 173, 183
  casualness and 145–6
  free will and 193 n.9
theosis 47, 49
Thérèse of Lisieux 69–70, 203
Thomas Aquinas
  on Christ's passion 82–4
  on divine causality and creaturely activity 83–4
  on God's justice and mercy 76–8
  on Job 75
  on merit 81–2
  on penance 78–80
  on providence and evil 73–5
  on sacrifices 81
  on satisfaction 80
Thomas of Celano 99
tragic world view 184–5
  contingency and 185
  depression and 161
  pessimism and 160
  sin and 157
transformation 200, 201, 204 n.34
Trinity 98, 191–2
truth-telling 138, 143–5
tumours. *See* cancer

undoing 110. *See also* injustice; purgation, spiritual
unsentimentality 186–7
uprootedness 118

van Leeuwen, Jan 62–3
Vann, Gerald 199, 205 n.36
van Ruusbroec, Jan 62
violent ideological groups
  disengagement from 106–7, 111–12
  personal transformation and 110–11
virtue 4, 34
vocation 194, 203, 205. *See also* fulfilment
vulnerability
  acknowledgement of 187
  affirmation of 175–7, 186–7
  contingency and 179–81
  definitions of 165, 178
  denial of 179–80
  divine 181–7
  as fundamental condition 178–9
  intensification of 178
  mastery and 186
  range of 180
  recognition of 176, 186–7
  self-securitization and 177–8
  solidarity in 177
  value of 176–7

Weil, Simone
  on affliction 117
  assessment of 129–31
  on divine mercy 85
  on rootedness 118
  on suffering 115
Wendel-Moltmann, Elisabeth 150
will 205–6
Williams, H. A. 197
Williams, Rowan 157, 160, 187
Wilson Gilmore, Ruth 179 n.4
Winslow, Donald 48
world views 156–7

www.ingramcontent.com/pod-product-compliance
Lightning Source LLC
Chambersburg PA
CBHW052041300426
44117CB00012B/1923